SHAHEED
BHAGAT SINGH

Harish Dhillon

SHAHEED
BHAGAT SINGH

Harish Dhillon

Indus Source Books
Indian Spirit, Universal Wisdom

Indus Source Books
PO Box 6194
Malabar Hill PO
Mumbai 400 006
INDIA
Email: info@indussource.com
www.indussource.com

ISBN 13: 978-81-88569-29-8

Copyright © Harish Dhillon, 2011

First edition October 2011
First reprint August 2012
Second reprint February 2013
Third reprint May 2014

All rights reserved

Printed at Decora Book Prints Pvt. Ltd., Mumbai.

This book is sold subject to the condition that it shall not by way of trade or otherwise, be lent, resold, hired out, or otherwise circulated without the publisher's prior written consent in any form of binding or cover other than that in which it is published and without a similar condition including this condition being imposed on the subsequent purchaser and without limiting the rights under copyright reserved above, no part of this publication may be reproduced, stored in a retrieval system, or transmitted in any form, or by any means, electronic, mechanical, photocopying, recording or otherwise, without the prior written permission of both the copyright owner and the above-mentioned publisher of this book.

To my grandchildren:
Avneet, Ibadat, Mannat, Abhey, Nanki,
Inaaya and Rehaan.

ACKNOWLEDGEMENTS

I owe a special debt of gratitude to Jasveen Bhinder who spent endless hours poring over the thousands of entries on Bhagat Singh on the net and sifting through the material available to download what she thought would help me, to Bhupinder Mann who unflaggingly and diligently scoured every possible library bookshelf to get me books on my subject and to Vinod Kumar without whose generous help the typing of the manuscript would never have been completed.

CONTENTS

Prologue   1

Chapter 1. Family Background   11

Chapter 2. Formative Years   30

Chapter 3. Birth of a Revolutionary   84

Chapter 4. Assassination of Saunders   126

Chapter 5. Bombs in the Assembly   167

Chapter 6. The Trial   202

Bibliography   242

PROLOGUE

The prisoners of Lahore Central Jail followed a set routine. They were allowed to leave their cells in the morning and remained outside in the courtyard till dusk, when they had to return to their cells. But over the years, their warden, Chattar Singh, had established a comfortable rapport with them and saw no harm in allowing them to linger on in the prison yard an hour or two longer than the prescribed hour.

But 23 March 1931 saw a sudden and abrupt departure not only from this well established routine but also from the normally tolerant attitude of Chattar Singh. At four in the evening, more stern than any of the prisoners had ever seen him before, he ordered them back to their cells. They had by now developed an extremely high regard for their friendly and kind warden and obeyed his unusual orders with little protest other than a few quiet murmurs. But once back in their cells, they could not help but wonder at this sudden and inexplicable departure from their usual routine. Was there perhaps a VIP visitor coming on an unscheduled visit which had forced the usually lax and friendly Chattar Singh to affect the stern demeanour of a strict disciplinarian? Or was there

1

SHAHEED BHAGAT SINGH

perhaps another rumour of the possibility of an attempted jail break in the offing, which had prompted the jail authorities to herd them back to their cells as a precautionary measure? But these speculations only lasted for a very short time. The prison grapevine reasserted itself very soon and the news spread like wildfire from cell to cell: Bhagat Singh, Sukhdev and Rajguru were going to be hanged the next morning, and the jail authorities, expecting some strong reaction to the news, had taken the precaution of confining all the prisoners to their cells so that any form of organised protest could be pre-empted.

A hush descended upon the prison and a palpable tension built up over the succeeding hours. The eerie silence that had descended over the entire prison compound heightened the tension with each passing minute. Alone in his cell, Bhagat Singh must have certainly felt this tension and understood the reason why it had built up to this exceptional pitch. But judging by the kind of person he was and the exceptional strength of character that he was gifted with, we can be sure that he was not unduly affected or perturbed by this understanding.

Ever since his sentence of death had been passed on 7 October 1930, he had been waiting for this day and expecting his death to come anytime with a remarkable calm and a complete sense of equanimity. It was a state of mind shared by his two fellow-conspirators, Sukhdev Thapar and Shivaram Rajguru, as they too waited in the silent solitude of their cells and recognised the reason for the tension that permeated all around them.

The news of the impending execution soon spread beyond the walls of Lahore Central Jail. Pran Nath Mehta, the defence attorney for all the three conspirators, hurried to the prison and approached the jail authorities for permission for one last meeting with his clients. He made it clear in his plea that all he wanted to do in this final meeting was to ascertain the last wish of the doomed men, a request so reasonable that the authorities, even in their state of extreme panic and heightened threat perception, could not deny.

Mehta stood at the barred gate of cell no.14, trying desperately to collect his thoughts and emotions as he watched Bhagat Singh pacing up and down his cell, as if impatient for the end. As he turned for the fourth time Bhagat Singh finally caught sight of the lawyer.

Bhagat Singh smiled his usual warm and generous smile and asked, "Have you brought my book?"

"How could I forget?" the lawyer answered with a wan smile, trying desperately to emulate his client.

Chattar Singh let the lawyer into the cell and left the two alone together. Mehta handed the book to Bhagat Singh. It was titled *The Revolutionary Lenin*.

Bhagat Singh flipped through the pages and said, without looking up from the book, "So, it's time."

It was a statement, not a question, and the voice was soft but firm. Mehta could not find anything to say. Bhagat Singh looked up from the book full into his lawyer's face. Under that intense scrutiny, Mehta could do no more than nod his head. He felt a lump in his throat and found it impossible to give voice to the myriad of thoughts and emotions that chased each other through his heart and mind. Finally he cleared his throat and said, "I have been permitted to see you to ascertain your last wish and desire."

Bhagat Singh's face lit up with a smile. "I have only one desire," he said, speaking again in that soft yet firm voice. "I desire to be born in India again so that I have another opportunity to serve my country." He turned back to his book.

Mehta stood there in silence, his awkwardness and

SHAHEED BHAGAT SINGH

helplessness building up within him. He realised that there was nothing really left for him to say. He searched for appropriate and adequate words to make his final farewell, but failed to find them. He looked once again at his client, absorbed already in his new book, as if determined to read as much of it as he could in the limited time that remained to him. Mehta turned wordlessly to leave the cell.

"And yes . . . ," Bhagat Singh said suddenly, looking up from his book. Mehta turned on his heels to face his client again. "I desire to convey my deepest gratitude to Pandit Nehru and Babu Subhas Chandra Bose for the great interest they have taken in my case and all the help they have tried to render me." With that he turned back again to his book and Mehta quietly left the cell for the last time.

His heart already heavy after his traumatic last meeting with Bhagat Singh, Mehta permitted himself to be escorted to the cell of his second client, Rajguru. Here too, he encountered the same stoic indifference to death. There was the same broad welcoming smile, the same absence of any trace of anxiety or fear. Rajguru embraced him warmly, thanked him for all that he had done for him, and then in farewell, said, "Don't look so grim, we will meet again soon."

With a heavy reluctant step, Mehta made his last call. Here too, he met with an almost identical reaction. Mehta realised that it could not have been any other way. The three had been completely bonded comrades-in-arms. They had shared the same total and intense commitment to their cause, the same reckless courage and total lack of fear and the same indifference to death. Mehta could find nothing to say, nothing that would break the intense awkwardness of the silence that hung between them. He went through the formality once again. "I have been permitted to see you, to ascertain your last wish and desire."

4

PROLOGUE

Sukhdev looked closely at his visitor for a long moment and then his face broke into his customary smile. "In a few hours I will die the death of a martyr in the cause of my country's freedom. What more could any Indian wish for?" He paused, his brow creased into a frown, and then he smiled again. "But yes, now that you remind me, there is one last wish left to be fulfilled. Please retrieve the carrom set that you so kindly lent me from the jailor. He seemed to feel that with death so close at hand, it was more befitting for me to spend my time in prayer and preparation for death than in frivolous pastimes like playing carrom. How was he to know that I had prepared myself so completely for death ever since I struck my first blow in my fight against the tyranny of the British rule, that ever since, anything other than the fight has been as frivolous to me as a game of carrom?"

It was not Mehta alone who had heard the news of the impending executions; it had spread beyond the walls of the prison. Other residents of Lahore had heard of it too. All through the evening groups of people began to congregate below the high walls of the prison to keep vigil through the night and, in these final hours, to be one in spirit with their heroes. By dusk the crowd had swelled to embrace many thousands; people from disparate sections of society, from different castes, from different religions and from different economic strata.

What united these people, who so rarely united in anything, was their reverence and love for the three who were about to die. They expressed this unity through the complete silence that they observed during the long hours of their tragic waiting.

The jail authorities watched this steadily increasing show of sympathy and support for the prisoners with a growing sense of alarm. Already panic-stricken, they realised that the

SHAHEED BHAGAT SINGH

quiet, peaceful demonstrators who had gathered to express their sympathy for the three martyrs were seething with suppressed emotions. It would take very little to ignite these emotions and cause a huge conflagration. The result would be either the forcible liberation of the three freedom fighters or the creation of another Jallianwala Bagh, outside the walls of the jail. To forestall such an eventuality, the jail authorities advanced the execution by eleven hours. Executions normally took place at six in the morning but the three executions would now take place at seven the previous evening.

The friendly Chattar Singh found himself thrust into the very unwelcome role of being one of the party that would escort the prisoners from their cells to be prepared for the hanging. He stood outside Bhagat Singh's cell, his bunch of keys rattling in his trembling hands as he fumbled to find the right key. Bhagat Singh looked up from his reading and quietly asked, "Will it be possible for you to wait a few minutes? It would be very kind of you to let me finish this chapter—I have only a few pages left."

Chattar Singh glanced at the other members of the party and seeing confirmation in their eyes, turned to Bhagat Singh again. He was too overcome to speak in the face of such overwhelming equanimity. He nodded his head in the affirmative. Bhagat Singh went back to his reading while the escort party stood outside the cell door waiting for him to finish. They waited in silence but they all felt a growing disquiet, a sense of discomfort in the face of such supreme courage. As he had promised, there were only a few pages left and he was indeed done in a few minutes. He turned the corner of the last page down as a marker, closed his book, put it aside and got to his feet. "Let's go," he said, walking to the cell door.

Popular stories, songs, plays and films have all combined to

PROLOGUE

leave in the public imagination, a highly dramatic vision of the succeeding sequence of events. But amazingly, though they have erred on other details of the Bhagat Singh story, they have all been absolutely true to all contemporary accounts, both eyewitness and otherwise, of the drama that followed.

Once all the three conspirators had been brought out of their cells, they locked their arms like true comrades-in-arms and walked through the narrow corridor, their firm, purposeful strides contrasting pointedly with the faltering steps of their escorts. And as they walked, as if on an unspoken cue, they broke into song. They sang one of their favourite compositions, a song which had always stirred strong patriotic fervour not only in their own hearts but also in the hearts of all those who heard them; a song that spoke of a future freedom and the immortality of those who laid down their lives in the cause of this freedom, an immortality that was not the immortality of cold stone monuments but the warm pulsating one of a life beyond death.

The other inmates at first clung to the bars of their cell doors in silence, too overcome by the enormity of the occasion. But then, as if in response to an invisible conductor, a single voice joined in the martyr's song. Soon it was joined by another and then another, until the entire prison reverberated with the echoes of the song and it was as if the very stones and mortar of the walls were one with the singers. A few fortunate inmates caught a fleeting glimpse of the three exceptionally brave men as they strode down the corridor, enough for their grandchildren to, in turn, tell their children: "My grandfather saw Bhagat Singh being led to his execution." And then, in a reverential whisper, "There has never been a braver man than him."

The three were first weighed and their weights meticulously recorded. They had all gained enough weight for one of them

7

SHAHEED BHAGAT SINGH

to joke, "At least history will not accuse the British of not having fed us well while we were in jail." But this last flash of humour elicited only a fleeting laugh. They then bathed and were asked to don the black robes that are customarily worn by prisoners being led to their deaths. Hoods were offered to them to cover their faces so they could be spared the final indignity of others being witness to their fear. Bhagat Singh shook his head. "If you please, none of us is afraid of death."

The three were led on the short walk to the gallows and as they walked they sang another of their favourite songs: "*Sarfaroshi ki tamanna aaj hamare dil mein hain*".

Once they reached the gallows they stopped their singing, and the other prisoners, craning their necks through the bars of their cell doors to catch every possible sound, heard the distant but strident calls of: "*Inquilab Zindabad*" and "*Hindustan Azad Ho*". Then there was silence for a while but soon there drifted out from the cells, in a faint voice that gradually grew into a full throated rendition, the strains of a popular freedom song which had captured the imagination not only of the Punjab but of the whole country: "*Mera rang de basanti chola*". It was like the fitting finale to a choral performance; the other prisoners were offering their tribute, making their farewell to the three men who had come to occupy the centre stage of their lives in Lahore Central Jail. And it was to the accompaniment of this finale that the final moments of the execution were played out.

The three nooses hanging side by side from the scaffold were tested for their strength to ensure that they would take the weight of an adult man. They were then put around the necks of the three condemned men and tightened. One by one, the planks from under their feet were kicked away and they were left hanging in the void long enough to ensure their death. Finally they were brought down and the prison doctor

8

PROLOGUE

examined and declared them dead.

As part of the procedure, a senior jail official was called upon to identify the bodies. He was so moved by the courage of the three martyrs that he wanted nothing further to do with the process of their death and refused to do the needful. He was suspended on the spot for this act of wilful insubordination and another officer had to be called forth to perform this duty. The certificates of death were signed by the superintendent of the jail and another British officer.

But the British were not yet done with the three martyrs. The sense of panic that had been growing in their hearts all through the proceedings of the evening, and which should have ended as they had hoped, with the three deaths, had now turned to total alarm. The prisoners had not ceased their chanting and singing for even a moment. If anything, it now seemed to be building up to a deafening crescendo.

Outside the walls the mammoth crowds were swelling by the minute and there were reports that some in this crowd were growing restive and raising anti-British slogans. The original plan had been to cremate the bodies in the premises of the prison and hand over the ashes to the next of kin the following day. But the fear of a violent reaction from the crowd, when it was learnt that the executions had already been carried out, made the British hastily change their plans. They did not think that cremation within the prison compound was now advisable. At the same time the van carrying the bodies out of the prison gates was bound to attract the attention of the crowd. The jail authorities feared possible retribution when the truth became known.

So late into the night, the rear wall of the prison was breached at a quiet spot far from the crowd outside. The bodies were carried out into a truck to the banks of the Sutlej to a remote and forlorn place outside Ferozepur. Here, under

SHAHEED BHAGAT SINGH

the watchful eyes of a strong police force, the three pyres were lit. But even in this obscure place the fears of the British came true.

In the pitch darkness of the night, the glow from the three blazing pyres caught the attention of the residents of the nearby villages like Gandha Singh Wallah, and aroused their suspicions. Armed with sticks and shovels and whatever else they could lay their hands on, they rushed to the spot. The police realised that the truth would be out soon with dire consequences to their personal safety and decided that at this time discretion was definitely the better part of valour. They ran back to their vehicles as quickly as they could and retreated to the safety of the walls of Lahore Central Jail. The large crowd of villagers, now sure of what they were witness to, sat in awed silence, paying wordless tribute to the three martyrs.

Chapter 1

FAMILY BACKGROUND

The saga that had ended so tragically in a remote area on the banks of the Sutlej in the early hours of 24 March 1931 had its beginning in Banga, in Lyallpur District, now in Pakistan, twenty-four years earlier, on 27 September 1907, with the birth of a boy child to Sardar Kishan Singh Sandhu and Bibi Vidyavati Kaur. The Sandhus had their origins in the village of Khatkar Kalan Khatka located in an area commonly referred to as the Doab Bist, the area lying between the rivers Sutlej and Beas. The people of this region are known for their supreme confidence and determination. They are also remarkable for their tolerance and for their compassion and kindness, especially to those in need. They are known to be very public spirited even to the extent of making the extreme sacrifice in a public cause. Swaran Singh, in *Path of Revolution*, his book on Bhagat Singh, says that this trait in the character of the people of the Doab "could have been due to some element in the geography and climate of the region, it could have been due to the openness and candour in their character

SHAHEED BHAGAT SINGH

and make-up" (p.12). Whatever the reason for it, the people of the Doab Bist, Jullundhur, have come to symbolise social awareness and a sense of patriotism, and the Sandhu family was a prime example of this.

The Sandhus were a prosperous farming family. They had over generations, established their own set of values, which had been concisely and succinctly set out by Sardar Fateh Singh, Kishan Singh's grandfather. Like other landlords of the Punjab, Fateh Singh had taken an active part in resisting the very aggressive designs of the British East India Company during its attempts to take over the Punjab in the aftermath of the defeat of the Sikhs in the Anglo-Sikh wars. And like other landlords, he too had been punished for his efforts to protect the independence of the Punjab—his lands had been confiscated. In 1857, when the rest of India was aflame with the fires of the First War of Independence, the British attempted to win over the Punjab to their side by offering to restore the confiscated lands to the Punjab landlords and also to give them awards of additional land holdings if they assisted the British in their attempts to crush the mutineers. To the eternal shame of Punjab, many landlords readily accepted the offer. Sardar Fateh Singh was amongst those who brushed the offer aside with angry impatience. In his public refusal of the British offer he said that his ancestors had chosen to become Sikhs and follow the teachings of the Gurus because of the example set by the ninth Guru, Guru Tegh Bahadur, who had sacrificed his life to protect the right of the Kashmiri Pandits to practise their religion. Drawing from this sacrifice, Guru Gobind Singh had preached that a true Sikh would always champion the cause of those who were fighting for their rights, even if it meant fighting side by side with them and sacrificing one's life in the fight. To oppose people who were fighting for their rights was tantamount not only to committing an act

12

of treason, but was also a betrayal of the Gurus and of the Sikh faith. If one had to choose between a principle and the gaining of material wealth, the choice was really a very simple one—the principle must always come first.

The public spurning of the British offer and all that it stood for became the defining credo, not only of his own life and the life of his son, Arjun Singh, but also of the lives of his three grandsons, Kishan Singh, Ajit Singh, and Swaran Singh. Ironically his other son, Surjan Singh, chose the easier way and by accepting the British offer, became one of their supporters.

In 1887, the British government in the Punjab created the Chenab Canal Colony. This was done by building an intricate system of canals which would divert the waters of the Chenab and provide perennial irrigation to an area which had till then been a barren wasteland in central Punjab and was transformed into rich, fertile farmland. By doing so they would be establishing the credentials of the British administration as a paternalistic administration. Fateh Singh's son, Arjun Singh, like hundreds of other farmers from eastern Punjab, migrated to the canal area and settled down in the village of Banga, Chak No.105, Gogera branch, in Lyallpur district, in what is now Pakistan.

During the early years, the canal area proved to be everything that the British had hoped for. The colony had brought prosperity to the settlers because of the enhanced agricultural production. It had brought together like-minded people and this had served to establish a harmonious community life. The standard of living was indeed higher than the settlers had known before. Sardar Arjun Singh, haunted by the tumultuous years that the family had seen during the post-1857 period and the conflict of values that had been created by the stand that his brother Surjan Singh had taken, channelised all his

SHAHEED BHAGAT SINGH

energies into giving his family a sense of harmony and culture in their new home. Arjun Singh was a great scholar and had devoted a lifetime to studies in various fields. He was fluent in Urdu, Persian, Punjabi, Hindi, and Sanskrit and was well read in the literature of all these languages. His special areas of interest were the Guru Granth Sahib and the Unani system of medicine. He was universally recognised within the community as an outstanding authority on the Sikh scriptures and also as a Unani *hakim* of exceptional skill. Many came to him with doubts and questions regarding the interpretations of the Sikh religious texts which Arjun Singh helped to resolve and many were the patients whose pain and suffering he eased with his medicines. He was particularly sought after as a *hakim*, by the poor and the needy, who could not afford the more expensive allopathic medicines. He not only gave them free medicines but often contributed to the cost of the nutritional supplements that they so desperately needed. He demonstrated his sense of social service in many concrete ways too. In the early days in Banga he constructed a gurdwara, a well, and a *sarai* for travellers. Not only did he organise the funds for this venture and get into the nitty-gritty of the design, but he also worked manually alongside the masons. He was a liberal in the true sense of the word. For him, faith and the practise of religion were not a mere observance of rituals. Faith and religion were a way of life to be lived according to the tenets laid down by the Gurus and the holy books. He had an intuitive ability to identify social needs and spent his entire life attempting to fulfil these needs.

In the Punjab it was Guru Nanak who had first brought social and political consciousness into the realm of everyday life. This political and social consciousness had been transmuted into a spirit of nationalism and patriotism by Guru Gobind Singh. A wave of political and social fervour

FAMILY BACKGROUND

was sweeping the country and Punjab provided the lead. The introduction of the English model of education in India in the 1860s had brought with it a great awareness of not only movements at home and abroad, but also of movements in the past. It brought with it new subjects and challenges to the people's way of thinking. People had to learn to cope intellectually with the influence of Western liberalism, the concept of individual freedom, the effects of the industrial and technological development, and literary and educational experiments which were now becoming a matter of course. There was, as a result, a kind of churning taking place, an attempt to bridge the gap between the British way of life and the Indian culture. It was obvious that a social revolution was in the making and, as usually happens, it was not long before a political churning also began to take place. Nowhere in India was this more obvious than in the Punjab. The Akali and the Singh Sabha movements with their emphasis on gurdwara reform were in the vanguard of other progressive movements in the country. The Arya Samaj, with its ideology of education and reform being the true agents for achieving freedom, fired the imagination of all educated Indians. The Indian National Congress and the Kirti Kisan Movement aroused intense patriotic fervour. Even Indians living abroad could not but be affected by the strong winds of change that were sweeping over their motherland and sympathised even with the extremism of the Ghadar Movement.

Sardar Arjun Singh sympathised openly with the Gurdwara Reform Movement and wore a black turban to show that he was an active member of the movement. But soon he felt himself being drawn towards the Arya Samaj Movement launched by Swami Dayanand. Though he was an authority on the Sikh scriptures and the Sikh religion, Arjun Singh, like some other Sikh landlords of the region, chose to align

15

SHAHEED BHAGAT SINGH

himself with the Arya Samaj, which was perceived to be a "Hindu" organisation rather than with the Singh Sabha, which was perceived to be an organisation for the Sikhs. He, like the others who had made a similar choice, had very valid reasons for doing so. He saw very clearly that the Singh Sabha, founded by feudal Sikh landlords, had the patronage of the British. The British were using it as a weapon to try to counteract the growing popularity of the Kuka Movement with its great emphasis on patriotism and nationalism. Because the Singh Sabha was started by feudal landlords, it was by its very nature and constitution, geared to protect their interests, often at the expense of the interests of the weaker sections of society. The Arya Samaj, on the other hand, propagated the view that the individual liberty of a member of a society was closely linked with the liberty of every other member of that society. In John Donne's immortal words, "No man is an island, entire of itself." The suffering of any one member of a society is the suffering of every other member of that society; the exploitation of any one member of a society is the exploitation of every other member of that society. As a result, the Arya Samaj not only preached and practised the removal of the caste system and untouchability but also humanism in its purest form. Arjun Singh practised this credo wholeheartedly and was able to instil a similar belief in his sons and grandson. Perhaps it was this strong sympathy for the ideals of the Arya Samaj that made Arjun Singh send all three of his sons, Ajit Singh, Kishan Singh and Swaran Singh to schools run by the Arya Samaj and years later, to advise his grandson, Bhagat Singh, to study Sanskrit. Arjun Singh was keenly interested in and sympathetic towards the activities of the Indian National Congress. In 1893 he participated as a Kisan delegate in the Congress convention held in Lahore, presided over by Dadabhai Naoroji.

FAMILY BACKGROUND

Against this background, it was inevitable that Arjun Singh's three sons would be drawn into what the British considered revolutionary activities. While Ajit Singh, the eldest of the three, was drawn immediately into the strong wave of political activity that was sweeping the country at that time, the two younger brothers, Kishan Singh and Swaran Singh found themselves contributing more to the social reforms being ushered in by organisations like the Arya Samaj, and to the cause of social service in general. However, such was the nature of the movements that were embracing the very fabric of life in India that they could not help but be drawn into the vortex of intense political activity that was taking place all around them.

While studying in the Sain Das Anglo-Sanskrit High School in Jullundhur, Kishan Singh came under the influence of Mahatma Hans Raj and went on to be actively involved in an extremely broad sweep of social activity. In 1898, part of Vidarbha, in what is now Maharashtra, was ravaged by a terrible famine. With the help of Lala Bishambar Das and Lala Amar Das, advocates from Ferozepur, he organised camps to help the people affected by the famine. In 1900, there was an equally bad famine in Ahmedabad and the surrounding areas. Kishan Singh and Lala Lajpat Rai not only organised relief camps for the famine-affected but also established an orphanage for the children who had lost their parents and had no one to look after them. Some years later, in 1904 to be precise, Kishan Singh worked diligently to repeat the relief bearing activity in the earthquake devastated Kangra district where he was unanimously elected as secretary of the committee that had been set up for the purpose. One year later, when the Jhelum was in spate and Srinagar and the surrounding areas were inundated by the flood waters, Kishan Singh once again rose to the occasion, rushed to the flood

SHAHEED BHAGAT SINGH

affected areas and provided tremendous help and relief to the flood-stricken Kashmiris.

With this movement between disaster-struck regions, Kishan Singh found himself coming into close contact with the political turmoil that had come to engulf India. Almost naturally he became a member of the Indian National Congress. Both Kishan Singh and Ajit Singh attended the Congress convention in Calcutta in 1906. Their enthusiasm and total lack of fear and inhibition in expressing their views drew admiration from Bal Gangadhar Tilak. He entrusted the brothers with the task of strengthening the movement in the Punjab. He became their inspiration and they gravitated towards the extreme faction led by him. Like their brother Swaran Singh, they had little sympathy for the moderate activity of the mainstream Indian National Congress and held views that came more and more into conflict with the views held by moderate leaders like Lala Lajpat Rai. They found themselves committed to the belief that the masses must be aroused to oppose the British at every opportunity that came their way no matter how radical a form this opposition may take. With the carving out of the North West Frontier Provinces in 1901 and the partition of Bengal in 1905, the brothers found themselves pushed to even more radical opposition to the British. They returned from the Congress convention and started a monthly paper in the Punjab called *Bharat Mata*, to propagate their views. They neither had enough finances to ensure the regular publication of the paper nor did they know people in sufficiently influential positions who could help them raise the necessary resources for this purpose. They found a unique and novel way out of their predicament. They went into one of the most central and crowded areas of the city and rang a bell. When they had collected a sufficiently large number of the curious, Ajit Singh

FAMILY BACKGROUND

delivered a rousing speech about the evil effects of the British rule on Indian commerce and industry. They announced that they would be conducting a meeting the following Sunday in the office of the *Bharat Mata* and invited all likeminded people to attend. After a tentative start over the first two weeks, the meetings became a regular weekly affair on every Sunday and attracted an ever increasing number of people who readily contributed to the expenses of publishing the paper. These informal gatherings were soon given a formal structure and the Bharat Mata Society was formed. Ajit Singh was elected as the president and Nand Kishore Mehta as the secretary of the society. Among the luminaries who became active members of the society and gave wholehearted support to the paper were Lala Lal Chand "Phalak", who was at that time regarded as the "national" poet of the Punjab, Lala Pindi Das, Dr. Ishwari Prasad and Sufi Amba Prasad.

The strong cultural and political environment of Arjun Singh's home was given an added dimension by Harnam Kaur, the wife of his eldest son, Ajit Singh. She was from Kasur, which had become the centre for studies related to the teachings of Baba Bulleh Shah, the renowned sufi saint. She brought these sufi teachings and all that they stood for in day to day life to her new home in Banga and enriched the already rich cultural environment there, making it a living example of how rich and composite Punjabi culture could be. It was a home where there was no hypocrisy, where there was no gap between what was professed and what was lived. There was great compassion and concern for the working people, for the downtrodden and the exploited; compassion and concern which found expression in affirmative activity for the uplift of the weaker sections of society. It was a home where every member reached out to other members of the community when they were in trouble, irrespective of caste, creed or personal affinity. It was a home where political affairs, regional, national, and international were discussed on a day to day basis and every member of the family, irrespective of age or gender, was encouraged to take part in the discussion. It was natural, and perhaps inevitable, that the interest in politics in a household like Arjun Singh's would not be limited to discussion but would translate into active participation whenever it was felt necessary. Corruption, graft, and nepotism were rampant in the administration of the colony. The early settlers were thoroughly disenchanted with the maladministration and some of them had even begun to talk of uprooting themselves and moving on again. The paternalism that the British rulers had sought to display through the running of the colony had become an obnoxious and unwarranted interference in the lives of the settlers. Fed up with the state of affairs, Sefaj-ud-din Ahmed, a retired postal official, was persuaded to start a paper called the *Zamindar*. Through this paper the settlers sought to give voice to their grievances and publicise their plight. It was hoped that the British rulers would recognise the need for some form of remedial measures and so avoid the political opposition that this discontent was bound to generate if left untreated. The British did nothing and the discontent built up. In October 1906, as if completely oblivious to the volatile situation that already existed, the British introduced the Punjab Colonisation of Land Bill in the local Legislative Council. Through the Bill, the British established conditions in the colony that can only be termed as retroactive, pertaining to sanitation, planting of trees, and construction. Any breach of these conditions would attract a heavy fine. To make matters worse, the Bill also established that the courts would have no jurisdiction in the colony. In other words, there could be no appeal against the decision of the administration. As if this was not bad enough, in November of the same year the government announced a drastic increase in the occupier rates, which was a charge for using the canal water imposed on all settlers. Till then the Bari Doab areas in Amritsar, Gurdaspur and Lahore districts had been charged lower rates because a large number of recruits (36%) for the Indian Army came from these areas and it was hoped that the lower rate would ensure their loyalty to the British. Now with the spectre of 1857 firmly behind them and the economic prosperity of the canal area before them the British deemed it fit to introduce this exploitative measure. Through this Act, the government not only increased the water rates and the land revenue, which the farmers with small landholdings could ill afford to pay, but also made it easier for money lenders to take over the lands of farmers who defaulted in the repayment of their loans.

As was to be expected there was a strong and volatile reaction to the introduction of the Bill. It was not surprising that having been one of the earliest settlers in the region and belonging to a family which was so strongly active in all matters political, Arjun Singh's son, Ajit Singh, should become one of the leading spokespersons for the settlers. On 22 and 23 March 1907, the *Zamindar* held a public meeting to launch the opposition to the Bill. Though the meeting was essentially a platform for the farmers to express their views, Ajit Singh sent delegates from his newly found Bharat Mata Society to launch an agitation against the exploitative measure in particular and against the British in general. The *Zamindar* called upon Lala Lajpat Rai, who had by now become a leading light in the fight against the oppressive British rule in the Punjab, to address the gathering.

Twenty-three years later, in October 1930, Bhagat Singh was to describe the meeting in his essay "Why I am an Atheist" and bring out the basic difference in the political ideology of Lala

SHAHEED BHAGAT SINGH

Lajpat Rai and Sardar Ajit Singh. Before leaving (for Lyallpur) Lalaji sent a message to Sardar Ajit Singh saying that the government should be thanked for (a previous) amendment and then asked to repeal the law. To this Ajit Singh is said to have replied, "We shall prepare the masses for a no revenue campaign. Also we can never thank the government." The meeting itself is described by Bhagat Singh thus: "Lalaji was received by a large rally and consequently reached the pandal two hours late. In the meanwhile, Sardar Ajit Singh gave a speech. He was an impressive speaker. His tireless style of speech made the audience enthusiastic and by the end he had a large following of people. By the time Lalaji reached the pandal, the masses were with the Bharat Mata Society . . . Lalaji was Punjab's finest orator but the style, the fearlessness and determination with which he spoke was something else. He received an ovation after every line. After the meeting many people dedicated their lives to the motherland."

N. Gerald Barrier also tells us of Lala Lajpat Rai's stirring speech on this occasion: "Lajpat Rai attempted to be moderate, but as happened frequently with his speech making, the crowd's frenzy drove him to use phrases and ideas verging on what the British termed 'sedition'" ("The Punjab Disturbance of 1907", *Peasant Resistance and the Raj*, edited by David Hardiman). It was at this meeting that Shri Banke Dayal recited a poem beginning with the line: "Pagri Sambhal O Jatta, Pagri Sambhal Oye". This poem was an instant hit with the audience and it went on to become an anthem for any form of resistance to the British and was sung and recited at every meeting with any kind of patriotic or nationalist colour.

After this historic meeting, Lala Lajpat Rai, having assumed the role of a nationalist leader of pan-Indian stature, moved on to the United Provinces where he had committed himself

FAMILY BACKGROUND

to address a series of meetings to mobilise public opinion. Ajit Singh was left to give shape to the new movement that had been launched in the Punjab. He addressed a number of meetings not only of the farmers but also of college students and army personnel, both serving and retired, in Amritsar and Lahore, and was instrumental in bringing them together. They passed a resolution pledging themselves to a total boycott of all British goods, and more pertinently, pledged not to pay the new water rate and also ensure that nobody else paid this rate either. If anyone was found going against this resolution, he would be ostracised by his caste, banned from all community activities and functions, and would also have to pay a fine of five hundred rupees. Lala Lajpat Rai continued his agitation against the Act by writing a series of articles condemning the unjust provisions of the Act. The fallout of Lala Lajpat Rai's very effective campaign against the Act and the results of Ajit Singh's efforts to mobilise the settlers against the new Bill alarmed Denzil Ibbetson, the lieutenant-governor of the Punjab. He perceived that the activities of Lala Lajpat Rai and Ajit Singh were promoting sedition along two fronts. He felt that Ajit Singh, through his revolutionary activities, especially through his personal meetings with groups of people, was spreading disaffection amongst the students and the soldiers; and that both Lala Lajpat Rai, through his inflammatory speech, and Ajit Singh, in organising the resistance of the farmers to the new Bill, were guilty of "corrupting" the farmers. He asked for permission to proceed against these troublemakers, so as to be able to strike terror in the minds of all such troublemakers. At this juncture riots broke out in Rawalpindi and it was generally felt that these had been caused due to the instigation provided by the vituperative campaign mounted by both Ajit Singh and Lala Lajpat Rai. As a result, permission was readily given by the government

23

to proceed against the troublemakers. Both Lalaji and Ajit Singh were arrested, but so great was Ibbetson's fear of a possible backlash against the arrests, that in the early hours of the morning the duo were made to board a special train to Calcutta from where they were put on a ship and deported to Mandalay. Though Kishan Singh and Swaran Singh had not played as prominent a part in the agitation as their brother, they had provided all assistance that they could in mobilising participation in the meetings that their brother conducted. They went from village to village and town to town, exhorting students, soldiers, and farmers to attend these meetings in as large a number as possible. As a result, they too came under the British scanner. There are conflicting accounts as to what happened to them. Kuldip Nayar, in his book, *The Life and Trial of Bhagat Singh,* seems to imply that both of them were arrested and imprisoned by the British, while Malwinderjit Singh Waraich in his book, *Bhagat Singh, the Eternal Rebel,* says that while Swaran Singh was arrested and imprisoned, Kishan Singh escaped to Nepal before he could be arrested by the British.

The movement against the infamous Act had taken on a life of its own, and even the extremely repressive measure of arresting and incarcerating all the leaders who had spearheaded the opposition to it could not suppress the movement. Questions were raised in the British Parliament about the Act and about the repressive measures that had been taken to snuff out the opposition to it, especially the arrest and deportation of Lala Lajpat Rai, the well-liked and well-respected leader even in British political circles.. The government made every effort to justify the Act as also the repressive measures that it had taken to wipe out all opposition to it. But for once it failed to convince the British Parliament and, in 1907, was forced not only to repeal the controversial Bill but also to release all

FAMILY BACKGROUND

the agitators that it had arrested, amongst them Lala Lajpat Rai, Ajit Singh, Kishan Singh, and Swaran Singh.

The child born to Kishan Singh and Vidyavati, a few months later in September of the same year, was fondly nicknamed "Bhagawala" by his grandmother. Coinciding with the time of his birth, three fortuitous events had taken place for the family: his uncle Swaran Singh had been released from the Lahore Jail, his father Kishan Singh had returned from Nepal, and orders had been given for his uncle Ajit Singh's release from Mandalay. Because of this happy coincidence, she firmly believed that he had brought good fortune to the family. The name was later formalised to Bhagat Singh.

Even after his release from Mandalay, Ajit Singh remained one of the most proactive leaders who promoted militant action against the British in spite of the many criminal cases that had been registered against him. He established contact with revolutionary groups and parties outside the country who could help the Indians in their fight against their rulers. He visited Iran and Germany to mobilise support for revolutionary activity against the British in India. After the defeat of Germany in the First World War, he went to Brazil, where he lived till 1934. During the Second World War, he moved to Italy where he established the Azad Hind Fauj. In 1946, through the sustained and determined efforts of Pandit Jawaharlal Nehru, the British were persuaded to drop all cases against him and he was permitted to return to India, though he lived out the next few months in what can only be termed as a loose house arrest in Dalhousie. In a tragic twist of irony he lived only to see the first few hours of the freedom for which he had so valiantly fought and for which he had sacrificed so much: three hours after Pandit Nehru unfurled the national flag from the ramparts of the Red Fort and delivered his historic and now legendary "Tryst with Destiny" speech,

SHAHEED BHAGAT SINGH

Ajit Singh passed away in the wee hours of the morning of 15 August 1947.

Bhagat Singh grew up in a household that encouraged a pragmatic and liberal attitude of mind and freedom of thought. Frank, open discussions on any subject, especially on subjects connected with politics, were an everyday affair and hence it comes as no surprise that at an age when other boys were playing marbles and fighting over who had won, Bhagat Singh's thoughts centred on matters of a far higher order.

There is a charming story from this period of Bhagat Singh's life that has come down to us through oral tradition. Kishan Singh, being a progressive farmer, was always looking for innovations that he could make in his agricultural practices. Though mango was a traditional and popular fruit in the Punjab, its cultivation was almost always limited to small groves of trees, breaking the monotony of vast stretches of wheat fields. The variety grown was limited almost entirely to the small, slightly sour variety called the "desi" mango in popular parlance. By one of those tremendous coincidences which end up bringing so much colour into our lives, Kishan Singh went to attend a relative's wedding at a farm in what was then called the United Provinces. The relative had taken the rather adventurous step of buying up a huge tract of land because he was getting it cheap, and settling down there. It so happened that Kishan Singh's visit coincided with the height of the mango season. He was amazed at the variety and richness of the fruit available and immediately began to consider the possibility of developing some of his land in Banga into a full-fledged mango orchard along the lines of the orchards he saw around him. He returned to the United Provinces at the appropriate time of the year, chose a few of the sturdiest varieties of mango for his experiment, carefully selected as

26

many healthy saplings of these varieties as he could carry, returned to his farm and planted them with the greatest care to create what was the first "professional" mango orchard in his region. Kishan Singh was justifiably proud of his orchard and never tired of showing it off, not only to his friends and relatives but also to the most casual of visitors. One day, a very dear friend, Nand Kishore Mehta, had come to visit the family. Nand Kishore arrived in the evening and after he had bathed and eaten his evening meal, the two friends chatted late into the night, catching up with each other's news. Inevitably, the conversation turned to Kishan Singh's orchard. Nand Kishore was keen to see the orchard and when the friends finally went to sleep it was with the promise that Kishan Singh would take his friend around first thing in the morning. So the next morning, after their ablutions and the customary glass of warm milk, the two made their way to the orchard. Bhagat Singh had not yet started attending school and liked to spend as much time as possible with his father and grandfather. The little boy was always curious about what the grown-ups were doing and saying, especially when there were visitors to the house. It was inevitable that he should follow his father and Nand Kishore Mehta. That morning, having gone around the orchard, the two friends soon became engrossed in a discussion on the merits and demerits of diversification in agriculture, and forgot about the little boy. It was only at the close of this discussion that they remembered that the boy had been with them and looked around for him. They saw him in the field adjoining the orchard. The field had been freshly ploughed in preparation for the next sowing and the child was completely absorbed in planting twigs that he had broken off from a small bush along the ridges of the furrows. The two friends walked quietly up to him. Kishan Singh caressed his son's hair and when the boy looked up into his face and smiled, asked him in a voice loaded with gentleness and love, "What are you planting, my son?"

"I am sowing guns," he replied firmly and turned back to his work. It was not an answer that either of the friends had expected and they looked at each other in surprise.

"Guns, my son?" Mehta asked. "You know that what you sow will multiply many times over. What will you do when you have harvested so many guns?"

Bhagat Singh looked Mehta straight in the eye and replied in a clear, firm voice, "I will use them to drive the British out of India."

Perhaps it is too precocious a statement for such a young child to have made, perhaps this incident never really happened, perhaps this is an apocryphal story, a mere accretion, like so many accretions that attach themselves to a legend long after the person is gone. But it does serve to bring home the fact that growing up in the environment that he did, Bhagat Singh would have imbibed the spirit of nationalism and patriotism from a very tender age.

All through these early years in Banga, Bhagat Singh was a source of great strength and comfort to his aunt, Harnam Kaur, wife of his uncle Ajit Singh. Ajit Singh had a number of criminal cases pending against him because of his extremely active participation in various revolutionary, and hence anti-British, activities. As a result, he was forced to go into self-imposed exile to escape prosecution. Harnam Kaur was forced to lead what was virtually a widow's existence with the additional anxiety of always worrying about the safety and well-being of her absent husband. She knew that the rest of the family was as worried for her husband as she was, and to spare them any anxiety on her account she put up a brave front. But in the quiet of the night, when she was sure that everyone was asleep, she would let the mask slip away from her and permit herself the luxury of softly weeping into her pillow. Bhagat Singh, ever sensitive to the pain and suffering that his aunt was going through, was the only one in the family who knew of Harnam Kaur's tears. He would slip quietly out of his bed and snuggle under the covers of his aunt's bed. In a reversal of roles, he would hold her head in his lap, caress her hair, wipe the tears away and say, "Chachi, don't cry. When I grow up, I will drive the British out of India and then Chachaji will come home and no one will be able to take him away from us ever again."

Chapter 2

FORMATIVE YEARS

The monsoons had hit Banga with unusual strength that year and it was through pouring and incessant rain that Arjun Singh took his grandson, Bhagat Singh, for enrolment at the district primary school. Vidyavati, his mother, had wrapped him in a thick *khes* which she had woven herself, and as a result, when they reached the rather stark school building, Bhagat Singh found himself in a fairly dry condition. The headmaster, apprised in advance of their visit, was expecting them. The boy was sharp and perceptive as ever and noticed the almost reverential tone with which the middle-aged headmaster greeted his grandfather and the deference that was so obvious in his attitude and manner. However, this came as no surprise to the little boy; that his grandfather was a highly respected and influential person in the community was something that he had long known and taken for granted.

For Bhagat Singh, the day had begun earlier than most other days. He had woken up at dawn, bathed, and been dressed in a brand new school uniform. He was both embarrassed and flattered to be the focus of all this special attention. When his aunt, Harnam Kaur, had finished fussing over his hair and tying his *jura* or topknot, he had stolen a glance in the mirror that fronted his grandfather's cupboard. He could not help feeling a thrill of pride in seeing himself accoutred in the school uniform. The family gathered around a small portrait of Guru Nanak, and in his deep, sonorous voice, Arjun Singh recited the *Ardas* and asked God to take care of the boy and direct him always to choose the right course in life. He asked for God's special blessing with regard to the child's academic career. As a concession to the special occasion, instead of the customary parathas at breakfast, Bhagat Singh was treated to a feast of *puri* and *aloo*. Before he left the house, his aunt fed him the mandatory spoon of curd and sugar to safeguard the auspiciousness of the occasion.

As Bhagat walked side by side with his grandfather through the pouring rain, the pure undiluted excitement and anticipation of the beginning of this new stage in his life slowly turned to apprehension. He had heard about how brutal school masters could be when they chastened and punished errant boys. He had heard how demanding they were when it came to homework. He had also heard how difficult study could be at school. Images of all the dreadful stories he had heard now came crowding into his mind and the bounce in his stride was replaced by a reluctance to take each next step. As the blurred image of the school building loomed large through the pouring rain, Bhagat Singh felt emptiness in the pit of his stomach and a rising sense of panic. He reached up and clutched at his grandfather's hand. The old man clasped the boy's hand firmly in a reassuring grasp and looking down into his face, gave him an affectionate smile.

Once they reached the school building and came face to face with the headmaster, the little boy's apprehension and

SHAHEED BHAGAT SINGH

anxiety faded quickly away. It was not only the deference and the respect with which his grandfather was treated that was responsible for this, it was also the attitude of the headmaster towards the child. He had an open, sunny face which lit up with a welcoming smile every time he looked at the child. While his grandfather completed the formalities, Bhagat Singh found himself feeling more and more at ease with the new surroundings, and by the time he said goodbye to his grandfather and was led to his class, all the fear had gone and there was once again in his heart the surge of undiluted excitement with which he had set out from home in the morning.

The only seat available was towards the back of the class and all through the hours before recess, Bhagat Singh was aware of the furtive glances that the other boys kept casting his way. A few smiled hesitantly. He knew that they were sizing him up, deciding whether it was worth their while to try and be friends with him. He knew many of them; some of them were his playmates at home. But young as he was, he knew that in the school environment things were bound to be different. He was afraid that these very playmates, caught up in a peer group of a different kind, might not be so accepting of him. He was soon swept away in the novelty of the lessons that were being taught and was surprised at how soon the bell for recess rang. Once the teacher had left the classroom and the other boys crowded around him, he was relieved to find his playmates displaying the same warmth towards him in school as they did at home. The others too, were keen to make friends with him and at the end of that first day it was as if he had always been in school.

The days drew into weeks, and weeks into months, and his teachers saw in the child qualities of head and heart and more so of behaviour that marked him out as being different

FORMATIVE YEARS

from the other boys. He was a happy, cheerful child who made friends easily and his sunny disposition won him easy popularity not only with his school mates but also with all the teachers. He was an integral part of all the games the children played and the childish pranks that they were involved in, and yet there was, even at this early age, an undefined quality of detachment, almost of aloofness, that marked him as being distinctive. Those who watched closely, as his teacher did, could not fail to observe that Bhagat Singh displayed a sharp mind, quick thinking, and a higher intelligence than most of his peers. It was soon clear that in spite of his active participation in all games and sports, he was a dedicated scholar as well. Where most of the other boys had to be coerced and bullied to turn to their studies, Bhagat Singh was drawn naturally and instinctively to his books. He was the ideal pupil that every teacher dreams of and it was not surprising that over the next four years he won the respect and affection of every teacher in the school.

Most people were amazed that even at the tender age of eight, he seemed to know more than most of the adults around him about the events happening at the state and national level and the effect they were likely to have on the day to day lives of the people. But those who knew his family and their involvement in politics and social welfare, and the company they kept, were not at all surprised by this precociousness in the young boy. They knew that this was a natural outcome of the influences that he had been exposed to.

Bhagat Singh had been in school in Banga for about five years. It was the season of the monsoons and again the rain was extremely heavy and came down in sheets. On one such day, when the bell rang for the school give over, it was pouring heavily outside. At the sound of the bell, the boys rose to their feet, snatched up their bags, and made to tear out of

33

their classroom and away from the school as all children do when school gives over. But the teacher was not willing to let them go into the pouring rain and risk catching cold.

"Where are you off to?" he shouted across the noise that the boys were making. The boys fell silent. "Sit down," he said in a quieter voice. "I am still in class and you must wait for me to leave." The boys sat down reluctantly and if there were groans and moans of protest they were too quiet and subdued to attract the teacher's attention. In any case, the history teacher, a seemingly harmless looking Sardar gentleman with a flowing salt and pepper beard and an untidy turban, was a strict disciplinarian, and all the boys knew from personal experience that he brooked no opposition to his order from the children placed in his care.

"I will hold you till the rain stops." The boys looked with one accord towards the windows and then exchanged apprehensive glances—it seemed to them that the rain would never stop and they would be stuck in the school room with this tyrant for the rest of the day. They settled back in their seats, sure that he would set them some tedious and difficult written work to fill up the time. But to their pleasant surprise he smiled at them and said, "Don't worry, I am not going to ask you to do some more work—you have done enough work for the day." He paused, thought for a while, and then said, "Each of you will tell me what you want to do when you grow up."

Each child in turn rose to his feet and, as clearly as such a young child could, voiced his ambition for his future. One child wanted to be a police officer, another wanted to join the army. One wanted to be a judge; another, a doctor. Each of them when asked the reason for his choice had more or less the same answer; they hoped to gain prestige, status, and a comfortable income by following their chosen profession.

FORMATIVE YEARS

When Bhagat Singh's turn came, he said in a firm, clear voice, "Sir, I don't yet know what I want to be when I grow up. But whatever it is I decide to do, it must contribute to my people and the good of my country." His answer was greeted with pin drop silence. Even the teacher displayed signs of uneasiness and discomfort in coming face to face with such maturity in one so young. To someone who did not know Bhagat Singh and his family, the answer would sound like something that the child had picked up from an adult at home and parroted in class. But the teacher and the other boys in the class knew Bhagat Singh well and many of them knew his family. They were aware of his reflective nature and were familiar with his ability to think way beyond his years. To them Bhagat Singh's answer seemed the most natural of answers and yet it left them feeling insecure and uncomfortable because it gave them an awareness of their own inadequacies, a sense of being far behind him. In his school circle, his premature sobriety and maturity were well recognised and it was acknowledged, often openly, that the boy was destined for great things when he grew up, that he was born to be a leader of men.

Bhagat Singh's father, Kishan Singh was at this time very involved in political activities as well as activities connected with social welfare. The impetus that had been provided when he worked to bring relief to victims of natural disasters spilled over into everyday life and continued to be the centre of his existence. He had realised over the years that to contribute to both politics and social welfare, he would have to, sooner or later, move to Lahore, which had become the hub for both these areas of activity in the Punjab. And opportunity came his way in 1916 when Bhagat Singh was nine years old. Kishan Singh secured an appointment as an agent with the Prudential Insurance Company, which involved his moving to Lahore. He set up residence in the Nehran Kot area of Lahore and

35

when Bhagat Singh completed his primary education at the district primary school in Banga, it was considered appropriate that he too, should move to Lahore for the next stage of his schooling.

Once again the young boy's mind and heart were besieged with conflicting thoughts and feelings at the prospect of having to leave Banga and move to Lahore. Banga was the place where he had been born and where he had grown up. It was the place where he had first been introduced to the joys of learning and reading. It was the only home that he had known. It was also the place which was home to his revered and adored grandfather, Arjun Singh. In many ways Arjun Singh had been the true anchor of Bhagat Singh's young life. It was Arjun Singh who had inculcated in the boy a supreme sense of self confidence, a proclivity to free and independent thinking, and a desire to be useful to his country and to his countrymen. Arjun Singh had, through the books he recommended to the boy, opened up to him the world of the thoughts of great men, especially of freedom fighters like Lala Hardyal, Sufi Amba, and his own uncle, Ajit Singh. Through a free exposure to the discussions with freedom fighters and revolutionaries that took place in his home, Arjun Singh gave him a first-hand experience of the revolutionary fervour that was sweeping the country. And above all, he had given the boy not only moral and ethical strength but also a very high degree of emotional strength. Bhagat was also loath to part from his aunt Harnam Kaur. It was she who, through her own need for emotional comfort, had stirred the sensitivity to the suffering of others that was to be the corner stone of his life. She it was too, who had lifted the little child on to her lap and regaled him with stories not only of his own uncle's resistance to British imperialism but also to the exploits of the other freedom fighters; stories that had aroused in the

FORMATIVE YEARS

young boy's heart strong and unabated indignation at what the British were doing to India and a burning determination to get India her freedom.

At the same time, as a true Punjabi, even as a young boy, he couldn't help but be excited at the prospect of going to Lahore. For all Punjabis the fabled city of Lahore is like a Mecca that must be visited at least once in a lifetime. Legend has woven innumerable stories around Maharaja Ranjeet Singh's capital city, some true, some totally apocryphal. In the Sikh psyche it represents everything that was glorious and wonderful and strong about their empire. In the modern context, Lahore had become not only the political and cultural capital of North India but also the epicentre of most revolutionary movement and activities. Finally the little boy also knew and understood that for the fulfilment of his father's dream the move to Lahore was absolutely necessary.

As the day for departure approached, the conflict in his heart and mind became more and more acute. Arjun Singh watched his once open and cheerful grandson becoming withdrawn and restless, and understood, as he understood most of the boy's troubles, the reason for this change. He knew that the boy was dependent upon him for some kind of resolution of the conflict that was churning within him. So over the rest of the boy's sojourn in Banga, the grandfather insisted that the boy accompany him daily to a post-dinner walk. Unlike earlier times when there was always a friend or two accompanying him, the old man chose to be alone with his grandson. And unlike his usual practice of stopping at a friend's place to indulge in a group session, Arjun Singh chose to stop at a *kotha* that had been built in the middle of his fields next to a well, a mile or two away from his home. Here the two would sit on a string cot and linger on in the dusk, well after darkness had gathered around them. With a sensitivity born ✕

out of a deep understanding of his grandson's personality, Arjun Singh chose to let the boy choose the moment of broaching the troubles of his mind and heart. As a result, the first few days produced little more than an uncomfortable silence between the two, interspersed by brief snatches of completely inane and inconsequential conversation. But once the routine of their evening walk had been established and the boy knew that he would be alone with his grandfather, as naturally as he had clasped his grandfather's hand on that first anxious day to school, he opened up his heart and gave word to all the troubles that lay in it. Arjun Singh listened patiently, offering only the briefest of comments because he knew that if the child unburdened his heart and mind as completely as possible it would be much easier for him to come to terms with his situation. And so it was, that first in bits and pieces and then in long rambling monologues, Bhagat Singh gave voice not only to his anxiety at leaving home and the sense of impending loss at being separated from the people he loved with all his heart, but also to his excitement at the prospect of all the possibilities that lay ahead of him in Lahore. One by one all his doubts and misgivings came out in the open and, just as his grandfather had known would happen, once they had been given voice to they no longer had the magnitude they possessed while they had been kept sealed within him. What was left of them was scaled down even further by the gentle but firm reassurance that the grandfather provided through his affectionate words. Lahore was not so far from Banga, they could meet each other as often as they wished, the old man said, putting his arms around the boy's shoulder. In any case Bhagat Singh would be coming home for all his school vacations and his grandfather and aunt would come to meet him in Lahore after every harvest, when there was lull in farm activity. His father would find greater happiness and

FORMATIVE YEARS

satisfaction, a greater scope for his work in Lahore than he could ever find in Banga.

"You are extremely fortunate," Arjun Singh said. "Other boys have only one home. You will now have two homes."

The grandfather dwelt at length on the wonderful opportunities that the boy would have both for academic and other pursuits in Lahore, which he would be denied if he remained in Banga. He described vividly the architectural and artistic splendour of the city. He described the colour and richness of the bazaars and the variety of street foods available in such vivid detail that Bhagat Singh could almost savour all the smells and tastes. Arjun Singh described the rich cultural tradition of the capital city. He talked about some of the leading literary figures who had made the city their home, and the wealth of books that were available in the libraries like the Dwarkadas Library. Above all, he described how wonderful Bhagat Singh's new school was; the Dayanand Anglo-Vedic School was considered one of the leading educational institutions in North India. Gradually, as the evening sessions rolled one into the other, the boy felt the uneasiness and anxiety that had consumed him slip away from him and found himself gripped only with anticipation of the heady, ecstatic phase ahead.

The last few days together were the culmination of the bonding between the two and it was during these days that Arjun Singh thought it appropriate to open up and offer the little boy some extremely valuable advice; advice that Bhagat Singh would hold close to his heart and follow as strictly as he could in what remained of his short life. "Do you remember the day you had to stay on in school because it was raining so heavily?" his grandfather asked him one day. Bhagat nodded. "Your history teacher asked you what you wanted to be when you grew up. Do you remember what you told him?" "How

39

SHAHEED BHAGAT SINGH

do you know about that? Who told you?" the little boy asked in surprise, because his grandfather had never before let him know that he had heard about that incident.

"Never mind," Arjun Singh said, reaching out and touching his grandson's cheek. "Do you remember what you said?"

Again Bhagat Singh nodded his head.

"You said, 'Sir, I don't know what I want to be when I grow up, but whatever it is I decide to do, it must contribute to the welfare of my people and the good of my country.' No one taught you that. Young as you are, you decided on it yourself. How you arrived at this decision, I cannot say. Perhaps it was listening to all the freedom fighters and revolutionaries who visited our home, perhaps it came from some very serious reading you have been doing. Perhaps it came from setting up your father and your uncle as your role models and aspiring to follow in their footsteps. Whatever the reason for your decision, I hope that having arrived at it so early in life, you will abide by it always."

On another day Arjun Singh told his grandson, "All that is of value to you in life and all that you hold most dear, you have learnt outside the classroom. What you have learnt in school is important because not only will this help you in getting employment but it also teaches you about the world at large. But all the lessons that are important in your day to day life are lessons that you have to learn for yourself. You have been good at following this process of self education and you must remember to follow it for all your life." Bhagat Singh did take this advice to heart and all through his life, and even till the very end, as we have seen, he continued the process of self education.

There were other long conversations that took place between the two and in all of them Arjun Singh re-emphasised various aspects of Bhagat Singh's upbringing and the values

40

FORMATIVE YEARS

he had imbibed, values that were so dear to his faith and to his family. He took the little boy back all the way to his great-grandfather's time, the life Fateh Singh had lived, the path that he had always followed: putting principles always before material wealth and comfort, always championing the cause of the oppressed and supporting the fight for righteousness and truth. He led the boy through his own life and the life that all his family had lived, where equality of all men irrespective of caste or creed was not a mere concept to be preached, but had been practised every moment of their lives as living reality.

Lahore was everything that his grandfather had said it would be and more. The first few days before he joined school were heady days. The very air exuded an aura of excitement and liveliness. The boy was overwhelmed with the richness he saw all around him. There was a pulsating whirl of activity everywhere, which was in sharp contrast to the leisurely, easy going lifestyle of Banga. As a young boy Bhagat Singh was caught up in the excitement and the novelty of his new surroundings and found that he did not miss his home and his family with the sadness that he had anticipated. Then when he joined school a few days later a sense of balance returned. His new school too, was exactly as his grandfather had said it would be. The Dayanand Anglo-Vedic Sanskrit School, situated on Mohan Lal road was indeed a very special school. S. R. Bakshi, writes in *Struggle for Independence: Bhagat Singh*, that by the time Bhagat Singh joined this school it had established its reputation as one of the premier educational institutions of the northern region in India. It was a well-deserved and well-earned reputation. Realising that the strength of the school came primarily from the strength of its faculty, the management insured that a very strict recruitment procedure was followed. All the teachers without exception were highly

SHAHEED BHAGAT SINGH

qualified and well trained with sufficient experience in the field of teaching. The management recognised the need for the teachers to constantly upgrade not only their knowledge but also their teaching skill. To ensure this, even in those days, the management invited eminent educationists to deliver talks to the faculty. They also gave their teachers opportunities to interact as much as possible with teachers of other outstanding educational institutions to ensure a constant exchange of thoughts and infusion of new ideas. The teachers were paid well and their problems, both personal and professional, were attended to with a great deal of compassion and sympathy. As a result, they were not only highly competitive in their field but were also extremely motivated. This resulted over a period of time in a situation where most of the leaders of Punjab, both in the freedom struggle and in the administration, were former students of the school. It was not surprising then that there were a large number of children both from among the very rich and the middle class, who were desirous of gaining admission to this school. Bhagat Singh found the first few days in his new school rather intimidating and very different from his first few days in his school in Banga. There most of the teachers had been family friends and even those who were not knew of Arjun Singh and his son and had great respect and admiration for them. In Lahore, the teachers were total strangers and if any of them had heard of the family, it was only as a passing reference to their contribution to the anti-colonisation agitation of 1906-1907. In Banga many of his classmates had been friends and acquaintances. Here in Lahore he was a total stranger and especially at the beginning, the other boys took pains to bring this fact home to him. The boys in the school in Banga had all come from rural and semi-rural backgrounds and had been rather simple and rustic in their speech and manner. In Lahore almost all the students were

42

FORMATIVE YEARS

from a rich urban background with a veneer of sophistication in their speech and manner, which Bhagat Singh found a little unnerving. Most of all, Bhagat Singh found himself a little ill at ease with the attitude of the teachers. In Banga the teachers had all been rather easy going and undemanding, tolerating casualness in the students' attitude to study. The errant boys were rarely punished for not keeping up with their work. In Lahore the teachers, though friendly and affectionate, were extremely demanding and exacting when it came to their expectations from their students towards academics. No laziness or shirking was tolerated and those erring in this direction were dealt with severely. It was quite common for the parents to be summoned to the school in connection with their child's poor performance.

After his initial apprehensions and doubts regarding his ability to adjust to the new environment, Bhagat Singh soon saw everything falling into place. His innate cheerfulness, his inherent qualities of leadership, and his skill in games soon broke through the wall of reserve that the Lahore boys had built between him and them. He found that he was soon as popular with all the other students as he had been in the school in Banga. With his natural interest in books, his sense of discipline, and his ability to work hard, he won the respect and admiration of his teachers. After the initial hesitation he found himself at par with most of the other boys who had been in the school far longer. He found himself enjoying the greater challenges that life in his new school offered. Within a few months it was as if he had always been there and the other students and the teachers would often forget that he had joined the school only a few months earlier. A short while after Bhagat Singh joined the school, it was upgraded to a secondary school with classes now going up to the matriculation level. Bhagat Singh realised that he was indeed very fortunate to

SHAHEED BHAGAT SINGH

have been admitted to this wonderful institution and worked exceptionally hard to justify his admission.

A postcard written to his grandfather on 22 July 1918, when he was only eleven years old, bears testimony to the fact that he was applying himself diligently to his school work. His sixth class examinations had concluded recently and results of some subjects had been declared. He tells his grandfather that he had scored 110 marks in Sanskrit, a subject his grandfather had asked him to pay particular attention to, and 68 in English. He adds that he had studied hard for the examination and hoped that his result in other subjects would be satisfactory too. The postcard is written in Urdu, which was the medium of instruction at the time. English was introduced very late in the non-English medium schools. Recognising the importance of both these languages, Bhagat Singh applied himself to learning English and as his writing bears witness, he was more than proficient in the language by the time he turned to revolutionary activities.

Even in Lahore, away from his grandfather, Bhagat Singh never forgot the advice that his grandfather had given him during those final days together. In addition to his studies in school, he listened attentively to the discussions that took place in his home when freedom fighters came to visit his father. He spent a lot of time reading books which praised activities of patriots and nationalists both in India and abroad. Bhagat Singh was a boy of tidy habits and every day when he finished studying he would carefully put his books away. But one night, when he had been reading till very late, he forgot to put his book away. In the morning, in his hurry to go to school, he again left his books lying on his table, one of them open at the page he was reading. After he had left for school, his mother came to tidy up his room and found the books on his table. She looked closely at them and realised that

FORMATIVE YEARS

they were not connected with his studies in school. She was particularly surprised at the notes that he had been making from the books. When he came home in the evening she came in to his room with his customary glass of milk. But where she usually left this on his table and went away, she now sat down on his cot and he knew that she wanted to talk to him about something. "What is it, Mother?" he asked when he had finished his milk.

She got up from the bed and pulled out the books from his bookshelf. "I found these books on your table this morning and I know they are not connected with your studies in school."

"They are about the lives of great men who fought for the freedom of their countries," he replied.

His mother sighed; the family had seen enough results of the active participation of so many of its members in anti-government activities. She was afraid that her son would follow in these footsteps and there would be more suffering for him and for the family. "Why do you sigh, Mother?"

"I worry that the reading is only a beginning. I worry that you will be inspired and motivated to follow their example and this will bring great suffering to yourself. I am afraid that when you are grown up you will be involved in anti-government activities and might even have to go to jail."

Bhagat Singh embraced his mother and said, "As Fateh Singh's great grandson, as Arjun Singh's grandson, as Kishan Singh's son and as Ajit Singh's nephew can there be any other way for me?" Vidyavati had no answer to this but after that day, much as she worried about her son's future, she accepted the inevitability of the course that his life would take.

Two of the strongest influences on Bhagat Singh during these early years were those of the Ghadar Movement and the Jallianwala Bagh massacre.

45

The Ghadar Movement was the brain child of a group of expatriate Indians living in the United States and Canada, who, as Indians, wanted to contribute to the cause of India's freedom. Unlike other anti-British movements of the time, the Ghadar Party was from its very inception clear that the only way to free India from the clutches of British rule was through the use of militant force. The impetus to the movement and to the process of uniting Indians living abroad was provided by Sohan Singh Bhokia, Lala Hardyal, Bhai Kesar Singh, Bhai Parmanand and Pandit Kansiram. On 13 April 1913, Baisakhi day, a meeting was organised at Astoria in Oregon and the Hindustan Association of the Pacific Coast came into existence. This was the precursor of the Ghadar Party. At the inaugural meeting all agreed that the objectives of the association would be to end British rule in India through the use of an armed revolution, following closely the methods adopted by the Bolsheviks during the Russian Revolution. When the association evolved into the Ghadar Party a few months later, the manifesto of the new party reiterated the same objectives in very clear terms: "What is our name? Ghadar. What is our work? Ghadar. Where will Ghadar break out? In India. The time will come when rifles and blood will take place of pen and ink."

The headquarters of the party were located at Yugantar Ashram, San Francisco. The party published a periodical also called *Ghadar* edited by Lala Hardyal. This was published in Urdu, Hindi, Punjabi, Marathi and Bengali. The first issue of the magazine carried under its mast head, the sub title "Enemy of the British". It was widely circulated among Indians living not only in India but also abroad.

The Ghadar Party advocated the separation of religion and politics. All discussion on religion was strictly prohibited. Members were free to practise their own religion as long

FORMATIVE YEARS

as they did not try to force their religious belief on other members. They believed that the corner stone on which free India would rest would be the stone of communal harmony.

The Ghadarites, as immigrants to America, had faced at first hand the harsh realities of not only class exploitation but also racial discrimination. As a result, their commitment to the belief that all men are equal was complete and unqualified. They rejected outright not only the concept of untouchability but all forms of discrimination. The dream of the Ghadarites was to establish a free India where equality of all citizens would be ensured and practised. Their belief in the equality of all men extended to the sphere of economics as well.

In the strong anti-imperialist stand the Ghadar Party adopted, they revealed an outlook which, with hindsight, we could term as being truly international or global. They appealed to right thinking people in all the countries of the world to unite in the effort to overthrow once and for all the system of imperialistic exploitation which had for centuries been ravaging a major part of the world. The party appealed to their brother Indians who were serving in the British army not to fight in wars which the British were waging in other parts of the world in order to extend their colonial domination. One of the Ghadarite poets wrote:

> Oh brother, do not fight a war against the Chinese.
> The people of Hind, China and Turkey are real brothers.
> The enemy should not be allowed to besmirch the brotherhood.
> (Quoted by Sohan Singh Josh, *Hindustan Gadar Party: A Short History*, Volume 2, p. 193)

The actual rebellion of the Ghadar Party can be said to have started with the famous "Komagata Maru" incident which occurred in 1914 on the eve of the outbreak of the First World

War. Baba Gurdit Singh, a prominent leader of the Ghadar Party, chartered the Japanese merchant ship Komagata Maru to sail from Hong Kong to Canada with 376 would-be Indian immigrants, mostly Sikhs, aboard. This ship became the first visible symbol of revolution. When it docked in Vancouver it was cordoned off. The Canadian authorities ruled that only 22 passengers would be allowed to set foot on Canadian soil. The others did not have the right to land. Baba Gurdit Singh was told that contrary to the procedure governing merchant ships, he would have to pay the charter dues in one lump sum. He pointed out that under the Canadian law he was permitted to pay the dues after selling his cargo. The authorities refused to relent. The Indian committees in Canada came together to demand and agitate for the release of the ship. The unfairness of the demands of the Canadian authorities caused many Canadians to come to the support of the Indians.

For two months a cold war persisted between Canadian government on one side and Baba Gurdit Singh and the Ghadar Party on the other. The Canadian government refused to relent and the passengers refused to turn back. The incident captured the imagination of the media and all newspapers and news reels of the time carried images of the ship accompanied by loud glaring headlines and dramatic commentary. The incident was discussed and re-discussed in political forums all over the world. Baba Gurdit Singh had succeeded in drawing the attention of the world and focusing it not only on the evils of the British imperial rule in India but also on the efforts of his party to free the country of this rule. Frustrated by the unfairness of the Canadian authorities and their discrimination against the Indians, there was a strong wave of sympathy for the Indian cause. Fitzgerald, a Canadian socialist, gave voice to this sympathy when he called upon the Indians: "Get up and arm yourselves and fight to regain liberty. Inspire your countrymen to return and sweep all the whites out of India" (Quoted by Kuldip Nayar, *Without Fear: The Life and Trial of Bhagat Singh*, p. 53).

It was a cry that Bhagat Singh was to repeat often in later years to his fellow freedom fighters. To the eternal shame of the viceroy in Delhi, he made no effort on behalf of the stranded passengers to procure permission for them to land in Vancouver, nor did he utter a single word to express his sympathy for their suffering.

Eventually, fed up of the glare that was focused upon them from all corners of the world and the hostility that was building up against the unfairness of their stand especially amongst their own citizens, the Canadian authorities trained the harbour guns on the ship and forced it to turn back. The ship was refused permission to berth at Hong Kong and Singapore where most of the would-be immigrants had their home and was finally allowed to dock at the Budge Budge Harbour near Calcutta.

But the Komagata Maru incident did not end there. There were two other far reaching scenes to unfold. In Vancouver, the Canadian government had hired William Hopkinson as immigration inspector and interpreter. Hopkinson had been in service with the Calcutta police force, spoke Hindi fluently, and could speak Punjabi quite well. As a result, he was ideally suited for this role. Unfortunately, Hopkinson's role was soon extended and he began using his expertise with the two Indian languages to monitor the activities of Indian extremists living in British Columbia. Within a short span of time he had developed a network of pro-British Sikh informants who spied on the activities of the revolutionaries and reported back to him. He passed the information on to the authorities. After the Komagata Maru incident, based on his familiarity with Indian immigrants, Hopkinson was called upon to testify in court against the ideology and activities of the Ghadar Party, which would provide the authorities with some justification for turning away the ship. While he waited in court, Mawa Singh, a *granthi* from a local gurudwara shot him dead, a small act of revenge on behalf of the Ghadar Party.

When the ship docked at Calcutta it was subjected to a thorough search for arms. Contrary to the rumours spread by the British and the Canadian authorities, there were no arms on board. The passengers were herded like cattle to a waiting train. Some of them asked for permission to deposit a copy of the *Granth Sahib* they were carrying in the local gurudwara. The permission was denied. The passengers formed a procession and forced their way through the police cordon. The police opened fire; eighteen persons were killed, many more injured, and two hundred were arrested and jailed. Baba Gurdit Singh and a few others escaped. The newspapers once again highlighted the incident which resulted in sympathy for the victims and anger at the British for mowing down harmless unarmed civilians. Since most of the victims were from the Punjab, there was strong anger and resentment there and it seemed as though insurgency would erupt at any time.

The Komagata Maru incident provided the spark to ignite the smouldering anger that Indians living abroad had for long harboured against the British rule in India. The anger now burst into flames and was waiting to be converted into positive action. An opportunity for this was provided by the outbreak of the World War. The Ghadarites realised that, preoccupied as they would be in their war efforts, the British would be in a vulnerable position in India. Taking advantage of the high pitch, to which anti-British feelings had been raised, the Ghadarites exhorted their countrymen to return to India to support the revolt against the British which now seemed certain. Thousands of Indians, especially Punjabis, living abroad, caught the first ship to India.

Though the time seemed ripe to strike a decisive blow against the British, the Ghadar Party was hampered by the fact that it did not have a leader of the stature that the situation demanded. In the aftermath of the killing of Hopkinson, there was a reaction against the party. The secretary-general of the party, Hardyal, had been disowned as an anarchist in San Francisco and had fled to Switzerland to escape arrest. Sohan Singh and Kartar Singh had already left for India. It was left to Ram Chandar, who Hardyal had appointed, to try and provide some direction to the party. He called upon all Indians to return to India and assemble in Moga in Punjab. He said, "Your duty is clear. Go to India. Stir up rebellion in every corner of the country. Rob the wealthy and show mercy to the poor. In this way gain unusual sympathy. Arms will be provided to you on arrival in India. Failing this you must ransack the police station for rifles. Obey without hesitation the command of your leaders" (Quoted by Kuldip Nayar, *Without Fear: The Life and Trial of Bhagat Singh*, p. 55).

Batches of Indians from San Francisco returned to India in Japanese ships. Most of them were arrested as soon as the ship docked. The few who escaped managed to reach Moga. The Ghadarites whose ships docked in southern India fared better. Most of them were able to evade arrest and made their way to the Punjab. The Ghadarites and their sympathisers who were returning to India from the East, from Hong Kong, China, Japan, Borneo and the Philippines, were able to make contact with the Indian troops serving in the area. That this did influence some of these troops was borne out by the response from the 26th Punjab Regiment stationed in Singapore, which revolted against the British commander. Unfortunately there was no co-ordination with the other Indian regiments and the

British were able to crush the rebellion before it spread to other units. By this time, the British were alarmed by the report of the great number of Ghadarites who were able to make their way to the Punjab in spite of the strong vigilance on the part of the police. On 19 March 1915 the British government passed the Defence of India Act. This Act gave extraordinary power to all civil and military authorities with regard to the entry and residence of anyone in the area of jurisdiction. If they had the slightest suspicion that the person concerned was likely to act in a manner, which might endanger public safety they could prohibit his entry and residence in any area and also restrict him to a specified area. By making full use of this new Act the authorities arrested and deported thousands of Ghadarites and suspected Ghadarites. Some of these were even killed.

In the face of this large scale repression, the movement faltered. In the absence of a strong leadership there was also a vacuum as far as any planned strategy of the movement was concerned. Realising this shortcoming, the Ghadarites turned to Rash Behari Bose to assume the leadership of their party. He was a well known Bengali revolutionary who had shifted home from Calcutta to Lahore. Seeing the tremendous opportunity, Bose accepted the leadership. From this point in time Bose and N. G. Pingle were behind the planning and execution of all the programmes of the party. They followed a two-pronged strategy. The first section of the Ghadarites would commit as many acts of violence as possible against the establishment. The second section of the party workers was to fan out and establish contact with Indian soldiers in all the major military cantonments located in the Punjab, like Ferozepur, Rawalpindi and Lahore, and incite them to rebel. In order to succeed, it had to be a well co-ordinated rebellion. The first section of the party was very successful in letting

FORMATIVE YEARS

loose a wave of terror directed against British authorities and those who worked for them. They raided arsenals, killed police men who had committed atrocities on the Ghadarites, derailed trains and committed a number of dacoities. In order to collect funds for these activities they robbed banks. They also set up factories in Amritsar and Jhabal, near Ludhiana, to manufacture bombs. Sir Michael O'Dwyer, lieutenant-governor of the Punjab at that time was later to admit in his autobiography, *India as I Knew It*: "Back by early 1915, Punjab had become the centre of Ghadarite activities and they had come to pose a big challenge to the authority of the government."

The second section of the Ghadarite workers set up anti-British secret cells in almost all the cantonments of the Punjab. They were also able to motivate the Indian soldiers stationed at Meerut, Allahabad and Lucknow to support the cause. 21 February 1915 was fixed as the General Uprising Day. On this day, the 23rd Cavalry stationed at Lahore was to shoot all the British officers, capture the armoury and the arsenal, and distribute the arms and ammunition among the revolutionaries. The successful completion of this revolt, which was not expected to take more than a few hours, would be a signal to all the other cantonments to follow suit. The revolt had been organised and planned extremely well, and would, in the normal course of events be successful enough to shake the British control in India. But it was doomed to failure because of that oldest military failing, treachery from within. Kirpal Singh Brar, respected member of the inner circle of the party, had been bought over by the British almost from the time he had joined the party. As a result, all vital information was passed on to the British authorities and they were able to take three pre-emptive steps well in time. The information that Kirpal Singh was not able to give the British

53

SHAHEED BHAGAT SINGH

was provided by Mula Singh, one of the local level Ghadarites who was picked up by the police. Under interrogation he told the police everything he knew, Armed with the information from these two sources, the British moved to first disarm and disband the regiments that had committed themselves to revolt. The ring leaders were all court-martialled and either imprisoned or shot. Then acting with amazing swiftness, the police swooped in similar fashion on a number of places and arrested thousands of Ghadarites. A large number of these were awarded life sentences and transported to the Andamans, Mandalay and other high security prisons. Many of them succumbed to the intense physical torture they were subjected to while in police custody. Still others just disappeared and were never heard of again. By the time the monsoon broke in the Punjab in 1915, the whole movement had been crushed. According to the official figures released at the time, "One hundred and forty five Ghadarites were hanged or killed, three hundred and six were sentenced to transportation for life, seventy seven to lesser period of imprisonment, three hundred were detained without trial and as many as 2455 were interred in their villages." Though the mutiny in the army was nipped in the bud, the influence that the Ghadarites had been able to wield in the army was tremendous. "Of the 145, who were hanged or killed, 62 were army men and out of those sentenced to transportation for life 190 were army men" (Harkrishan Singh Surjit, *Lessons of Punjab*, p. 52).

On 16-17 November 1915, the Ghadar Party chapter in the history of the Indian freedom struggle was finally closed with the hanging of six Ghadarites in what has come to be called the *First Lahore Conspiracy* case. The hanging rocked Punjab, and Kartar Singh Sarabha, at eighteen the youngest of those hanged, immediately became a national hero.

Bhagat Singh was immensely moved by the courage and

FORMATIVE YEARS

sacrifice of the young man and came to look upon him as a role model. He referred to him often as his "mentor, brother and friend". At some point during this period he took to always carrying a small photograph of Sarabha. His mother once found this photograph in his pocket when she was taking his clothes to be washed. She had seen Sarabha once when he had come to her husband for financial support and she recognised him now in the photograph. But she could not understand why her son was carrying his photograph in his pocket. When she questioned him about this he replied, "He is everything that I want to be." Vidyavati felt a chill run up her spine. She thought of Sarabha's death and wondered if her son was preparing for a similar fate.

In 1928, when Bhagat Singh wrote a short, high spirited, and moving biography of his hero, he stressed the fact that before his hanging Sarabha had been totally fearless and had refused to relent from his stand against the British in any way.

In March 1921, when Bhagat Singh, Sukhdev, and Bhagwati Vohra, founded the Naujawan Bharat Sabha, the proceedings of the inaugural session began with the unveiling of Sarabha's portrait. "Kartar Singh Sarabha has said, 'Our struggle will continue as long as a handful of men be they foreign or native, or both in collaboration with each other, continue to exploit the labour and resources of our people. Nothing shall deter us from this path.' This was in many ways to be the beacon that guided Bhagat Singh throughout his remarkable life" (P. M. S. Grewal, *Bhagat Singh: Liberation's Blazing Star*, p. 28).

What chiefly attracted Bhagat Singh to the Ghadar Party was its secular character, which made a clear cut distinction between politics and religion and propagated that the two should never be allowed to mix. Many of the members of the Ghadar Party moved to form the core of the new Babbar Akali Movement which was to mount a murderous campaign

SHAHEED BHAGAT SINGH

along Ghadar lines in Jalandhar, Ludhiana and Hoshiyarpur. Bhagat Singh was to publish an article on the heroism and glorious sacrifices of the Babbar Akalis in the *Partap* on 15 March 1926. He expressed his admiration for the oath taken by the Babbar Khalsa to sacrifice all in the service of the country and to die fighting.

With its anti-imperialist outlook and the great sacrifices its members made, the Ghadar Party laid the foundation for the rise of the left group parties, which set out more clearly the ideology that the Ghadar Party had formulated. Many of the Ghadarites went on to join the Workers and Peasants Party and the Communist Party. In the light of this progression, it is understandable why Bhagat Singh in later years came to have such a deep interest in Marxism and Lenin. A more immediate influence on the course of action that Bhagat Singh chose to follow was the Jallianwala Bagh massacre.

The early years of the twentieth century had seen rising discontent against the British in India. The discontent was particularly active in the Punjab. The end of the war had resulted in a steep rise in prices, especially of food grains. A large number of soldiers who had been discharged from the army at the end of the war were left without a means of livelihood. There had been war time taxation, which had added to the burden and suffering of the people. The relationship between the British bureaucrats and the Indians was coloured by racial hostility and deep distrust. The Punjab government had over the years established a tradition for ruthless governance, which was nourished by the policies followed by Sir John Lawrence, Sir Denzil Ibbetson, and Michael O'Dwyer.

During the war the government of India had enforced the Defence of India Rules according to which the authorities were entitled to take extreme steps to enforce law and order.

56

FORMATIVE YEARS

In spite of this, the moderate leaders who were in the majority had pledged support to the British in their war efforts, in the hope that in return the British would make some concession to the Indian aspiration for greater role in self governance. These hopes proved to be futile because even while the war was drawing to a close and as the limit of the Defence of India Rules was ending, the government looked for ways and means to continue with similar repressive measures. In 1918, the government of India appointed a Sedition Committee to consider what means could be taken to counteract revolutionary activities in India. On the recommendation of this committee, two bills were introduced which were as repressive as the Defence of India Rules. These came to be better known as the Rowlatt Act. According to the provision of this Act, any person suspected of criminal conspiracy connected with the revolutionary movement in India, could be arrested and imprisoned without trial for an indefinite period of time or could be sentenced to an indefinite period of imprisonment after a secret trial. In other words, the authorities were free to pick up any one they chose and imprison him without permitting him legal help of any kind. As was to be expected, this Act aroused deep resentment and anger among the Indians. There were wide spread protests and demonstrations. People, irrespective of their caste, creed, or community, came together in an unprecedented show of unity to oppose the Act. Gandhiji threatened satyagraha if the Act was not repealed. The centre of the storm of protest against the Rowlatt Act was Amritsar. Peaceful demonstrations were held on 30 March and 6 April in the city. On Ram Navmi, 9 April 1919, a procession was taken out through the more important streets of Amritsar and according to the report of the Hunter Committee, which was later set up to enquire into the Jallianwala Bagh massacre,

SHAHEED BHAGAT SINGH

Muslims in large numbers came out to participate in what was essentially a Hindu function. Tempers were high and there were a few incidents of mob fury expressing itself by causing damage to government buildings and property, which alarmed the authorities. Dr. Saifuddin Kitchlew and Dr. Satya Pal, two prominent leaders from Amritsar, were detained and taken to an unknown detention centre, which only served to incense the people even further.

On 10 April 1919, people turned out in large numbers to protest against the arrest and detention of their leaders. It was a peaceful demonstration, but the numbers were so large that the British authorities panicked and resorted to firing on the mob. All hell broke loose; the mob turned violent and attacked post offices, banks, the railway station and even the town hall. Five Englishmen were killed by the mob. As the news spread to other towns and cities, they too were convulsed by disturbances. The disturbances were particularly severe in Amritsar, Lahore, Gujranwala, Gujrat and Layallpur. O'Dwyer, the lieutenant-governor of Punjab, realised that the situation was rapidly springing out of control. Martial law was declared by which civil authority in the Punjab was transferred to the army. Brigadier General Reginald Dyer was given control of Amritsar. He had been born in Shimla and through his long association with the country would have been expected to understand the psyche of the people and to have shown some consideration. But he displayed British contempt for Indians. It is said that he harboured a particularly strong grudge against the people of Amritsar and an opportunity to display his authority came his way soon enough—in a matter of just three days.

13 April 1919 was Baisakhi, a very important day for all Punjabis. It was the harvest festival but it was also a day, which marked the birth of the Khalsa. It was a day which

58

FORMATIVE YEARS

was sacred to both the Hindus and the Sikhs. Like Diwali
and Holi, it embraced people of all religious communities
and castes in the Punjab. As a result every one turned out
to celebrate the festival and rejoice through song and dance
at the abundant harvest they had reaped. 1919 had yielded
a particularly rich harvest and it is said that the strong smell
of *snogra* and *sarson* pervaded even the streets of Amritsar.
There was usually a big *mela* held on the outskirts of the city.
This year, however, the air was thick with discontent, anger
and hostility. As a precautionary measure, General Dyer had
declared all assemblies of people unlawful. Unfortunately the
declaration had come only three days prior to the festival and
there had not been enough time for the order to reach all the
people, especially the ones living outside the city limits. As a
result, the people descended as usual by the thousands to take
part in the celebration. The centre of the gathering was at
the Jallianwala Bagh. It was not really a *bagh* in the traditional
sense of the term, but a large open rectangular ground. There
were no trees or bushes. There was a high wall all around
the ground. There was one main gate and one or two small
entrances. There was an unused well on the property. By mid-
morning almost twenty thousand people had collected there.
The people from nearby villages, dressed in their best clothes,
had come to see the sites, to visit the nearby Golden Temple
and then go to the *mela*. They were a little disappointed to find
that the usual gaiety which marked the occasion was missing.
They joined unhappy disgruntled city folk who had assembled
to listen to their leaders as they explained the implications of
the terrible Act. It was Hansraj who was addressing the crowd
when Dyer decided to swing into action.

It was a carefully co-ordinated and particularly brutal course
of action. In Kuldip Nayar's words, "Dyer set the police on
the gathering like the hunter unchaining his ferocious hounds

59

SHAHEED BHAGAT SINGH

to bring the pursued animals to bay." All exits to the Bagh had been sealed off. The point that Dyer chose for the action was higher than the rest of the ground. While Hansraj was addressing the crowd, Dyer led two files of soldiers into the Bagh through the narrow lane on the Jallianwala Bazaar side of the ground. The soldiers were mainly Gurkhas and Baluchis; perhaps Dyer felt they would feel no affinity for their victims.

There were some English soldiers with them as well. Without any warning the soldiers opened fire at the crowd of innocent men, women and children. At this stage they aimed above the crowd. Hansraj, like many others, did not believe that even the British could be so brutal. He called upon his listeners to stay calm and not panic, saying, "They are only firing blanks."

This remark angered Dyer and he called upon his soldiers to fire down into the crowd. The soldiers reacted to the officer's order and trained their guns and machine guns onto the helpless crowd without a break. With the main gate barred by two armoured guards and the other exits also blocked, the victims had no route of escape. They were easy targets for the bullets being fired at them. According to the Hunter Report, the firing lasted without a pause for a full ten minutes. In all, 1650 rounds were fired. Some 400 people died on the spot and over 1500 were injured but these figures are official figures and open to question. Eyewitness accounts sum up the horror of the situation. Mothers frantic to save their children from the rain of the bullets threw them into the well only to have them perish there.

All eye witness accounts by the survivors agreed that anyone attempting to get to the gate was especially targeted. Blood drenched the walls and the ground of the Bagh and flowed into the drains of the adjoining streets. There were bodies

FORMATIVE YEARS

everywhere. One account would be sufficient to sum up the horror of the situation. Ratan Devi, widow of one of the victims, came to look for her husband. She came into the compound in the gathering gloom of dusk and spent hours looking for him. The whole scene was catastrophic and the sight of so many dead bodies was appalling. When it was almost too dark to see, she finally identified her husband's bullet ridden body, dragged it as far as she could, and spent the long night in lonely vigil, waiting for someone to help her find a cot on which she could carry the body home and perform the last rites. "It is impossible for me to describe what I felt. Heaps of bodies lay there, some on their backs, some with their faces upturned. A number of them were poor, innocent children. I was alone that whole night, nothing but the bark of dogs or the braying of donkeys was audible. Amidst hundreds of corpses, I passed my night in crying and watching" (Quoted by Omesh Saigal, *Shaheed Bhagat Singh*, p. 179).

The entire nation was shocked by the horror and brutality of the massacre and many right minded people in London were equally horrified. The Hunter Commission was set up to enquire into the disorder in the Punjab. The "Butcher of Amritsar" showed no remorse or regret. "My mind was made up as soon as I came along in my motor car. I had made up my mind that I would do all the men to death." He said that he did not consider it necessary to ask the crowd to disperse or to give them any warning before giving the order to fire. He also said that he had felt no need to refer to the deputy commissioner before resorting to the extreme step. He concluded by saying that he had only been doing his duty when he fired at the unarmed. "I wanted to teach them a lesson so that they might not laugh at me. I would have fired and fired longer, if I had the required ammunition. I had

SHAHEED BHAGAT SINGH

taken an armoured car but found that the passage to Bagh could not admit it. I thought I should shoot well and shoot straight so that I or anybody else should not have to shoot again." He boasted privately that he had not wasted a single bullet. The commission did not find any fault with his actions and did not admonish him. In fact, to add insult to injury, Sir Michael O'Dwyer, in a telegram, approved his actions.

In spite of the clean chit given to him by the authorities, the government felt that in view of the tremendous pressure mounted by the people in England, it would be prudent to recall Dyer. An indication of Dyer's attitude and state of mind can be gauged from the reply he gave Justice Rankin when asked if he had extended any help to the wounded: "No, certainly not. It was not my job. The hospitals were open and they could have gone there." An indication of the attitude of the British establishment is provided by the fact that the House of Lords refused to pass a motion to condemn Dyer. Though Dyer was stripped of his command and lost his pension, the British community in India publicly presented him with a purse of 20,000 pounds. The British ladies in India presented him an ornamental sword for having protected their honour. In London a public reception was arranged for him where he was hailed as a hero. The *Morning Post,* one of the leading papers in England, collected an amount of 26,000 pounds for Dyer as a reward for his devotion to duty. Some British officials even went so far as to publicly state that Dyer's action had saved the Punjab from anarchy. When the Punjab tragedy was raised in the Supreme Council, the government regretted the atrocity, especially of Jallianwala Bagh, but made no reference to any kind of punishment.

Though Bhagat Singh was only twelve at the time of the massacre, he was deeply affected by it. The day after the event he did not go to school, but went to Amritsar instead. One can imagine the boy going around the ground, finding his way amongst the bodies that were still unclaimed, looking closely at the wounds that had been inflicted, examining each inch of the blood soaked ground, running his hand over the bullet scarred, blood splattered walls and pausing at the edge of the well to peak in and try to count the number of innocent children who had lost their lives. One can see him close his eyes so that he could hear more clearly the rapid burst of machine gun fire, the screams of the terror of the unsuspecting victims, the cries of agony of the wounded and the dying. One can see him crinkling up his nose and taking deep breaths so that he would never in his life forget the smell of the blood of the innocent and the acrid smell of gunpowder. One can feel the lump that must have formed in his throat and the tears that must have come to his eyes. One can feel the sadness and pain give way to a seething hatred, a rage that demanded action. He must have touched the walls again and looked at his hand streaked faintly with the still wet blood. A steely resolve must have slowly grown in his heart, a resolve that India must no longer remain under that barbaric rule.

Bhagat Singh bent down and scooped up a handful of the still wet red soil and tied it up in a corner of his handkerchief before putting it carefully into his pocket. He walked slowly to the now unmanned gate and then turned to look once more at the scene of the terrible carnage that would be etched forever in his mind and in his heart. Then he bent down again, touched the ground, folded his hands and paid a silent tribute to those who had laid down their lives.

When he reached home he went straight to his room, lay down on his bed and wept into his pillow. Later in the evening, when his mother came to call him for the evening meal, she saw him lying on his bed, staring up at the ceiling. He got up when she came in. "I am sorry, Mother. I know you have all been very worried about me. I should have told you, but I was afraid you would not permit me to go."

She smiled and brushed the stray stand of hair away from his forehead. "Seeing what the aftermath of yesterday's happening has been here in Lahore too, yes, I would have forbidden you to go. But when did my forbidding stop you when you have made up your mind to do something?" He smiled back at her and she put her arms around him and held him close. No matter how much he pretended to be a man, she knew that at the age of twelve he was still only a boy. After a while, still holding him close, she asked, "Was it really bad?"

Once again he lived through the day and told her all that he had seen. And she was glad that he had been able to talk about it, glad that he had achieved some catharsis. He would now be able to put it away and take it all in his stride. But when she went to tidy his room the next day, she was not very sure. She found a bottle in which he had put the bloody mud, prominently displayed on his table and in front of it there was an offering of two fresh flowers. Over the years, that bottle of soil and fresh flowers were to become a permanent part of her son's life and of her own and she came to realise that he had not put it away from him, that he was deliberately and firmly holding on to it. She realised that the daily offering of those flowers was part of a ritual, part of a prayer that a day would come when the soil of his motherland would no longer be stained by the blood of his countrymen.

Dyer's lack of remorse and regret, the arrogance he had displayed, O'Dwyers' congratulatory telegram, the attitude of the British establishment and the press, all ensured that it was not only Bhagat Singh who failed to put the Jallianwala Bagh massacre away from him. It stayed in the minds of all

Indians and stoked fresh fires of anger and hatred. Punjab was engulfed by open revolt, while the rest of the country seethed with anger. Motilal Nehru called upon his countrymen to respond to the pain and the suffering of the Punjab.

Not content with the massacre in Amritsar, the government retaliated brutally against every expression of anger and discontent. Military courts were set up in the Punjab and throughout the country. 852 men were tried on charges of sedition and of these 582 were convicted. No one knows how many hundreds were executed.

Every Punjabi became a soldier and every home was turned into a fort (Omesh Saigal, *Shaheed Bhagat Singh*, p.150). There was a mushroom growth of secret societies all pledged to the cause of independence through revolution. The greater the repression that the British resorted to, the more committed the Indians became to the cause of freedom. There was a global reaction against the Jallianwala Bagh massacre and the repressive measures adopted by the British against the peasants of Punjab. (Lenin, in a letter dated 10 April 1920 to the editor of the *Amrit Bazar Patrika*, predicted the doom of the British rule in India.) Martial law was declared in the districts of Lahore, Amritsar, and Gujrawala. There followed a rein of terror. So much so that, at Lahore, bombs and machine guns were used to disperse the rebels. The British showed their inventiveness and came up with even greater means of humiliating the Indians.

Thousands of students were forced to walk sixteen miles a day for roll call: school children of five and six were compelled to attend parade and salute the British flag. Owners of property were ordered to bear the responsibility for safety of the Martial Law posters stuck on their property. Open cages were constructed and placed in central places where arrested men were confined like animals. Persons

SHAHEED BHAGAT SINGH

were handcuffed together and paraded in public places. In an attempt to mock the Hindu-Muslim unity, this was most often done to a Hindu and a Muslim. In Amritsar more than two people were not allowed to walk together on the sidewalks. "Langar", such an essential part of the Sikh way of life, was forbidden. Anyone on suspicion was made to crawl on his belly. Flogging became commonplace. When the Martial Law notices were seen torn on the notice board of one college, the whole staff and the Principal were arrested and interned in the Fort. A village headman was publicly flogged and then tied to a tree.

(Omesh Saigal, *Shaheed Bhagat Singh*, p. 80)

A reign of terror had been let loose and it brought in its wake a wave of anger which threatened to burn up the whole of Punjab. At Gujranwala, the railway station and the railway bridge were set on fire by an angry mob. There were several instances of arson at Wazirabad. Lahore, too, witnessed indiscriminate shooting and firing. Rabindranath Tagore wrote his now famous letter renouncing his knighthood in protest against the massacre of Jallianwala Bagh.

The aftermath of Jallianwala Bagh did not spare even highly respected and eminent journalists in India. M. G. Horniman, editor of the *Bombay Chronicle*, was deported because he had publicly condemned the government's repressive measures, especially the Jallianwala Bagh massacre. Babu Nath Kohli, the editor of the *Tribune*, Lahore, was taken into custody. On 21 July 1919, Gandhi issued a statement demanding a commission of inquiry into the Punjab happenings. On 17 October 1919, when the order against his coming to Punjab had been removed, he came to Punjab. Motilal Nehru and Jawaharlal Nehru were already there and they were joined by Purshottam Das Tandon and C. F. Andrews. A glimmer of light appeared on the horizon at this juncture because the government did seem to accede to Gandhi's desire by

FORMATIVE YEARS

appointing the Hunter Commission to enquire into the happenings in Punjab in April 1919. But, as we have seen, the hope of some kind of justice being meted out was belied when the commission submitted its report.

The Congress session in Lahore took place in December 1919. It was decided to build a memorial at Jallianwala Bagh to perpetuate the memory of all those who had been killed in Dyer's action and the Bagh was bought for the nation for this purpose. The session was a crowded one and was attended by fifty thousand delegates. As many as fifty resolutions were passed, among these one condemning mob frenzy and violence. Gandhi spoke as the leader of all nationalists when he said: "I say do not return madness with madness but return madness with sanity and the whole situation is yours." The final ode to the Jallianwala Bagh tragedy was written by Udham Singh twenty-one years after the tragedy. It is said that like Bhagat Singh, Udham Singh too, when he was twenty-one years old, had visited Jallianwala Bagh almost immediately after the massacre. Amongst the dead he saw forty-one children, including a baby, an infant barely a few weeks old. In November 1919 he had heard Dyer testifying before the Hunter Commission. His heart burned with the injustice of it all. Twenty-one years later on 13 March 1940, at a public meeting, he shot dead Michael O'Dwyer, who had started it all. In his statement at the time of surrender he said that he had no personal enmity against O'Dwyer. It was just that he happened to be the lieutenant-governor of the Punjab at the time of the Jallianwala Bagh massacre and had to be held responsible for it.

Fed up with the eye wash response that the British had made to his demand for an enquiry into the happenings in the Punjab and their failure to take suitable action against those who were guilty of crimes against the Indians, on 2 August

67

SHAHEED BHAGAT SINGH

1920 Gandhi found that he could not remain a moderate any longer. He took the extreme step of returning all the honours that the British had bestowed upon him—the Kaisar-i-Hind and the Zulu war medal. The fact that he took so long to follow Tagore's example was due to his continued belief that the Indians could hope for some justice at the hands of the British, a belief that had finally received a mortal blow after the Jallianwala Bagh tragedy.

At the Nagpur session of the Congress in August 1920, the Non-Cooperation Movement against the British was formally launched. It was decided to return and renounce all honours and awards received from the British, to boycott all British-made goods, especially British-made cloth. This boycott was extended to embrace all British institutions including courts and even educational institutions. Lala Lajpat Rai had opposed the last on the plea that it would be counterproductive in the long run as the children's education would suffer. But since most of the leaders were keen to go along with Gandhi on this matter, he accepted, but decided to set up national schools and colleges where children would be given a liberal education with a strong emphasis on their culture and heritage.

The Non-Cooperation Movement was a huge success and even Bhagat Singh, still only in class nine at the DAV school, abandoned his studies in April 1921 and joined wholeheartedly in the movement. The scars of Jallianwala Bagh and all that it stood for were still fresh and painful for him and he welcomed this opportunity to hit back at the tyrants. He went from door to door to mobilise support for the movement and many who would otherwise have stood as spectators were moved by the passionate intensity of this boy and were motivated to participate in the movement. In a postcard dated 14 November 1921 written to his grandfather in Banga, Bhagat Singh mentions that the railway employees had also decided

FORMATIVE YEARS

to support the movement by going on strike and hoped that this would happen as early as the following week.

Prior to the call for the Non-Cooperation Movement and the attendant call of "Swaraj in one year", Gandhi had taken the very appropriate measure of meeting all the revolutionaries and requesting them to suspend all revolutionary activity against the rulers for one year. So great was the respect he commanded in all sections of the freedom fighters that the revolutionaries readily acceded to his request and agreed to suspend all their anti-British militant activities. The Non-Cooperation Movement was a thundering success. Millions of people from all walks of life came out to offer a peaceful protest against the British rule, using the highly effective tool of non-cooperation. The movement received a particularly eager response from the peasants, who saw in the struggle for independence an opportunity for the successful resolution of issues that concerned them—issues like rent, taxes, eviction by landlords, appropriation of their land by money lenders, etc. Because the Congress had extended full support to the Khilafat Movement, the Muslim masses also came out in support of the movement, and a strong sense of Hindu-Muslim unity pervaded this stage of the struggle for freedom. The masses looked upon the movement as the opportunity that they had been waiting for, for generations, to free themselves from the British Raj and the hold that the stooges of the British, the landlords, exercised over them. This explains why they contributed so much more than the one crore that Gandhi expected to the Tilak Swaraj Fund and why the number of volunteers was many times the one lakh that Gandhi had called for.

The Non-Cooperation Movement swept the country with such vigour and passion that it left the British administration in a total state of panic. But they were not the only ones who were unnerved. Many of the moderate leaders of the Congress felt themselves shaken to the core by all the fury that they saw around them. They were afraid that once the masses were truly aroused, they would break the limits within which the movement was intended to function. This did indeed happen. Within a very short time of the launching of the movement, the masses did break all controls. In 1922, the peasants of Chauri-Chaura launched an agitation, both against the British control and the exploitative control that the landlords exercised over them. The authorities ordered firing on the mob in which many peasants were killed. Incensed by this act of undeserved brutality, the mob lost all control, and set fire to the local police station. Seeing the mood of the mob, the police had fled to what they had thought was the safety of the police station. The police station was razed to the ground and twenty-two policemen were burnt to death. Gandhi, who firmly believed that the struggle for independence had to remain free from all violence, was saddened by the incident, as according to him it had violated the basic tenet of his political philosophy. He gave a call for the withdrawal of the movement, accepting full responsibility for its failure, and announced that he would no longer be taking part in active politics. One hundred and seventy-two peasants of Chauri-Chaura were sentenced to death for their role in the attack, on what was regarded as a universally hated symbol of British rule in India. Nineteen of them were actually hanged, the others being transported for life. Amazingly, neither Gandhi nor any other leader of stature raised his voice against this punishment.

The Congress Working Committee met at Bardoli on 12 February 1922 and passed a resolution formally withdrawing the Non-Cooperation Movement. Accordingly, the peasants were asked to pay all taxes that were due to the government and suspend all activity of any offensive nature. It also reminded the peasants that refusal to pay their rent to the landlords (zamindars) was against the resolution of the Congress and went against the best interests of the country. The resolution also assured the zamindars that the Congress had never intended nor would ever intend in the future to interfere or impinge on their legal rights through any movement, that the Congress had always advocated the resolution of differences between the zamindars and their tenant farmers through a process of mutual discussion.

Nehru was to admit later that Gandhi's decision to suspend the movement was resisted by almost all the leaders of the Congress. But so great was Gandhi's control over the party at that point that the resistance was never very openly voiced. The revolutionaries, of course, regarded the withdrawal of the movement as an act of betrayal. They felt that the movement had been a great success because it had mobilised the entire country and brought all the suffering Indians together in one united movement against the British. By abandoning it at this vital stage, Gandhi had played straight into the hands of the British and betrayed all those who had so vigorously participated in the movement, in the certainty that it would at last bring them the much desired liberation from the British yoke. They also felt that in the instructions given to the peasants and the reassurances provided to the landlords, the Congress had betrayed the interests of the suffering peasants and shown clearly that it was on the side of the exploitative landlords. This sense of betrayal is best summed up in the words of Shiv Verma: "Instead of welcoming the incident and asking for a thousand more Chauri-Chauras, Gandhi quietly and on his own withdrew the movement and retired from politics. It was against this background that the revolutionaries, who had laid down arms at the Mahatma's request, decided to reorganize themselves and take up arms again" (Quoted by P. M. S. Grewal, *Bhagat Singh: Liberation's Blazing Star*, p. 35, 36).

The fourteen-year-old Bhagat Singh, like all the other revolutionaries, was angry and disgusted at Gandhi's unilateral revoking of the movement. He was certain that if India was to achieve freedom, it would not be through the now on, now off struggles that the Congress had been practising. It would have to be through a sustained, unswerving resistance. He was also convinced that the non-violent path proposed by Gandhi and the Congress would not prevail against the harsh brutality practised by the British to crush all forms of resistance.

Soon after the suspension of the Non-Cooperation Movement, Bhagat Singh decided to resume his studies. As we have seen, one result of Gandhi's call to boycott all British institutions, including educational institutions, was the setting up of national colleges and schools all over the country. Among these institutions were the Kashi Vidyapith in Benaras, the Gujarat Vidyapith, and the Bihar Vidyapeeth in Patna. Lala Lajpat Rai had set up one such institution in Lahore called the Tilak School of Politics, popularly referred to as the National College. The college was affiliated to the Punjab Qaumi Vidyapeeth. "It was set up to provide an alternative to the institutions set up by the government, bringing the idea of Swadeshi to the field of education. The philosophy behind the setting up of this establishment was to produce self-reliant men and women that new India needed" (Kuldip Nayar, *Without Fear: The Life and Trial of Bhagat Singh*, p.13).

This institution now became the favoured institution for students who had abandoned their studies to take part in the Non-Cooperation Movement. Bhagat Singh, too, turned to the National College for admission. Unfortunately,

FORMATIVE YEARS

only matriculates were admitted to the college and he had abandoned his studies while still in class nine. Jai Dev Gupta, one of Bhagat Singh's classmates, who was sailing in the same boat, tells us how they were able to secure admission. Bhai Parmanand who along with Lala Lajpat Rai had set up the college and now managed it, was convinced of the earnestness of the two boys to pursue their studies. He gave them a period of two months to prepare for a special examination in lieu of the matriculation examination. They were both dedicated students and applied themselves to the preparation for the examination with great determination and zeal. They were both successful in clearing the exam and Bhai Parmanand was only too happy to offer them admission to the college. According to Manmathnath Gupta, "Parmanand invented his own method of testing this young man who posed something of a challenge. He gave him a list of books and asked him to read them. He saw him two months later, asked him a few questions, and was satisfied that Bhagat Singh had the right calibre" (*Bhagat Singh and His Times*, p. 81).

His stint at the National College was to have a far reaching effect on Bhagat Singh's character and political ideology. The influence came from a variety of sources. It came from the curriculum that was taught, from his fellow students and most of all from his teachers, most of whom were to have a lasting effect on his young mind.

Many details of Bhagat Singh's life in college and his college career are provided by Chabildas in his autobiography: *Meri Inquilabi Yatra* published in 1985. Chabildas had been an outstanding student but had decided to leave college while pursuing his postgraduate studies to devote himself to the service of the nation. He had joined Lala Lajpat Rai's "Lok Sewak Mandal" and written a number of articles on subjects of national concern. When the National College was set up,

73

SHAHEED BHAGAT SINGH

Lala Lajpat called upon him to join the institution. "There I started teaching English to the college class. Next year, on the retirement of the Principal, Acharya Jugal Kishore, I was made Principal and started teaching History in addition to English . . . In the beginning Lala Lajpat Rai used to come himself and teach the students. Education in the National College was different from other colleges. History, Economics and Politics were the subjects taught here. Although education was imparted through the medium of Hindi or Hindustani, students were also taught English because all the books were in English" (Quoted by Omesh Saigal, *Shaheed Bhagat Singh*, p. 52).

All the students of National College were young men who had responded to the appeal of Mahatma Gandhi. When these students learnt about the events of European history, as taught by Bhai Parmanand, they became sceptical of how Mahatma Gandhi could claim that he could secure independence through peaceful and non-violent means, when other countries of the world had to resort to armed violence to shame off the bridle of slavery. The students often asked themselves the question, Why was Mahatma Gandhi building castles in the air? . . . While Bhagat Singh was a fervent revolutionary he was also a good student. As his teacher I can say with confidence that he enjoyed his studies. He greatly enjoyed reading. Whenever the name of a book was mentioned he wanted to read it at once. Although Bhagat Singh had read numerous books on history I still remember the book he liked the best: "Cry for Justice". He had marked many portions of this book with red pencil. This shows how strong was his desire to fight against injustice.
(Quoted by Omesh Saigal, *Shaheed Bhagat Singh*)

That reading was a burning passion with Bhagat Singh is borne out by accounts from his friends. They claimed that if

FORMATIVE YEARS

he hadn't been a revolutionary he would in time have been an out and out bookworm or perhaps a university professor. He always seemed to be carrying a veritable library with him. Shiv Verma says, "I do not remember a single occasion when he was not carrying books. I have seen him ill clad and almost in rags, but even then I was sure he carried a book in his pocket. Bhagat Singh was also a lover of music and art. When Sukhdev and Bhagat Singh came to our Agra hideout I saw them lost in speculation or discussion on the in fights, moves and countermoves inside the Punjab Congress, the work of the Naujawan Bharat Sabha, the ups and downs of intellectuals, the problems of the party and the working class. They also compared notes about the latest reading, had discussions of the latest films, the actors and actresses" (Quoted by Manmathnath Gupta, *Bhagat Singh and His Times*, p. 85).

It was the study of history that was the burning passion of most of the students of that time. One of the history teachers, Jaichandra Vidyalankar, who had affiliations with the Bengal revolutionaries, was of particular importance to Bhagat Singh and the other like-minded students because he acted as a link to the revolutionary party. In addition to being a great scholar, he was an excellent teacher. He laid great stress on the revolutions in different parts of the world. The success of the revolutions, especially of the Russian Revolution, were studied and discussed in great depth. He also made them aware, with a degree of immediacy, of the activities of the Indian revolutionaries. He did not believe in half measures. In addition to the course of studies, he monitored the books that the students read, engaged them in discussions, both individually and in groups, and dwelt at length on their objectives in life. He encouraged them to continue their discussions when he took them out for recreational activities

75

SHAHEED BHAGAT SINGH

like moonlight picnics and boating on the Beas. Through these persistent methods he ensured that most of his students would adopt a revolutionary way of thinking.

Bhai Parmanand also exercised a deep influence on the minds of his students. He was at that time also teaching at the DAV College, Lahore. Earlier in his life, Parmanand had been sent by the Arya Samaj to spread the Vedic religion in South Africa. On the way back he had stopped in England, and using the material available in the main research library in London had written a history of India, which the government of India found most offensive. The book was banned and the government of the Punjab implicated him in a case of political conspiracy for which he was awarded capital punishment. On the intercession of Pandit Madan Mohan Malviya and C. F. Andrews, who appealed to the viceroy, the death sentence was commuted to life imprisonment and Bhai Parmanand was deported to the Andaman Islands. Better sense, however, prevailed and he was released after five months. Against this background, it was no surprise that the history that Parmanand taught was based entirely on wars, revolutions, and bloodshed. The kind of influence that Parmanand could wield on young minds is provided by an account given by Kartar Singh Sarabha. He tells us that it was Parmanand who motivated him to join the revolutionary movement. (V. N. Datta, *Gadar and Bhagat Singh*, p. 21). From the books that he read and the notes that he made while in jail, it is easy to deduce the tremendous influence that Parmanand had in shaping Bhagat Singh's mind.

In college Bhagat Singh was universally liked by students and teachers alike. He is remembered as an intelligent, hardworking, extremely disciplined young man, always showing the greatest respect to his teachers and affection to his fellow students. He was devoted to his studies and his results were

76

FORMATIVE YEARS

always good. His favourite subjects were history and political science. Though the curriculum in the National College did not lay much emphasis on sports and co-curricular activities, it did encourage debating as a means for the students not only to give a clear expression to their own ideas, but also to exchange ideas with other students. Bhagat Singh took an active part in all debates and soon made a mark for himself as an excellent debater with his powerful voice and the depth and scope of his reading and knowledge. More often than not, he sourced material for his debates from the Dwarkadas Library, which was just a stone's throw away from the college. The library had been set up by Lala Lajpat Rai and had a tremendous collection of books on history, political science ,and the social sciences. But more to the purpose of Bhagat Singh, it was rapidly becoming a repository for revolutionary books, journals, and magazines from all over the country. Bhagat Singh and his fellow students like Sukhdev, Bhagwati Charan Vohra, Shiv Verma, Ram Kishen, and Yashpal, not only borrowed and read this literature but also fiercely debated the issues that were raised by their reading. Rajaram Shastri, who was later to become an important labour leader, was the librarian and was to say in later years that he remembered that Bhagat Singh was an avid reader, especially interested in the works of Marx and Bakunin.

In order to propagate and popularise revolutionary ideas, Bhagat Singh and his friends, with active support from their teachers, set up the "National Dramatic Club". Sometimes under the garb of dealing with historical subjects like Maharana Pratap Singh and Chandragupta Maurya, the plays would propound thoughts and ideas which were relevant to India's then-current political situation. At other times, plays would be staged on the themes of Hindu-Muslim unity and the bane of superstition. Bhagat Singh proved to be a natural actor and,

SHAHEED BHAGAT SINGH

with his commanding physique and powerful voice, would often play the part of the protagonist. After one performance of "Chandragupta", it is said that Parmanand climbed onto the stage and hugged Bhagat Singh and announced to the audience: "He will be a Chandragupta in real life too." The plays were staged not only in Lahore, but also in Lyallpur, Gujranwala, and Rawalpindi. As a result of all these activities, Bhagat Singh became well known not only in his own college but also in all the other colleges of the Punjab, and acquired a large circle of fans and admirers even before he got involved in revolutionary activities.

After completing his Intermediate year, he joined the undergraduate classes with more or less the same circle of teachers and the same group of fellow students. The influence of these two groups and the constant interaction with them aroused deep and abiding feelings of patriotism, nationalism ,and a revolutionary fervour to win freedom at any cost. An example of this is provided by Yashpal in his narration of one such interaction with Bhagat Singh:

> We two were alone in a boat. There was no third person present. I do not remember now how it all came about. I remember that finding ourselves alone, I said with full confidence, what Bhagat Singh was also feeling and burst out in English, "Let us pledge our lives to our country." Bhagat Singh suddenly became serious and said in English, "I do pledge." We clasped one another's hands and remained quiet for some time. The sun was just sinking and the sky was still crimson. As it began to grow dark, we went to the bank and returned the boat to the owner. While plodding back we were both so full that we did not speak. All this happened in such an emotional atmosphere, that this event still lingers in my memory. Perhaps the conversation that we were having with the professors had something to do with the pledge.
> (Quoted by Manmathnath Gupta, *Bhagat Singh and His Times,* p. 82-83)

78

FORMATIVE YEARS

It was at this time that Bhagat Singh made his first foray into the field of writing. Bhagat Singh was sixteen years old and Punjab was caught up in a debate on the official language issue. The popular opinion was to choose between Urdu and Hindi. But there was also a section of the intelligentsia and the media that was advocating the use of Punjabi. It was against this background that the Punjab Hindi Sarmaya Sammelan invited people to write about their views regarding the language and script for Punjab. It offered a prize of fifty rupees for the best article. Bhagat Singh sent in an article and won accolades for it. It stated quite emphatically the need for a national language and was clear that ultimately Hindi would become the national language. In the interim, Punjab should like all other states, give importance to the mother tongue, Punjabi. Punjabi could be made universally acceptable by adopting the Devnagari script for its usage. In this way Punjabi and Hindi would come to stand side by side.

This phase of Bhagat Singh's life was brought to an abrupt end by a letter from his father. It was 1924 and Bhagat Singh was seventeen years old, an age which at that time was considered most suitable for marriage for boys. Since Bhagat Singh was considered a very eligible bachelor, there had been many proposals of marriage which he had impatiently brushed aside with the statement: "I don't want to get married, Mother." His mother had smiled indulgently with each rejection and let the matter rest. She knew that all young men went through this phase and was certain that it was only a matter of time before her son accepted the necessity of marriage and children and settling down in life. But when almost a year had gone by and Bhagat Singh had turned down dozens of suitable proposals on no other grounds than his desire not to get married, it caused great anxiety in the family. The parents would have been content to let the matter rest for another year or two.

But it was Bhagat Singh's grandmother, Jai Kaur, who insisted that the matter be dealt with urgently and firmly. "I am old now and do not know how much longer I have to live," she said over and over again. "And before I go I want to see the next generation of my family so that you can seat me on a silver 'piri' and my funeral ceremonies will be a celebration."

The family could find no fault with her argument. She was old and frail and it was perfectly understandable that she should have this urgency to see the birth of a great-grandson and participate in all the attendant celebrations when her grandson was in a position to fulfil her wish. She clinched the matter by referring to Jagat Singh, Kishan Singh's first born, who had died as a young boy. "If Jagat had lived, my wish would have already been fulfilled. But now it is only Bhagat, my bhagawala, who can give me my greatest desire, who can let me go in peace."

In the face of such strong emotional blackmail, there was little that Kishan Singh could do except force this decision on his son. Through intermediaries known to both families, negotiations were begun between Kishan Singh's family and a wealthy Mann family from Mannawala in Sheikhpura district. Kishan Singh, Vidyavati and a small group of relatives went to see the girl at Mannawala and found her to their liking. At this stage Bhagat Singh again voiced his opposition to marriage. But this time Kishan Singh brushed it aside firmly. The family was at the time living at a little distance from Lahore and Kishan Singh communicated his decision to his son through a letter.

Dear Bhagat Singh,

We have settled your marriage. We have seen the bride. We approve of her and her parents. I myself and yourself will honour the desire of your old grandmother. Therefore it

FORMATIVE YEARS

is my order that you should not create any difficulty in the celebration of your marriage and must prepare for it gladly. (Quoted by Gurdev Singh Deol, *Shaheed-e-Azam: Bhagat Singh*, p. 17)

Bhagat was greatly perturbed by the peremptory and final tone of the letter. Since this was an extremely grave matter, Bhagat Singh turned to Principal Chabildas for help and advice. He stated as clearly and objectively as he could that his sole purpose in life was to work for the freedom of his country and to serve his fellow countrymen. He voiced his conviction that marriage and all the attendant duties that go with it would distract him from this simple purpose. Chabildas, with his usual good humour, pointed out that a wife need not be an impediment in his goal. In fact, it was quite likely that he would get a like-minded partner who would be of great assistance to him in the goal that he had set for himself in life. He went on to quote the examples of Sun-Yat-Sen, Lenin, and Karl Marx. It seemed on the surface that young Bhagat Singh's doubts and anxieties on the subject of marriage had been allayed by Chabildas' arguments because he smiled wryly at his principal and said, "Guruji, who can beat you in an argument?" and went his way.

According to Virinder Sandhu, he even went home with the girl's brother, Teja Singh Mann, who had been deputed by his father to see the prospective bridegroom as part of the marriage process. "All day Bhagat seemed to remain very happy. He was bubbling with joy and he himself harnessed the horse to the tonga and drove the tonga to escort his visitor back to his village. The bride's brother had liked him and before leaving, had fixed the date for the engagement ceremony" (Quoted by Omesh Saigal, *Shaheed Bhagat Singh*, p. 65).

But inwardly Bhagat Singh still remained troubled and as

the day for the engagement drew closer, he became more and more certain that he could not go through with the marriage. He shared his thoughts and feelings with Jaidev Gupta. He said the path he had chosen for himself was beset with many difficulties. He had the example of his two uncles always before him. His uncle, Swaran Singh, had died in jail, leaving his wife to live the anguished life of a widow. His uncle, Ajit Singh, because of his revolutionary activities, had been forced to live the life of an exile in foreign countries thus also condemning his wife, Harnam Kaur, to the life of virtual widowhood. He did not wish to ruin the life of another young girl.

We also have a first-hand account of his conversation on the issue with the revolutionary Sachindra Nath Sanyal, which seemed to have clinched the issue for him. In the wake of the disillusionment caused by Gandhi in calling off the Non-Cooperation Movement, Sachindra Nath Sanyal launched an all-out effort to bring all revolutionaries under the umbrella of a common organisation called "The Revolutionary Party". Both Bhagat Singh and Jayachandra Vidyalankar had joined the party.

Sanyal says, "I had also had a talk with Bhagat Singh, who told me that his father was serious about his marriage. I myself was married, but I felt that marriage was a serious handicap and I had committed a great blunder. I warned Bhagat Singh that if he married, he would not be able to do much. Bhagat Singh said that he did not want to marry. It was my custom to test revolutionaries to find out how far they were ready. We only accepted a man as a full-fledged revolutionary if he was ready to leave the security of home. Accordingly I asked Bhagat Singh: 'Are you ready to leave your home? If you marry you will not do much work, and if you stick to your home you will be compelled to marry.' Bhagat Singh immediately agreed to quit home. I had thought of meeting Sardar Kishan Singh because I had known him, but knowing

that Bhagat Singh had agreed to leave home there was no point in seeing his father. At my request Bhagat Singh left home and went to U.P."
(Quoted by Manmatnath Gupta, *Bhagat Singh and His Times*, p. 85)

Before he left Lahore, he left a letter addressed to his father in a drawer of his father's writing table. In this letter he said, "The mission of my life has been devoted to the attainment of freedom of my motherland. Therefore I do not give any preference to lust and worldly desire." In the second paragraph he went on to say, "You must remember when I was a child, my grandfather announced that my life would be dedicated to the cause of the motherland. I am therefore fulfilling the commitment made at that time. I trust you will forgive me" (Quoted by Dr. L. P. Mathur, *Bhagat Singh, the Prince of Martyrs*, p. 25).

Chapter 3

BIRTH OF A REVOLUTIONARY

There are conflicting accounts regarding Bhagat Singh's arrival in Kanpur. One account would have us believe that armed with the introductory letter from Jayachandra Vidyalankar, Bhagat Singh came straight to Ganesh Shankar Vidyarthi, who was running the Pratap Press and the paper with the same name. Another better documented account tells us that with a letter of recommendation from Sachindra Nath Sanyal, Bhagat Singh first came to Suresh Chandra Bhattacharya, who was the leader of the revolutionaries in Kanpur.

Bhattacharya tells us: "Bhagat Singh came to me with a letter from Sachin Da. I arranged for his stay in my mess. As Bhagat Singh had to remain all alone in the house in the afternoon, I introduced him to Batukeshwar Dutt. He started learning Bengali from Dutt and within a very short time had learnt by heart the famous poem *Vidrohi* written by the poet Nazurul Islam."

It is interesting to note that in later years, Bhagat Singh was to use the pen-name "Vidrohi" for many of his articles.

BIRTH OF A REVOLUTIONARY

Bhattacharya goes on to say: "He rarely went out of the mess, yet I noted that the constables of the CID had started moving around the house at number 221, in Ram Narain Bazar. I also came to know that Durga Prasad, the Deputy Superintendent of the CID and Yatin Das had been making frequent trips to Kanpur looking for members of the Revolutionary Party.

"Somehow Ganeshji (Ganesh Shankar Vidyarthi) came to know about the arrival of Bhagat Singh. Bhagat Singh's father and Ganeshji knew each other; both had been members of the All India Congress Committee. One day Vidyarthi asked me, 'Suresh Babu, is Bhagat Singh staying with you?' Although it took me a few seconds to answer this straightforward question, I gave a clear reply and said, 'Yes.' 'You bring him to the Pratap Press,' Ganeshji directed me. 'He is being closely watched by the police. Will it be proper to take him there?' I asked. 'You need not worry at all about it. And I would teach him journalism. You know recently there have been serious riots at Daryaganj in Delhi. I have to send him there to bring the correct news.'" (Quoted by Omesh Saigal, *Shaheed Bhagat Singh*, p. 67).

This account does not tell us how Vidyarthi came to know about Bhagat Singh's arrival in Kanpur. Perhaps Vidyalankar not having got any news from Bhagat Singh had addressed an enquiry to Vidyarthi about the young man. Perhaps Vidyarthi had read an advertisement inserted by Kishan Singh, Bhagat Singh's father in the daily *Vande Mataram*, asking Bhagat Singh to return home and since Kanpur at that time was the ideal place for aspiring revolutionaries to be in, had deduced that Bhagat Singh may have come there.

Be that as it may, the fact remains that within a short time of his arrival, Bhagat Singh was working for Vidyarthi at the Pratap Press. His meeting with Sachindra Nath Sanyal and his training under Vidyarthi were to define his political career.

85

SHAHEED BHAGAT SINGH

Sachindra Nath Sanyal had been arrested and transported for life in the *Lahore Conspiracy* case. He was later released. Like most other revolutionary leaders he had responded to Gandhi's call and suspended all militant and revolutionary activity on the eve of the launching of the Non-Cooperation Movement and had worked diligently to ensure the success of the movement. As a result, like all other revolutionaries he was extremely hurt and disappointed when in the wake of the Chauri Chaura incident, Gandhi had called it off. He had seen how effective a united effort against the British could be, and he now spent all his efforts in forming a united all India revolutionary party. As a result of this effort, the Hindustan Republican Association was formed in 1923. Bhagat Singh became a member of this association in 1924. Sanyal wrote a manifesto of the party aptly titled "Revolutionary", which was distributed in all the metropolitan cities of the country on New Year's Day, 1925. In the manifesto Sanyal clearly and concisely stated the objectives of the association. The association would work, not only to rid India of foreign rule but would also work to establish a Federal Republic of the United States of India through an armed and organised revolution. The association had to go far beyond the mere overthrow of the British rule and the gaining of political freedom. The manifesto stated that all the systems that had made possible the exploitation of man by man would be nationalised. Amongst these systems were listed the railways and all other means of transportation and communication, the mines and other major industries like the manufacture of steel and ships. It stated that in the new republic, preference would be given to cooperative over private business. The manifesto also pledged itself to the cause of communal harmony.

The manifesto made it clear in no uncertain terms that it was in favour of the use of terror to further the cause espoused by the Hindustan Republican Association. "The official terrorism is surely to be met by counter terrorism. A spirit of utter helplessness pervades every strata of our society and terrorism is an effective means of restoring the problem in the society without which progress will be difficult. Moreover the English masters and their feudal lackeys can never be allowed to do whatever they like, uninterrupted, unmolested."

The social slant of the philosophy of the HRA was emphasised again in the constitution of the association which was also framed by S. N. Sanyal and released in 1924. The constitution stated that the intention of the organisation was, "To start peasant and labour organisations, for which suitable men must be engaged to organise labourers in different factories, the railways and the coal field and instil into their minds that they are not merely a tool for revolution, but the revolution will take place for their benefit" (Quoted by P. M. S. Grewal, p. 42, 43).

The peasants also had to be organised like the workers. The HRA thus gave a new dimension to the nationalist movement. It was no longer merely a struggle to attain political freedom from British rule but it was also a socialist struggle to secure the emancipation of the proletariat. The purpose of the nationalist movement according to Sanyal was both to create a new nation and a new civilisation.

It was the belief of the HRA, held not only by its leaders but also subscribed to by all its members, that the strongest weapon against British imperialism was retaliatory action against all the obvious symbols of imperialism. This action would inevitably be militant and revolutionary action, and would involve a large scale use of arms and ammunition. One of the avowed purposes of the organisation was that "Suitable persons should be sent abroad for military training and education in science so as to make them capable of taking charge of arms factories and army operations at the time of revolution" (Quoted by Omesh Saigal, p. 69).

This philosophy and call to militant and terrorist activity directed against the hated ruler had immediate appeal to all the youth belonging to the middle and lower middle classes, who were seething with anger at what they saw as conciliatory measures being adopted by the Congress and other moderate parties and who saw in Gandhi's action of calling off the Non-Cooperation Movement, a gross betrayal of the trust they had so willingly reposed in him. They joined the new association in overwhelming numbers and led to what came to be a universally held belief: that if freedom was to be gained by India, it could only be gained through the efforts of the youth. "The middle class youth alone are capable of giving lead, while workers and peasants would supply the soldiers for the revolutionary army" (S. N. Mazumdar, quoted by P. M. S. Grewal, p. 42).

The manifesto and constitution of the HRA accorded with Bhagat Singh's own political philosophy and ideology down to the letter and it was inevitable that he should become a very active member of the association. One of the driving forces of the HRA was Chandra Shekhar Azad and Bhagat Singh became very close to him. Kanpur, the biggest industrial centre of North India had become the centre of the activity of all revolutionary leaders with Marxism leanings. During the early days in Kanpur, Bhagat Singh also came into close contact with many other revolutionary leaders like Suresh Bhattacharya, B. K. Dutt, Shiv Verma, B. K. Sinha and Ajay Ghosh.

Ajay Ghosh described his first meeting with Bhagat Singh: "I believe it was some time in 1923 that I met Bhagat Singh ... he was introduced to me by B. K. Dutt in Kanpur. Tall and thin, rather shabbily dressed, very quiet, he seemed a typical village lad, lacking smartness and self confidence. I did not think very highly of him and told Dutt so when he was gone" (Quoted by Kuldip Nayar, p. 15).

It was an opinion that Ghosh was soon to revise and he came to admire and respect the young man for his sincerity and dedication. Bhagat Singh in turn was soon drawn into subscribing wholeheartedly to Marxist ideology. During the first few months he had little work at the press and he was able to devote much of his time to the study and understanding of a vast amount of revolutionary literature including Marxist literature.

During this time Bhagat Singh was deputed by Vidyarthi to go to Delhi and cover the communal riots that were rocking Daryaganj. Bhagat Singh spent some time in Delhi, collected all the information regarding the riots and on his return wrote a two-column story which was published in the *Partap*.

Apart from publishing the *Partap* every week, the press also secretly printed inflammatory, revolutionary literature, which was then distributed in a clandestine manner among the masses. Bhagat Singh joined the group of young revolutionaries involved in the task. The most opportune occasions for the purpose were the weekly markets and the various fairs that were organised on a regular basis not only in the small towns around Kanpur but also in the villages. These assured a very high degree of anonymity for Bhagat Singh and his colleagues, as they could easily mingle with the large crowd bent on their weekly purchases or enjoying themselves in the *melas*. The anonymity was highly desirable because all the pamphlets preached that armed revolution was the only weapon that could dislodge the British. These occasions, involving as they did a constant movement from village to village and town to town, provided Bhagat Singh and his colleagues with an ideal opportunity to recruit young men and women to the association. "As a member of the association, Bhagat Singh actively engaged himself in propagating its views and programs. He used to visit several villages in the United Provinces to meet peasants and labourers. He explained to them the aim of the association and tried to prevail upon them to join their organisation and work wholeheartedly for the independence of the country" (Dr. L. P. Mathur, p. 33).

Through this entire action, thousands of members were recruited to the HRA, who pledged themselves to further the cause with every means available to them.

Gurdev Singh Deol, in *Shaheed-e Azam, Bhagat Singh* narrates one incident where Bhagat Singh and his colleagues came close to being caught by the police while they were in the process of distributing seditious literature. The occasion was a *mela* organised in connection with the celebration of Dussehra, in the fields outside the settlement of Pratapgarh. The weather was mild. The heat of the summer had become a distant memory and the cold of the winter lay in the future. Crowds of gaily dressed men, women and children thronged the fields, moved not only by the religious fervour of the occasion, but also by the plentiful harvest which they had just reaped. There were all the usual stalls selling the colourful trinkets that are so dear to the simple villagers' hearts and there were also stalls selling all kinds of eatables, sweets and sherbets. There were games of skill and chance and there were the freak shows like a bull with three horns. Adding to the joyful din of hundreds of people in the serious pursuit of enjoying themselves, were groups of performers singing devotional songs in praise of the god king Ram, who had vanquished the demon king Ravana. Crowds of people collected around the singers and Bhagat Singh and his colleagues found easy recipients among these people. Most of them glanced at the pamphlet in Hindi, entitled *Jago Mere Desh Ke Logo* (Wake up, the people of my

BIRTH OF A REVOLUTIONARY

country), read a few lines, then slipped them into their pockets to be perused later at home. A few having read the first few lines were compelled to read the pamphlet through to the very end. There were some policemen too among one such crowd of music lovers. In their zeal to distribute the pamphlet to as many people as possible and in the confusion caused by the packed crowd, two of Bhagat Singh's colleagues made the mistake of handing over the pamphlets to two policemen as well. The moment the policemen read the heading of the pamphlet, they pounced upon the youngsters and clutched them firmly by the collar.

Bhagat Singh, who was a short distance away from where this incident took place, heard the commotion and realised at once what had happened. With remarkable presence of mind, he threw the remaining pamphlets in the air and began shouting: *"Congress Party wala agaya hain. Dekho kya baant rahe hai."* (The Congress Party workers have come. See what they are distributing.) The curious crowd began to pick up the scattered pamphlets and most of the policemen, distracted by the commotion, ran to try and control it. Bhagat Singh took the lead and fell upon the policemen who were still holding on to his colleagues. With help from some members of the crowd, he was able to free them and disappear into the confusion that he had helped to create. Some accounts of the incident say that he fired a few shots of his pistol in the air and thus "persuaded" the policemen not to come in pursuit.

Bhagat Singh had already come under the police radar and with this incident, he was thrown into the limelight. It was at this point that Vidyarthi asked him to go underground and lie low for a while. Bhagat Singh assumed the name of Balwant Singh and according to some sources, moved away from Kanpur to take up a job as headmaster of a National School in Saidpur in Aligarh district. (Jagmohan Singh, Bhagat

91

Singh's nephew, who is considered an authority on his uncle's life, says that this happened later, on a subsequent visit by his uncle to Kanpur). Whatever the facts, we know that Bhagat Singh made an excellent headmaster. He not only endeared himself to the students but also through his own example of selfless devotion and dedication, created within a very short time a highly motivated team of teachers.

There was unprecedented torrential rain on 26 and 29 September 1924 and as a result the first week of October saw heavy floods in the Ganga, Jamuna and the Ramganga. These floods were of record breaking magnitude and brought in their wake devastation of life and property, causing unspeakable misery and suffering. Almost as a parallel to what his father Kishan Singh had done in the wake of the Kangra earthquake, Bhagat Singh threw himself wholeheartedly into the relief operations. He played a major part in organising not only the distribution of food, medicines and clothing, but also in setting up camps for the victims. It would be no exaggeration to say that Bhagat Singh single-handedly brought relief and succour to hundreds of families who had lost everything in the calamity.

Bhagat Singh's escape from Kanpur had been kept a closely guarded secret by the few who were party to the event. They also kept this information from his family because they were afraid that if his whereabouts were revealed, pressures would once again be mounted on him to get married. Quite understandably, the family was filled with anxiety and worried to death about his welfare. When Kishan Singh's advertisement in the *Vande Mataram* failed to elicit any response, his worry knew no bounds. They were well aware of the cause that he had espoused and the activities that he would have to involve himself in because of this espousal. They also knew the attention these activities would draw

BIRTH OF A REVOLUTIONARY

from the British government and the consequences of this attention. His continued absence from home and the total lack of information about his whereabouts made them fear the worst. To make matters worse for the family, Jai Kaur, Bhagat Singh's grandmother, fell ill at this time. She compounded this illness by refusing all medication. No amount of begging and cajoling would make her relent in this refusal. Their entreaties elicited only one response: "Bring my Bhagat, my bhagawala. He is all the medicine that I need." Her condition deteriorated rapidly. The family became alarmed and doubled their efforts to trace the prodigal son. But once again all their efforts were in vain.

Then destiny decided to take the matter in hand. At this time Bhagat Singh's mind returned over and over again to a childhood friend, Ramchand from Junjar village, in the district of Rawalpindi. He found himself consumed with the desire to get in touch with this friend again. Finally, not able to live with this longing anymore he wrote a letter to his friend, still unaware of his grandmother's illness. Also afraid that his family were still seeking to get him married, he begged Ramchand not to tell anyone of his whereabouts and not to disclose to anyone that he had received a letter from Bhagat Singh. But the joy and relief of getting a letter from his friend whom most had considered lost was too much for Ramchand to conceal in his heart. When he met Jaidev Gupta, another close friend of Bhagat Singh, he could not help but share the news of their friend's well being with him. Jaidev knew of the grandmother's illness and of the intense anxiety that the family was suffering on account of Bhagat Singh's prolonged absence. He felt it was his duty to share the news that Bhagat Singh was safe and well, with Kishan Singh, Bhagat Singh's father.

Dusk was fast falling when the two friends reached Kishan

Singh's house in Lahore and all the members of the family were in the courtyard of the house savouring the stillness that comes at the end of a hard day of work. Vidyavati was busy giving the finishing touches to the evening meal and Kishan Singh sat on Jai Kaur's cot doing his best to distract her mind from the absence of her grandson by indulging in trivial chit-chat about the day's happenings. The two youngsters were greeted with great joy and Jai Kaur sat up and drew each into a warm embrace when they bent to touch her feet. It was as if through them and their great affection for Bhagat Singh, she was being given some vicarious connection with her grandson, an opportunity to lavish some of her pent up love on him. The two friends looked at each other not knowing where to start and Kishan Singh sensing the uneasiness behind that glance knew at once that their visit had something to do with his son.

"It is Bhagat Singh, is it not?"

A hush descended on the household. The friends looked at one another again and their continued silence told the family that they had indeed come with news about the missing lad.

"Tell me," commanded Kishan Singh and there was impatience in his tone, the suspense now beyond anyone's bearing. "He is well," Jaidev said. Kishan Singh closed his eyes and said a silent prayer of gratitude. Jai Kaur began to moan and Vidyavati cried with relief.

When the excitement had died down a little, the friends gave all the details. The letter was passed from hand to hand. Vidyavati pressed it to her bosom; Jai Kaur kissed it and pressed it to her forehead. But having expressed their relief at knowing that he was well and the joy of seeing his familiar, well-loved handwriting again, the family was impatient to see Bhagat Singh himself in flesh and blood. The two friends were at the receiving end of lavish hospitality and the next morning entrusted with the task of going to Kanpur and bringing their friend back with them.

"Tell him," Vidyavati and Kishan Singh said in turn, over and over again. "Tell him that he has nothing to fear. We will never again insist on his marriage."

"Tell him that all I wish is to see him once again so that I can die in peace," enjoined the grandmother.

That should really have been the close of this chapter. But unfortunately when the friends reached the Pratap Press in Kanpur, the address that Bhagat Singh had given in his letter, Bhagat Singh was away perhaps attending to his duties as headmaster. Some accounts say that he was present but deliberately hid himself. But this behaviour is so uncharacteristic of the Bhagat Singh that we know that most biographers discount it. Vidyarthi was not sure that this was not just a ruse to lure Bhagat Singh back to Lahore and into matrimony. He was not sure that Bhagat Singh would like his whereabouts to be known even to two such close friends. So he took the safe way out and said, "I do not know where your friend has gone. I do not know when he will return. But you can be sure that when he does return, I will convey your message to him, the news of his grandmother's illness and the promise that his family has made regarding not insisting on his marriage."

Both Jaidev and Ramchand knew that Vidyarthi was not telling them the truth but in the face of his implacable stand to withhold this information from them there was little that they could do. They returned to Lahore and admitted to Kishan Singh that they had failed in their mission to bring their friend home.

The Communist Party was due to hold its inaugural session in Kanpur in 1925. Kishan Singh's old friend Maulana Hasrat Mohani had been asked to chair the Reception Committee.

The Maulana was at that time a distinguished and leading political figure in the country. He was a firm believer in Islam and also a poet of great repute. This unique combination of political leader, religious leader and eminent poet won him great respect and popularity. He was greatly influenced by the Russian Revolution and felt that non-violence should not be insisted upon as a tenet of the Non-Cooperation Movement. In one of his most famous couplets, composed at this time he said,

> We shall not sit quietly spinning on the charkha like Gandhi,
> We shall rock the world as Lenin did.

Hearing of the Maulana's prospective visit to Kanpur, where his son was said to be, Kishan Singh wrote to him to ask him to persuade Bhagat Singh to return to Lahore. He also promised, this time in writing, that no further effort would be made to persuade Bhagat Singh into marriage. The Maulana did meet Bhagat Singh on the sidelines of the convention and showed him Kishan Singh's letter. When Bhagat Singh still remained a little reluctant, the Maulana prevailed upon Vidyarthi to join him in his efforts at persuasion. "Take this letter with you," the Maulana said. "My friend Kishan Singh will never go back on his promise to me with that written pledge staring him in the face."

So it was that Bhagat Singh returned home to Lahore. It was as Jai Kaur had said; his presence was all the medicine that she needed. She recovered from her illness and Bhagat Singh spent the succeeding months nursing her back to health. As Jai Kaur regained her strength and was able to move around, Bhagat Singh felt increasingly free to resume his revolutionary activities. At this stage the resumption took the form of visiting Banga, Lahore and the neighbouring cities and villages, meeting young people both individually and in groups, and bringing them over to the cause. So great was his power of motivation and his personal charisma that he was able to recruit a large number of new members to the HRA.

During the early twenties, a movement had started building up against the corrupt practices of the *mahant*s or custodians of the Sikh religious shrines. The *mahant* or *sarbrah* of the sacred Nankana Sahib Gurdwara had like many *mahant*s of other important gurdwaras, become a law unto himself. Like the others he too, had raised a private army of mercenaries and was able to enforce his will and his authority at the point of the gun. The terrorised people were at first forced to submit to the will of the *mahant*s even when they found the acts being committed in the name of religion totally repugnant and against their conscience. But soon a movement sponsored by the Akalis, started against the desecration of sacred religious shrines and the gross misuse of religious authority. The *mahant* at Nankana Sahib over the years had become the symbol of all that was despicable and hateful in the institution of the *mahant*s and the anger that the devotees felt. It was felt that if reform could be effected at Nankana Sahib it would be easier to effect it at other shrines. The anti-*mahant* movement took the form of *jatha*s of devotees travelling to Nankana Sahib, camping outside the gurdwara and indulging in peaceful demonstrations against the management of the gurdwara and the autocratic control that the *mahant* exercised. The *mahant* at first secure in the arrogance of power, contemptuously ignored the protestors, sure that the movement would fizzle out and the *jatha*s would stop coming to disturb his peace. But the movement did not fizzle out but grew in strength from day to day. The government, wary of the Akalis and afraid that the movement might take on a political anti-British tone,

97

SHAHEED BHAGAT SINGH

threw in its lot with the *mahant* and unleashed measures of repression against the demonstrations on the plea that these measures were necessary to ensure law and order and public peace. But this repression proved to be counterproductive and the movement was now continued with greater vigour. In March 1924 the demonstrations finally got under the skin of the *mahant* at Nankana Sahib. In an act of diabolic cruelty and barbarity, reminiscent of Dyer's act at Jallianwala Bagh, he ordered his mercenaries to fire upon the *jatha*s that were demonstrating outside the gurdwara. One hundred and thirty-nine peaceful devotees were killed in the firing. No action was taken against the *mahant* and it was discovered that the *mahant* enjoyed the support of the deputy commissioner. People realised that the British, through their support to the *mahant* had added another dimension to their repression of the Indians. Not only were they repressing the masses through the use of brutal means themselves, but they were also now encouraging their stooges to do the same.

A day of mourning was declared and large crowds gathered outside the gurdwara, not only to pay homage to the martyrs who had been so brutally killed in the gruesome incident, but also to voice their protest against the atrocities and excesses of the *mahant* and the government's refusal to take action against him. The Akali organisers of the demonstration prevailed upon everyone to wear black bands as a sign of protest. The crowd was surprised and more than a little pleased to see the Raja of Nabha, Raja Ripudaman Singh, amongst them, also voicing his protest against the incident and the British attitude by wearing a black armband. The surprise was caused by the fact that till now the Sikh rulers of the five major states of the Punjab: Patiala, Nabha, Kapurthala, Jind, and Faridkot, had always been strong supporters of the British, even to the extent of endorsing all the repressive measures that the

98

BIRTH OF A REVOLUTIONARY

British had taken to suppress the voice of the people. The genesis of their stand is not far to seek. After the Anglo-Sikh Wars, which had seen the disintegration and annexation by the British of the Sikh empire, which Ranjit Singh had so assiduously built, these five rulers had been allowed to retain their kingdoms with a fairly high degree of independence. In return, the British expected their unqualified support and loyalty. They proved their loyalty by opposing any progressive movement, which caused discomfort to the British and were regarded with suspicion by the people of India. It was expected that they would as was their wont, strongly oppose the reformist movement that the Akalis had launched simply because the British were against it.

Against this background one can well imagine the complete and utter surprise of the Akalis and the general masses when they saw Raja Ripudaman Singh standing amongst them wearing the black armband which was a symbol of both mourning and protest. The British were not only surprised but shocked and angry. They reacted in their usual manner.

To them this was an act of sedition and betrayal. They now looked upon Ripudaman as a traitor. The viceroy issued orders and Ripudaman was deposed and held in detention in Dehradun. For the Akalis and for the supporters of the gurdwara movement, Ripudaman's case became a cause célèbre. Now the movement gained an additional dimension. The movement now sought not only to abolish the institution of the *mahant*s but also to secure the reinstatement of Ripudaman as the Raja of Nabha. As a result the destination of the *jatha*s now became Jaiton town in Nabha rather than Nankana Sahib, as it had originally been. Jaiton town took on a stature of historical proportions and magnitude. Every village that the *jatha*s passed through would turn out in full strength to greet and welcome them. All the hospitality that the villagers could muster would be lavished on the *jatha*s. Through the warm welcome, the villagers were voicing their support for the Akali movement and adding to its strength. The government used all the means at its disposal to try and suppress this show of affection and support. If the *jatha* had to pass through quiet, empty streets, it would affect their morale and make them feel that the common man was against the movement. All the pro-government *jagirdar*s were summoned and given orders that there must be no show of welcome in their villages for the *jatha*s that passed through. In villages where the *jagirdar*s refused to carry out the government orders, efforts were made to replace them with more complaisant *jagirdar*s.

The thirteenth *jatha* was due to pass through Banga, Bhagat Singh's village. The *jathedar* or the group leader, in order to counter the repressive orders passed by the British government to douse the warmth that the masses were lavishing on the delegates, now began to seek out people of prominence and influence in the villages enroute, to help them counter the British action. The *jathedar* of the thirteenth *jatha*, Jathedar Kartar Singh accompanied by Jwala Singh, came to Lahore to meet Kishan Singh for the purpose. Kishan Singh was not an Akali but he like all right-minded Sikhs, was staunchly anti-mahant and supported the Akali reform movement. He greeted his visitors with the respect they deserved and listened politely to their request.

"Kishan Singhji, you are well aware how important it is for us to counteract the measures being adopted by the British to demoralise our *jatha*s. They hope that faced with a lukewarm welcome from the villagers, the whole movement will lose steam and people will stop volunteering as members of the *jatha*s. This will in turn result in the end of our movement. You and your family are well known all over Punjab for the

BIRTH OF A REVOLUTIONARY

brave stand that you have always taken against the imperialistic designs of the British. You are highly respected and regarded in the entire region. Our next *jatha* will be passing through Banga. We would like your help in ensuring that the *jatha* receives a rousing welcome from the people of Banga."

Kishan Singh reached out and held the *jathedar's* hand and shook it warmly. "Have no fear. The *jatha* will receive such a rousing welcome when it passes through Banga that the members will never forget it." He paused and thought for a while. Then the crease on his brow eased and he said, "Unfortunately during this period, I have to be away in Bombay on some urgent business connected with my insurance work. But have no worry, my son Bhagat Singh, who is a very capable young man, will take charge and ensure that everything is taken care of."

Fortunately Bhagat Singh was in Lahore at the time and when he came home in the evening, Kishan Singh introduced him to the visitors. They found that the young man was indeed as his father had claimed, an extremely capable young man. They talked late into the night, finalising details of the requirements and the *jathedar* was gratified to see that Bhagat Singh was very enthusiastic about the impending visit of the *jatha* and was determined to ensure, as his father had said, that the delegates would remember their short sojourn in his village for the rest of their lives.

There was little time left and Bhagat Singh left for Banga the next day. But there was trouble in Banga that he had not anticipated. As we have seen, Surjan Singh, the elder son of Sardar Fateh Singh and brother of Bhagat Singh's grandfather, Arjun Singh, had fallen prey to the temptation that the British had offered to the landlords of Punjab and accepted the return of his land in exchange for a pledge of loyalty to the British. This loyalty had remained intact through

SHAHEED BHAGAT SINGH

every generation of that branch of the family. Dilbagh Singh, the son of Surjan Singh had been given the title of Sardar Bahadur in recognition of his devotion and services to the British Empire. He was currently the *jagirdar* of the area which included Banga. He was also a first class honorary magistrate. He used his official position to decree that no village in the area should extend any kind of welcome to the members of the thirteenth *jatha*. This decree was conveyed to the people by public announcements made from street to street and village to village, with the accompaniment of drums. No food or drink was to be offered to the *jatha*. Since the magistrate had the authority to enforce his orders with the help of the police, which was always at his command, the people listened to the announcement of the decree with a high degree of apprehension and a growing fear. All wells traditionally have a rope with a bucket at the end of the rope, by which the thirsty passerby can draw up water to slake his thirst. Dilbagh Singh, taking a page out of the book of the repressive regime of the British, now ordered that all such buckets from all the wells in his area should be removed; in this way the *jatha* would be denied even the basic amenity of drinking water.

It was against this negative background that Bhagat Singh returned to Banga to try to organise an appropriate reception for the *jatha*. Dilbagh Singh had ensured that the police had gone around the area threatening people with dire action if they went against the decree of the magistrate and most of the people had decided that it was in their own interests not to have anything to do with the *jatha*. It was a truly uphill task for Bhagat Singh to go from house to house and from village to village trying to convince people to ignore the threats held out by Dilbagh Singh and the police, to make them see that in the long run, it was in their interest to ensure the success of the Akali movement. He was helped in the task of motivating

102

BIRTH OF A REVOLUTIONARY

people in favour of support for the *jatha*, by the fact that he was Arjun Singh's grandson, Kishan Singh's son and Ajit Singh's nephew, and the help of the cadre of HRA members he had recruited, who now came forward to help him actively. Dilbagh Singh, secure in the knowledge of the fear that he had been able to instil in the people did nothing. He least suspected that Bhagat Singh was working assiduously to undo his work.

Bhagat Singh and his team organised the reception along the lines of a military operation. Tents were set up in an open field surrounded by sugar cane fields, away from the eyes of Dilbagh Singh's stooges. People came forward with offerings of milk, atta, vegetables, dal, ghee, and spices, all of which had been transported to the site under cover of darkness. By the time the *jatha* arrived it was to find a full-fledged camp waiting for them. Volunteers had lit cooking fires and while the members of the *jatha* drank tumblers of warm milk, the evening meal was prepared for them. Villagers from the neighbouring village of Roda worked side by side with the residents of Banga and matched their efforts in every way, both in spirit and in action. Once the members of the *jatha* had been suitably fed and arrangements had been made for their rest, Bhagat Singh surprised everyone by setting up a fireworks display. On and on the fireworks went to light up the night sky in brilliant showers of sparks and colour. As if the fireworks were a signal for them to do so, people from Banga and the neighbouring villages streamed out of their homes to the camp to welcome the *jatha*. There was much laughter and shouting and rejoicing and even before Dilbagh Singh's stooges could react and take any suppressive action, the members of the *jatha* had been given a rousing welcome they would not in every likelihood forget for the rest of their lives.

The evening concluded with a moving speech by Bhagat Singh in which he welcomed the members of the *jatha*, congratulated them for making such a valuable contribution to the Akali movement and explained how the movement was so important to the larger movement for freedom from British rule. During the course of this speech, Bhagat Singh narrated the story of martyrdom of Gopinath Saha, one of the band of young firebrand revolutionaries who had been inspired and motivated by Sachindra Nath Sanyal and the HRA. He had taken it upon himself to rid the people of the notorious police inspector Charles Traggart, who had perpetrated untold atrocities on innocent people and had tortured revolutionaries. He decided to kill him. Unfortunately by mistake another innocent Englishman was killed. After his arrest, he boldly stated his original purpose and regretted the loss of an innocent life. He was subjected to unspeakable torture in order to get him to provide information about other revolutionaries and other revolutionary activities. But he gave nothing away. He was sentenced to death and went to the gallows with a smile. Scratched on the wall of the cell, in which he had been imprisoned prior to his hanging, were found the words: "Non-violence has no place in Indian politics." Years later, one of those who had been present that night was to declare that he had wept when he heard Bhagat Singh's narration of the story of Gopinath Saha.

Earlier in the evening he had been surprised to see that a large number of the delegates, after having washed off the dust of their long journey, had sat with whatever source of light they could get hold of, lanterns, battery powered flashlights and even the cooking fires, to read the Rehraas Sahib from their *gutka*s. Early next morning, too, so many of them sat and read the Japji Sahib. The image of so many so-called uneducated, semi-literate villagers, reading the difficult language of the

BIRTH OF A REVOLUTIONARY

prayer book so fluently, aroused in Bhagat Singh's heart the desire to learn his mother tongue. The *jatha* was given a warm farewell and as they walked away they sang: *"Laaj rakh laye, Bhagat Singh pyare ne laaj rakh laye"* (Omesh Saigal, p. 84).

By the time he returned to Lahore a few days later, the details of the reception accorded to the *jatha* at Banga had already preceded him and by the time Kishan Singh returned from Bombay, there was a letter waiting for him from *Jathedar* Kartar Singh, thanking him for the warm reception that the *jatha* had been accorded in Banga, congratulating him for having such a wonderful son and praising the tremendous effort that Bhagat Singh had made and the great organisational abilities that he had displayed. The letter ended with the prediction that Bhagat Singh was destined for great things and one day would take his place amongst the handful of leaders who would shape the destiny of the nation. When Kishan Singh turned from reading the letter to shower praise on his son, it was to find him absorbed in copying out the letters of the Punjabi alphabet from a Punjabi primer. Kishan Singh smiled indulgently. How typical of his son—the great achievement of having given a rousing welcome to the *jatha* in the face of stiff opposition, was already a thing of the past, to be put away and forgotten. The mind and the heart had already moved on to the next objective—to gain mastery and fluency over his mother tongue. Kishan Singh was sure that in this too, Bhagat Singh's efforts would be crowned with success.

Dilbagh Singh when he heard of what had happened seethed with anger at the failure of all his efforts and felt that he had been greatly humiliated in the eyes of his British masters. It was not possible for him to punish the entire population of Banga and Roda, who he knew had contributed to the success of the reception. They had broken no laws and it was not possible for him to single them out and trump up charges against them.

105

SHAHEED BHAGAT SINGH

It was Bhagat Singh, his close relative, who had given all the directions for organising the function and without his efforts and motivation the reception would not have taken place at all. If he was to make a point at all he would best make it by punishing Bhagat Singh. So all his desire for revenge, for what he considered a great humiliation, was focused on Bhagat Singh. Action against Bhagat Singh would deter others from disobeying his decrees in the future. He trumped up charges against Bhagat Singh, which in his position as magistrate was not difficult for him to do. But by now Bhagat Singh had admirers both in the intelligence and the police departments, and information about the impending arrest was leaked out to Kishan Singh well in time. At Kishan Singh's behest, Bhagat Singh returned to Kanpur and went underground. It was also at this time that he once again assumed the identity of Balwant Singh and spent a few months in Delhi working for the *Veer Arjun*. According to Omesh Saigal it was during this sojourn in Kanpur that Bhagat Singh served as the headmaster of a National school.

The revolutionaries needed money for their activities. Not only did they incur expenses in all the travelling that members of the HRA had to do in connection with their activities, there were also the day to day expenses to be met as far as housing, feeding and clothing the members was concerned because most of them had given up their regular means of livelihood in order to devote themselves entirely to the activities of the association. There was also a major expense involved in the printing and distribution of revolutionary literature and the procurement of arms and ammunition to carry out terrorist activities. Generous contributions were received from sympathisers and patrons, prominent among them Shivaprasad Gupta, Purshottam Das Tandon, the novelist Sarat Chandra Chatterji, A. N. Sircar the advocate

BIRTH OF A REVOLUTIONARY

general, and even Motilal Nehru, who frequently helped Chandra Shekhar Azad with money. But even though the revolutionaries kept a strict control of the money and lived virtually, the lives of ascetics, the money was always running short. In order to finance their activities they resorted to robberies and dacoities. Manmathnath Gupta, who himself participated in these activities, suggests that Bhagat Singh too may have been involved, and they were perhaps together in one dacoity. He points out that even though Bhagat Singh's niece, writing about this period of her uncle's life, mentions that Bhagat Singh participated in these activities only half-heartedly and against his will, she is really offering an apology where no apology is necessary. Bhagat Singh, like all revolutionaries, believed that the ends justified the means and if the robbing of a few British toadies and the looting of a few government institutions helped to hasten the departure of the British from India, so be it. The revolutionaries were convinced that this was a perfectly legitimate method of raising funds. Revolutionaries in Russia and Ireland had in the past resorted to hold-ups to garner funds for their activities and Sachindra Nath Sanyal, in the constitution of the HRA, refers to the levying of a forced contribution, a phrase first used by the Irish revolutionaries. In fact the report of the Sedition Committee mentions an incident where in a village dacoity, the revolutionaries had left behind a receipt for the exact amount of money taken, which the victim could encash when India gained her freedom. As part of this "criminal" drive to raise funds, the revolutionaries committed what was perhaps their most daring and most publicised raid. Members of the Hindustan Republican Association stopped the 8 Down from Hardoi to Lucknow, one mile from the Kakori railway station on 9 August 1925. A safe containing government funds was broken open and a sum of Rs. 4679, 1 anna and

SHAHEED BHAGAT SINGH

6 pies was taken away by the revolutionaries (Gurdev Singh Deol, *Shaheed- e- Azam, Bhagat Singh*, p. 23).

In the process one passenger was killed. The British, aware of the ripple effect this daring act of robbery would create, reacted swiftly and effectively. Most of those connected with the raid were arrested and what came to be called the *Kakori Conspiracy* case was opened. Amongst those arrested were Ram Prasad Bismil, Ashfaqullah Khan, Thakur Roshan Singh, Rajendra Lahiri, Sachindra Nath Sanyal and Jogesh Chandra Chatterji. Only Chandra Shekhar Azad and Kundan Lal Gupta escaped the snares of the dragnet which the British had cast. This daring dacoity, which received tremendous publicity, provided a great impetus to the revolutionary movement.

Almost as soon as the arrests had been made, machinery was set in motion to secure the release of those arrested. A committee was set up to fight the case in court. The prominent members of the committee were Ganesh Shankar Vidyarthi and the two Nehrus, Motilal and Jawaharlal. But in spite of this high powered committee, the revolutionaries themselves had little faith in British justice and knew that left to the courts to decide, the outcome of the trial was really a foregone conclusion. So a behind the scenes scheme was set in motion to try and help those arrested to escape from jail. Bhagat Singh was actively involved in this scheme and made frequent trips to Kanpur in connection with this effort. The first attempt made in November 1925 failed because someone connected with the scheme had been indiscreet and details of the attempt had somehow been conveyed to the jail authorities. The second attempt in January 1926 met a similar fate.

The growing disillusionment with the Congress, especially amongst the youth, provided the ideal breeding ground for the spawning of another militant organisation to fill the

108

vacuum created by the arrest of most of the leading figures of the HRA. In April 1926, Bhagat Singh and his comrades, Bhagwati Charan Vohra, Sukhdev, and Ram Krishen put their heads and their efforts together and set up a militant youth organisation which they named Naujawan Bharat Sabha, with Ram Krishen being elected as president of the fledgling organisation and Bhagat Singh as its secretary. It was formed with the aim of motivating young men, especially students, to channelise their energies towards the service of the nation and of humanity. As a result, at the beginning, the sabha's activities and programmes concentrated on the conducting of debates connected with moral, literary and social subjects. It also worked towards popularising swadeshi goods and encouraging people to abjure the use of foreign, especially British goods. The effort was to inculcate in the members a spirit of brotherhood, plain living and high thinking, a desire for physical fitness and an interest in the Indian languages and in the rich Indian cultural heritage. There was a particularly strong emphasis on secularism and in fact each new member, as part of his enrolment procedure, had to sign a pledge that he would always place the larger interest of his country before the narrower interests of his own community. It was emphasised that no person should be discriminated against on the grounds of the community that he belonged to. To the modern student of the history of this period, the emphasis that the NBS laid on secularism may seem overly exaggerated. But when we consider the background against which this emphasis had its genesis, it appears to be both natural and inevitable. 1924 had seen a veritable nightmare as far as communal violence was concerned. There had been incidents of communal violence in Delhi, Gulbarga, Nagpur, Lucknow, Shahjahanpur, Allahabad, Jabalpur, and worst of all, in Korhat. The Korhat riots tore apart the very fabric of Indian secularism. So great and awful was the carnage spread over 9 and 10 September that in order to control it four thousand Hindus were forced to board special trains and leave. Of these two thousand were lodged in camps in Rawalpindi and the others scattered in camps in other places, where they remained till law and order was restored and they could return to their native place without causing any further conflict between the two communities.

But soon after coming into existence, as was perhaps inevitable, the NBS adopted a political agenda. Bhagwati Charan framed and wrote a manifesto for the sabha. In this he exhorted the young men and women of India to follow the example of the Russian youth, who readily laid down their lives to secure the emancipation of their motherland from the tyrannical and imperialistic rule of the czars. The political aims of the sabha were clearly enunciated in the manifesto. These aims were:

a) To establish a completely independent republic of the labourers and peasants of India.

b) To infuse a spirit of patriotism in the hearts of the Indian youth in order to establish a united Indian nation.

c) To express sympathy with and to assist the economic, industrial and social movements, which being free from communal sentiments, are intended to take us nearer the ideal, namely the establishment of a completely independent republic of labourers and peasants.

d) To organise the labourers and peasants.

(Quoted by Gurdev Singh Deol, p. 24)

The manifesto is also an important historical document because it shows us the growing influence of socialism on the minds of the revolutionaries. It states:

The future programme of preparing the country will begin

with the motto: "Revolution by the masses for the masses." This meant that the struggle for freedom must not be limited to a few groups of people, but must involve the active participation of at least 99% of the citizens of the country. The youth had a very important role to play in the process because they would be the main instrument, which would awaken the masses and bring a desire for revolution in their hearts and minds, by making them understand that the revolution would not mean that there would be a change of masters, a set of Indian masters replacing the British masters. It would mean the birth of a completely new state and a new order of things where all men would be equal. The manifesto made a specific attack on religious bigotry, where members of one community carried deep rooted prejudices against members of other communities in their hearts. It stated that religious bigotry was one of the biggest hurdles in the way of progress. This narrow mindedness, this communal prejudice had been exploited to their advantage by the foreign enemy much to our own detriment.

If we were to sum up the aims of the Sabha in one sentence, it would be: to establish and promote secularism and socialism. In order to promote secularism and remove all distinctions caused by communal traditions, the Sabha adopted the practice of community dinners, where, very much like the gurdwara *langar*s of the Sikhs, not only was the food cooked by people irrespective of their caste or creed, but also people of all castes and creeds sat together to partake of the food. As a result, Hindus, Muslims, Sikhs, Christians, Brahmins, Jats, and people from the so-called untouchable castes all came together as one community. But these community dinners went one step further than the *langar*s in order to remove all distinctions of community. In order to get rid of the tradition where the kind of meat, *halal* or *jhatka* that a community ate created a divide, both kinds of meat were cooked together and everyone ate of the same dish. (Dr. L. P. Mathur, p. 36)

Most declarations of secularism at that time seemed half-hearted and did not succeed in breaking down the superstitions that separated one religion or one caste from the other. Bhagat Singh wanted to bring people together on a rational basis, a basis that would eschew all superstitions and meaningless rituals. He wanted them to have a complete change of heart and provide immediate and dramatic proof of this change. Therefore, in addition, lectures were arranged where leaders from each community spoke openly against the orthodox rituals and mindless superstitions that were practised in their own religion and which came in the way of a true realisation of God.

The sabha not only aimed to bring together the uneducated masses, the labourers and the peasants, and organise them in a movement against imperialistic and capitalist exploitation, it also aimed at arousing the sensibilities of the so-called privileged class and the intelligentsia. Much energy was expended in publishing and circulating weekly papers in different provinces and the publication of booklets and pamphlets, which sought to inform the educated reading public about the course of events and the thought patterns that were now taking place and emerging in different parts of the world.

From the beginning, the sabha evolved a two level programme to further its ends. On one hand there was what can be called an open programme, which consisted of activities like debates and seminars, and publication and circulation of literature which was mainly political in nature, with the aim of enlightening and educating the masses. But there was another programme, which, because it was extremely subversive in nature, had to be carried on in the utmost secrecy. This programme included the setting up of a secret press, which published literature that was so subversive and inflammatory that if it had been published under the open programme, it would have immediately invited repressive action against the sabha. This programme included the collection of funds for terrorist activities, the sending of suitable persons abroad for military and scientific training, especially in the manufacture and use of weapons like bombs, importing arms and ammunition and also the setting up of factories for their manufacture. The secret programme also included establishing a network of Indian revolutionaries abroad. The penetration of the army by members of the sabha was another item on the agenda.

One of the pioneers of communism in India, Muzaffar Ahmed, met Bhagat Singh during this time and wrote an article on him. In this article he makes a reference to the sabha:

My acquaintance with Bhagat Singh was rather short-lived. Naturally I hesitate to write about him as it amounts to writing on a subject on which one knows very little ... I went to Lahore in December 1926, intending to spend the whole of December and January there. I saw Bhagat Singh for the first time in the house of comrade Abdul Majid. Abdul Majid introduced him to me. Later Bhagat Singh became known to the public through thousands of photos in a particular pose. In these photos, he appears clean shaven, with closely cropped hair, wearing a hat, a shirt and half-pants. The country knows Bhagat Singh in this form. But I saw Bhagat Singh differently, as a Sikh young man He had long hair and was turbaned. His face had a sparsely growing beard and he wore pyjamas, a shirt and a coat. In my memory sits this lovely face.

The Naujawan Bharat Sabha was already in existence before my visit to Lahore. I do not remember when it had actually started. What I felt as an outsider was that it was a loosely knit organization and its leaders belonged to various shades.

It contained nationalists, communists and, of course Bhagat Singh and his friends. This means that Naujawan Bharat Sabha was open also to revolutionaries who believed in terrorism. Many of its members were just 20 years of age. On the other hand, people of 40 too, like Kedarnath Sehgal, were to be found among the members.

Now with the hindsight of time, it would seem that Muzaffar Ahmed's interaction with Bhagat Singh and the sabha was so cursory that he indeed knew very little on the subject. In spite of the "loose" coming together of various ideologies that Ahmed perceived amongst the members of the sabha, they were all committed firmly to their faith and belief to communism. They believed firmly that the class struggle between the peasants, workers and Indian capitalists on one hand, and the Indians and their imperialistic foreign rulers on the other, was inevitable.

Though on the surface the sabha appeared to be loosely knit, it had, in fact, a very tightly established structure, without which it would not have been able to carry out its secret programme. First and foremost, the sabha demanded complete selfless dedication from its members. No member was permitted to join any other organisation without prior permission from the district head. He was expected to devote all his time to the activities of the sabha and be ready, always, to lay down his life for his country. The members were sworn to complete secrecy in order to prevent the exposure of any of its anti-British activities to the authorities. The programmes of the sabha were controlled by a Central Council, which was the governing body of the sabha. The council was constituted by including representatives of all the provinces of India. Any decision arrived at by the council had to be unanimously agreed to by all its members. As far as the sabha was concerned, the Central Council had absolute power. The

BIRTH OF A REVOLUTIONARY

council was responsible for chalking out programmes of various activities, which would further the goals and objectives of the sabha. It would also supervise and co-ordinate the activities in the different provinces. The council also carried the direct responsibility for the sabha's programmes being carried on abroad. The second rung of the hierarchy was the Provincial Committee. This committee comprised five members, each representing a different area of the sabha's activities: propaganda, enrolment of members, collection of funds, storage of arms and ammunition, and foreign connections. The function of the Provincial Committee was to regulate the activities of the sabha at the provincial level, including directions as to the use of arms and ammunition. All decisions arrived at by the committee had to be agreed to unanimously by all the five members.

At the third level was the District Organiser, appointed by the Provincial Committee. The organiser was expected to establish branches of the sabha in all the villages and towns of the district. Not only was the District Organiser expected to be tactful and intelligent and extremely skilled at inter-personal relationship, but he was also expected to be familiar with the social, political and economic conditions prevailing in his district.

Shiv Verma, in his memoirs, writes:

In 1926, Bhagat Singh, Sukhdev, Bhagwati Charan, Yashpal and others founded the Naujawan Bharat Sabha in Lahore. It was a sort of open wing of the revolutionary party. Under its auspices meetings were held, statements were issued, and leaflets published to inculcate and publicise revolutionary ideology. After a study of worldwide exploitation, poverty and inequality, these men had come to the conclusion that complete independence of India could only be fruitful if it was supplemented by an economic independence. One of

SHAHEED BHAGAT SINGH

the works of the Sabha was to hold magic lantern shows of the pictures of the revolutionary martyrs with a running commentary on the history of the revolutionary movement. The Sabha was a very powerful organ of publicity.

Whenever Bhagat Singh came to Kanpur, he brought along some Naujawan Bharat Sabha literature. Association with Radhamohan Gokulji and Satyabhakta had made Kanpur comrades prone to socialism, Bhagat Singh strengthened this tendency and inspired us to study and discuss socialism.

He used to say that the assault on British imperialism would have no meaning unless it was also accompanied by the end of exploitation by man of man or of one state by another. That is why, he said, we must rear the grassroots, the masses, in every possible way. The Naujawan Bharat Sabha's trade unions and in the series of articles in periodicals, in magic lantern shows, in leaflets and booklets, were all attempts related in this direction.

Bhagat Singh was the first revolutionary to undertake the work of mass contact on such a massive scale. Even after his arrest he utilized the courtroom as a venue for the propagation of revolutionary ideology. He was not only a good fighter but an astute propagandist.
("Samsmritiyam", quoted by Manmathnath Gupta, p.101-102)

During the summer of 1926, the sabha held a series of meetings which were attended by large numbers of people and was a great success. No wonder Muzaffar Ahmed categorically states that no other youth organisation attained the political eminence that the sabha did.

"The NBS played a big role in popularizing anti-imperialism and socialist ideas, especially in Punjab and Sind and was to outlast both the HRA that preceded it and the Hindustan Socialist Republican Association that came after. Its

116

BIRTH OF A REVOLUTIONARY

popularity can be gauged from the fact that many prominent Congressmen like Saifuddin Kitchlew found it prudent to associate with it and speak from its platform, as a means of reaching out to wider sections, despite the fact that several aspects of the politics and policies of the NBS militated against the Gandhian paradigm of the Congress. Its socialist orientation and mass character were also to facilitate the association of many of its members with the Workers and Peasants and Communist parties in the future" (Quoted by P. M. S. Grewal, p. 44).

With such a tremendous sweep of popularity, it was inevitable that the NBS should be on the radar of the secret police. The reports of the police filed at that time are now available to us and we know that the sabha and its activities had, for the British, become highly suspect. Sohan Singh Josh tells us: "British intelligence hounds came to know about its real activities. The principals of colleges in Lahore were told the real motives of the Sabha and the Sabha was excluded from the use of their college and hostel halls . . . no college staff member was to lecture for the Sabha on social topics, civics etc. This order gave a death blow to the Sabha" (Sohan Singh Josh, *My Meetings with Bhagat Singh*, p.12-13).

The centre of this suspicion was, of course, Bhagat Singh. In May 1927, while he was walking through a garden in Lahore, Bhagat was picked up by the police. He was kept in a lockup of the Railway Police for a month till the British could come up with adequate charges against him. Finally they accused him of throwing a bomb on a crowd during the Dussehra celebrations the previous year. He was shifted to the Lahore fort and then to the Borstal jail. Finally, the superintendent of the CID, one Newman, arrived in his cell and advised him to confess that he had thrown the bomb or else he would be framed for the *Kakori Dacoity* case for which the CID had

117

SHAHEED BHAGAT SINGH

sufficient evidence to ensure his conviction and consequent hanging. When the case finally came to court, in spite of all the bluster and manipulation, there was no evidence against Bhagat Singh and he was released, though a bail of Rs. 60,000 was imposed upon him. This bail was jointly furnished by Barrister Duni Chand and Daula Ram of Lahore. In a letter to a friend, Amar Chand, a student in America, written shortly after this incident, he writes about the case and about the bail, specially the fact that with the passage of time the bail has not been withdrawn, which indicates that he is still being suspected of involvement in the case. (Virender Sandhu, Shaheed Bhagat Singh p. 28-29).

On 17 December 1927, Rajindra Lahiri, one of the accused in the *Kakori Dacoity* case was hanged and two days later Ram Prasad Bismil, Ashfaqullah Khan and Thakur Roshan Singh were also executed. Sachindra Nath Sanyal and J. C. Chatterji were sentenced to life imprisonment. Of those who had taken an active part in this episode of India's freedom struggle, only Chandra Shekhar Azad and Kundan Lal Gupta managed to escape. The Kakori martyrs have all become part of Indian folklore. Just before his execution Ram Prasad Bismil said, "We seek to be born again, shall meet again and shall jointly fight once again for the cause of the motherland as comrades-in-arms."

Ashfaqullah Khan told his nephew: "You must remember that the Hindu community has dedicated great souls like Khudiram and Kanailal. To me this is my good fortune that belonging to the Muslim community, I have acquired the privilege of following in the footsteps of the great martyrs."

It is said that as the three marched to the gallows they sang the song that was to become the anthem of the freedom struggle: *"Sarfaroshi ki tamanna ab hamare dil mein hai."*

In April 1928, during the Young Men's Conference in

Amritsar, Bhagat Singh came into contact with Sohan Singh "Josh" and through him with the Workers and Peasants Party, the Punjab unit of which was called the Kirti Kissan Party. The Workers and Peasants Party had been set up by the communists when the Communist Party had been banned and subjected to tremendous repression. In order to continue their activities and yet escape the eyes of the authorities, this new party had been founded in 1926 and in two short years had become a well organised all-India party, now called the Kirti Kissan Party in the Punjab. It had its headquarters in Lahore and published a weekly magazine called *Kirti*. When they first got to know each other, while attending the conference, Sohan Singh told Bhagat Singh that his party was organising a special conference to commemorate the martyrs of Jallianwala Bagh. Bhagat Singh said that he and his friends of the sabha would also like to be a part of this conference. Bhagat Singh was able to use this association to give the sabha a second lease of life. The Naujawan Bharat Sabha was now named the Naujawan Bharat Sabha, Punjab and the Kirti Kissan Party became, more or less, a subsidiary of the sabha.

The two associates, the sabha and the Kirti Kissan Party, soon found an occasion for launching a fresh agitation against the British. The wheat crop had failed in the Punjab and many farmers were ruined. Yet the government had not provided them relief with any degree of seriousness. The little relief that had been provided was sadly inadequate. A few Congress members also came to attend the meeting that had been called to launch the agitation. The meeting was held on 23 May 1928. Although the official declaration stated that the agitation had been sponsored by the Congress, everyone knew that it was the brainchild of Bhagat Singh's sabha. The meeting was held in Ghaman village in Lahore district. Among the many speakers who delivered excellent speeches on the

SHAHEED BHAGAT SINGH

occasion, were Satyapal, Kedar Nath Sehgal and M. A. Majid, who were universally recognised to be extremist leaders. There was a great deal of excited anticipation for what was recognised to be a fresh phase in the freedom struggle. But for once the British showed some compassion and wisdom by granting extremely generous remissions in revenue to the victims of the crop failure and thus, effectively took the wind out of the sails of the proposed agitation. But the meeting did serve to strengthen the bonds between the sabha and the Kirti Kissan Party and also to bring extremist leaders from different parties onto a common platform. For a short period the leaders seemed to find a common denomination in their support to the various meetings that the Congress organised at the time.

During this time Bhagat Singh also joined the editorial staff of the *Kirti* and contributed articles to the weekly under the pen name "Vidrohi". An article was published in the weekly titled "Students and Politics", which advocated the participation of students in politics. Though it did not carry his usual signature of "Vidrohi", it is now universally accepted, from the tone of the letter, that it was written by Bhagat Singh. The periodical also carried a series of articles under the heading "What is Anarchism?" which sought to define and justify anarchism. Though these articles did not carry the name of the author, their authorship is now generally ascribed to Bhagat Singh. During this time he also translated into Hindi the work of his favourite revolutionary, Danbril of Ireland. The work was titled "Fight for Irish Freedom" but was in actual fact little more than a biography of Bhagat Singh's hero.

Bhagat Singh's association with the Kirti Kissan Party, fruitful as it was both for the party and for the sabha, did not last very long. This was because, unlike Josh, he did not have much faith in the gradual development of revolution, both political and social. He believed that as long as the end of political and social revolution was achieved quickly it did not matter if the means adopted were violent or non-violent. In fact, given the then situation in India, he was a firm believer in the "politics of militancy". But the influence of Josh, who was later to become one of the most prominent communist leaders in India, remained dominant during this time and brought his ideology around from anarchism to socialism.

The Hindustan Republican Association had been the only revolutionary association of national importance. With the execution and imprisonment of most of its prominent leaders in the wake of the *Kakori Dacoity* case, a void in this area had been created. But the revolutionary spirit of firebrands like Bhagat Singh and Chandra Shekhar Azad would ensure that this void did not remain for very long. The Kanpur group of revolutionaries began to re-form under the leadership of Chandra Shekhar Azad, one of the participants in the *Kakori Dacoity* case, who had escaped the police dragnet, ably assisted by Kundan Lal Gupta, who had also participated in the dacoity and managed to escape, Shiv Verma, Bejoy Kumar Sinha, Jaidev Kapoor, Gaya Prasad and others. In Lahore it was Bhagat Singh, Bhagwati Charan Vohra, Sukhdev, Kishori Lal, Yashpal and others, who had emerged as the main leaders of the movement. Shiv Verma tells us that even though the revolutionary movement was passing through a transitory period as it were, this constant thinking and rethinking of ideology continued to churn in the minds of the leaders. He tells us of the great influence that the Communist leaders like Sohan Singh Josh and Radha Mohan Gokulji in Lahore and Maulana Hasrat Mohani and Satyabhakta in Kanpur had on the minds of the leaders in drawing them closer to the cause of socialism ("Introduction", *Selected Writings of Bhagat Singh*, p. 26).

SHAHEED BHAGAT SINGH

The influence and tilt towards socialism was further strengthened by a series of developments in the country. The Workers and Peasants Party had formed units of their organisation in a number of states. There was also a spate of strikes of industrial workers led by the communists in the period 1921-1928, which influenced the minds of the revolutionaries. Sympathy for socialism was further aroused by the Peshawar and Kanpur cases against the communists.

Bhagat now took the initiative to try once again to bring all the different revolutionary groups together to form an all-India revolutionary party. To this end, he organised a meeting of all the leading revolutionaries at the Ferozeshah Kotla Ground in Delhi on 8 and 9 September 1928. In the meeting about sixty revolutionaries from Punjab, the United Provinces, Bihar and Rajputana took part. Prominent amongst these sixty were Bhagat Singh, Rajguru, Sohan Singh Josh, Sardul Singh Kavishar, Chandra Shekhar Azad, Yashpal, Bhagwati Charan, Bijoy Kumar Sinha, Surendra Pande, Jaidev Gupta, Brahm Dutt Mishra, Shiv Verma, Jitendra Nath Das and others. Bengal, for some reason, went unrepresented.

Bhagat Singh placed a number of proposals before the meeting for discussion:

• A time has come to boldly declare socialism as our ultimate goal.

• The name of the party should be changed accordingly, so that our people would know our ultimate aim.

• We should undertake only such action which might have direct relationship with the demands and sentiments of the people, and that we should not fritter away our time and energy in killing petty police officials or informers.

• For our funds we should lay our hands on government money and avoid as far as possible, actions on private houses.

122

• The principle of collective leadership should be strictly observed.

After due deliberations spread over two days, the proposals were accepted by a majority vote. The name of the Hindustan Republican Association was now changed to the Hindustan Socialist Republican Association.

Through his proposals, Bhagat Singh revealed a very important shift in his political ideology. Where, before, he had been a strong advocate of individual acts of terrorism as a means of fighting British Colonial rule, he now stated that acts of violence must be linked to specific problems of the people in order to have the maximum effect.

The following decisions were also taken at the conference:

a) To take an active part in the boycott of the Simon Commission and to throw a bomb at the train carrying its members.

b) To open bomb factories in Calcutta, Saharanpur, Agra and Lahore.

c) To arrange a good instructor to give training to the members in making bombs.

d) To murder the informers in the *Kakori Dacoity* case and to free J. C. Chatterji from jail. (Gurdev Singh Deol. P. 29)

The headquarters of the Party were also shifted from Jhansi, where they had been located after the Kakori Dacoity case, to Agra. Though these discussions spread over two days, the revolutionaries had taken the first active step towards adopting Marxism as the road to achieving their goal, though they still did not seem to have a clear understanding of the use of Marxism and Leninism as a weapon against the imperialistic British rule in India.

According to Ajoy Ghosh, who was at that time one of the leaders of the UP group of revolutionaries:

SHAHEED BHAGAT SINGH

As for the most important question, it was the question in what manner the fight for freedom and socialism was to be waged. Armed action by individuals and groups, was, however to remain our main task. Nothing else, we held, could smash constitutional illusion, nothing else could free the country from the grip in which fear held it. When the stagnant calm was broken by a series of hammer blows, delivered by us at selected points and on suitable occasions, against the most hated official of the government, and the mass movement unleashed, we would link ourselves with that moment, act in its armed detachment and give it social direction. (*Bhagat Singh and his Comrades*, p. 4)

Thus we see that within the span of a few short years, from the time he abandoned his studies and the formation of the HSRA, Bhagat Singh had grown and evolved from a soldier, fighting in the cause of freedom, willing to take direction from the leaders, into a great revolutionary leader himself, who had not only taken the lead in organising the conference at Ferozeshah Kotla in order to bring all other revolutionary leaders together, but had also given direction to the common programme that had resulted in a unity of purpose being forged between the leaders. An illustration of this transformation is provided by Ajoy Ghosh, who had met Bhagat Singh when he had first set out on the path of revolution and who met him again after an interval of several years.

One day in 1928, I was surprised when a young man walked into my room and greeted me. It was Bhagat Singh, but not the Bhagat Singh that I had met before. Tall and magnificently proportioned, with a keen, intelligent face and gleaming eyes, he looked a different man altogether. And as he talked I realized that he had grown not merely in years ... All those who met Bhagat Singh then and afterwards have testified to his remarkable intelligence and to the powerful impression he made while talking. Not that he was a brilliant speaker.

124

But he spoke with such force, passion and earnestness that one could not help being impressed. We talked the whole night . . . It seemed to me that a new era was dawning for our party. We knew what we wanted and we knew how to reach our goal.

(Kuldip Nayar, *Without Fear: The Life and Trial of Bhagat Singh*, p. 16)

Chapter 4

ASSASSINATION OF SAUNDERS

One of the provisions that the Montague Chelmsford Reforms of 1919 had made was that a commission would be set up every ten years to review not only the working of the Montague Chelmsford Reforms, but also to assess the need for any further action in this regard. The provision was not regarded with any seriousness either by the British rulers or by the leaders of the Indian freedom struggle, because everyone saw it for what it was—a sop to the growing political aspirations of the Indian people. There was grave unrest in India after Gandhi aborted the Non-Cooperation Movement. All across the country there had been widespread communal riots, a large number of strikes by industrial workers and also a spurt of terrorist activities sponsored by the revolutionaries. But what the British government must have regarded as its greatest threat was the increasing restiveness within the Congress. Ever since it was founded by Allan Octavian Hume in 1885, the Congress had been regarded by the British as a loyal ally. In those early years the government kept the Congress happy by doling out to it an occasional crumb in the form of some little concessions. Though no one either recognised or admitted the fact, the Congress was, at that time, little more than an instrument in the hands of the British rulers, which could be used, when needed, to control public opinion in India and manipulate it to the advantage of the rulers. The Indians came to look upon the Congress as their conduit to the British rulers. As a result, the rich and the important in India, all sought to curry favour with the Congress leaders. But by the turn of the century there were those within the Congress who were no longer content with the role that the British rulers had assigned to the Congress and the faithfulness with which the Congress, over the years had fulfilled this role. There was the growth of a liberal ideology within the Congress and it was no longer satisfied with the crumbs that the rulers were content to throw its way. The demand was now for self-rule. Bal Gangadhar Tilak famously declared, "Freedom is my birthright and I mean to have it." But even while voicing this demand, the Congress remained faithful to the rulers.

Gandhi had led and won many rights for the Indians settled in South Africa by adoption of non-violent methods. He returned to India and advocated that Indians too should adopt such methods to get the rulers to accede to their demands. His political philosophy found a ready voice and platform through the politics of the Congress and he soon became the voice and life of the Congress, and through the Congress, the life and face of the rebellion against the British, which was now at the core of political life in India. Gandhi was no revolutionary and did not talk in words that were fuelled by violent hostility. He was in favour of a cooperative method in the struggle and eschewed the use of violence, which for him was self-defeating. His desire was to quietly wean the British to sympathise with the Indian cause. Gandhi had great charisma and through his speeches and through his own example, won the heart of every Indian. But with the withdrawal of the Non-Cooperation Movement, Gandhi lost the support, not only of the radicals like Bhagat Singh, but also of a section of his own party. Motilal Nehru and C. K. Das moved away from the mainstream Congress and formed a new party, the "Swaraj Party" whose avowed aim was to gain complete freedom. The move won sympathy amongst more and more Congressmen and in the 1927 session of the Congress, held in Madras, a resolution was proposed seeking that the Congress should now state that its avowed goal was complete independence. It was with the greatest difficulty that the moderates were able to defeat the passing of the resolution and to keep dominion status as the goal of the Congress.

Alarmed by all these developments, the British felt that it would be an appropriate time to pull out the sop of further constitutional reforms provided by the provisions of the Montague Chelmsford Reforms and use it to try and counter the deteriorating civil and political situation in the country. Therefore, using the 1929 elections in England as an excuse, the British government advanced the setting up of the commission for the purpose of examining the need for constitutional reform in India by two years and the commission was set up in 1927 rather than the statutory 1929. The commission consisted of Sir John Simon and six British members of Parliament. This purely white composition of the commission was immediately suspect in the eyes of all sections of the Indian people. The exclusion of Indians from the commission would have only one consequence—the report would minimise the need to make any real concession to the political aspirations of the people. Inevitably there was a strong reaction in India when the composition of the commission was announced, and the people rose as one against the blatantly unfair and prejudiced action. Gandhi, who had till now hoped that the British would grant dominion status by 31 December 1929 and that he could persuade the Congress to accept dominion status, regarded the appointment of the commission as an anti-climax. In this appointment Gandhi saw that the British had little intention of giving the Indians any meaningful political power. He saw the move for what it was: an effort to win the moderates over by throwing a sop their way. In his belief that he would be able to win the British over to a step by step transfer of political power, he had lost the respect and support of many Indians. This loss was now being compounded by what he regarded as an act of betrayal. A thoroughly disillusioned Gandhi now persuaded the Congress to call for a total boycott of the Simon Commission. Lala Lajpat Rai voiced the Congress opposition to the commission and its decision to boycott it when he rose up in the Central Legislature Assembly in February 1927 and moved the following resolution:

"The present constitution of the commission and its terms of reference are unworthy of acceptance by the House. Therefore, this House advises the Government that it should have nothing to do with the Commission."

He also made an extremely moving speech justifying this resolution. As it was a foregone conclusion that the many English members of the assembly would vote against Lalaji's resolution, he directed his pleas towards the Indian members in the following words: "Let the members understand that they are slaves in the eyes of the British Government and of the world. When they vote on the resolution let them remember that in 1919, because of a single epidemic many people died in our country. Let them remember that in this country ten crores of people do not have even one meal a day." Lalaji questioned the right of the British Parliament to frame a constitution for India. He reiterated that this right belonged to the Indian people alone. The people were determined that they would not let a constitution be thrust upon them by their rulers. Lalaji's resolution was the spark that lit a blazing fire.

Bhagat Singh and his comrades had parted ways with Gandhi and the moderates much earlier. They believed that the ends justified the means and every method used in their cause was a just method. This was diametrically opposed to Gandhi's firm belief that wrong means would not lead to right results. Because of this basic difference in belief, Gandhi eschewed violence in any form while the revolutionaries believed that the acts of violence alone would have any effect on the rulers.

Another basic difference was that while Gandhi had for long harboured faith in his ability to persuade the British government to adopt a step by step devolution of power to the Indians, and as such had advocated dominion status as the first goal. The revolutionaries were not ready to accept anything other than complete independence, not even as a stop gap, interim measure. In spite of the radical difference in approach and philosophy, the revolutionaries, as we have seen, supported Gandhi's call for a complete boycott of the Simon Commission. They believed that any move which stirred up the people against the British was a welcome move because it would serve to build up awareness amongst the people of the shackles by which the British kept them bound. As a result, the revolutionaries decided to lend their wholehearted support to the Congress and even stand side by side with it in any agitation that it launched.

As both Gandhi and Bhagat Singh had hoped, the call to boycott the Simon Commission struck a chord in every Indian heart and there were protests and demonstrations all over India. The Congress leaders fanned out all over the country and made rousing speeches against the inequity that the British government had imposed upon them. Right from the moment that Simon and his colleagues stepped off their ship in Bombay they were greeted by crowds of protestors who waved black flags at them and shouted in one voice, "Simon Go Back."

The strongest impact of the anti-Simon Commission movement was felt in the Punjab. The commission was expected in Lahore on 30 October 1928. Expecting a very strong protest to be made against the commission on its arrival, the government had taken the strongest precautionary measures. Prohibitory orders banning gatherings in public places and movement of processions had been put in place. It was generally expected that Lala Lajpat Rai would lead these protests and in spite of the fact that he was suffering from one of his frequent bouts of ill health, Lalaji was determined to live up to these expectations.

Lalaji had for many years exercised a strong influence on Bhagat Singh's family. Bhagat Singh's father, Kishan Singh, and uncle, Ajit Singh had together with Lala Lajpat Rai played a leading role in the agitation against the Punjab Canal Settlement and the Transit Bill of 1907, for which both Ajit Singh and Lalaji were deported and jailed in Mandalay. And when the Congress had been strongly divided between the hardliners and the moderates, Lalaji had thrown in his lot with the hardliners. For a while it seemed that he had given up his membership of the Congress to devote himself entirely to Arya Samaj activities. He re-entered the Congress in 1912. Bhagat Singh's father and Lala Lajpat Rai had worked side by side in all Arya Samaj activities connected with social welfare, providing relief to the victims of natural calamities like drought and famine and the earthquake in Kangra. They had

SHAHEED BHAGAT SINGH

together worked with the orphanage set up for the children of the victims of these calamities. Bhagat Singh had studied at the National College in Lahore of which Lalaji was one of the founder fathers. But over the years Kishan Singh and Ajit Singh had fallen out with Lalaji because of the sharp differences that had crept between them due to the divergent political ideologies that they had chosen to follow. While both Kishan Singh and Ajit Singh, and later Bhagat Singh, were committed to freeing India from the yoke of the British rule at any cost and by whatever means possible, Lala Lajpat Rai sometimes flirted with the Congress, sometimes seemed to espouse the cause of the revolutionaries and sometimes chose to go into political retirement. He had begun his career as a revolutionary and had been, if not an active member, at least a strong supporter of the Ghadar Party, participated vigorously in the Non-Cooperation Movement launched by Gandhi and had even been jailed for his role in it. This was the period when he set up national schools and colleges as an alternative to the government controlled educational system. When Gandhi suddenly called off the movement, Lajpat Rai like a large number of other leaders had been greatly disillusioned with this abrupt abandonment of what was an extremely successful movement. In the wake of the Hindu-Muslim riots, there was a rise of Muslim-only associations. Lajpat Rai saw this development with alarm and to counteract its fundamental and extremist elements, launched two Hindu-only movements: the Shuddhi and Sangathan movements which were aimed at bringing about the purification of Hinduism, and unity and co-operation between the various denominations of the Hindus. He had till now held blemish-less credentials as a secular leader. Now through the launching of these two movements, he was perceived to have done a complete turnabout and become a communal leader. This

132

new avatar that he had taken was anathema to Bhagat Singh who was completely and wholeheartedly committed to the cause of secularism and had done everything that was possible to eliminate all divisions along communal lines in his own association.

Lala Lajpat Rai went a step further in his efforts to promote Hinduism, along with Madan Mohan Malviya, the founder of the Hindu Mahasabha; he formed a Hindu-only group and decided to stand for election to the Central assembly. He decided to stand in opposition to Chaman Lal, a candidate who had been sponsored by radical stalwarts like Motilal Nehru and Satyamurti. Prominent revolutionary figures like Bhagat Singh, Bhagwati Charan Vohra and others decided to oppose Lala Lajpat Rai.

Sukhdevraj writes: "A meeting in support of Lala Lajpat Rai was advertised, where inter alia Madan Mohan Maliviya was to speak. While Malviya was speaking, a leaflet in English, entitled 'Lost Leader' was distributed, in which it said, 'The lion of Punjab has turned chicken-hearted.'

"The leaflet was based on the famous poem of Browning entitled 'Lost Leader'. The leaflet began with the paraphrase of the famous lines:

Just for a handful of silver he left us,
Just for a rebind to stick in his coat.

"The leaflet abounded with sentences that spoke ill of the Lala. I remember very well that this leaflet was being distributed by a man who stood in a sort of a pit and he was besieged by Lala's admirers. I also remember that Bhagat Singh was one of the persons distributing the leaflet . . .

"Lala Lajpat Rai mentioned this leaflet in his speech and said that this had been distributed by his sons. This was true, because those responsible for the leaflets were students or former students of the National College" (Quoted by Manmathnath Gupta, *Bhagat Singh and his Times*, p. 95).

But now in 1928, appreciating the need to present a united opposition to the Simon Commission, these acrimonious differences were pushed firmly into the background by both sides. Bhagat Singh, in spite of what he perceived as Lalaji's failures and his apparent betrayal of the revolutionary and secular cause, had great regard for Lala Lajpat Rai and his services to the nation in the past. He also knew that because of his services Lalaji had assumed such a stature in the eyes of the people that he more than anyone else stood as a symbol of the people of Punjab. Bhagat Singh and the other revolutionaries decided to give Lalaji wholehearted and unconditional support to make this act of opposition to the Simon Commission a great success.

One day before the proposed visit of the Simon Commission to Lahore on 29 October 1928, a meeting was called in the municipal garden. This meeting was chaired by Sirajuddin Ahmed. Lala Lajpat Rai made an impassioned speech and appealed to all sections of people to come together as one united force to oppose the Simon Commission. Sardar Kharak Singh expressed the hope that through their strong opposition to the Simon Commission, they would be striking another blow against British imperialism. People gathered for the meeting, expressed their strong resentment against the visit of the Simon Commission to Lahore and were sure that every individual in Punjab shared this resentment. It was decided at this meeting to organise a protest rally against the commission the next day and then to move out in a procession to show their solidarity and their anger against the visit. Word of this decision spread like wild fire and the next day more than five thousand people collected in a garden just outside the Lahore railway station, to take an active part in the proposed demonstration. Though Lala Lajpat Rai was the undoubted leader of the demonstration and thus always in the forefront, there were a host of other important leaders standing side by side with him and adding to the stature of the demonstration. There was Bhagat Singh offering all the moral support of the revolutionaries to the protest. Beside Bhagat Singh and his comrades, the other prominent leaders were Sir Mangal Singh, Duni Chand, Durga Das Khanna, Sardul Singh Kavishar, Raizada Hansraj, Lala Bodh Raj, Maulana Zafar Ali, Gopi Chand Bhargava, Abdul Qadir Qasuri and Dr Mohammad Alam. Bhagat Singh and his comrades ensured that every demonstrator wore a black armband as a mark both of protest and of mourning. Slogans of "Simon Go Back" rent the air. At about one o'clock in the afternoon, on the direction of Lala Lajpat Rai, the demonstrators moved out in a procession from the garden and headed towards the railway station.

The police had taken every conceivable step to try and prevent the demonstrators from reaching the railway station. The large police contingent, which had been allotted duty at the station for the occasion was being personally commanded by the senior superintendent of police of Lahore, J. A. Scott, who appreciated the gravity of the situation and was determined to do everything to ensure that the arrival of the commission was not impeded in any way. The commission, on its arrival, must have been dismayed by the sheer strength and volume of the slogan shouting demonstrators. As the members of the commission stepped off the train, the demonstrators surged forward to prevent them from leaving the station. Where before there had been the single, almost universal chant of "Simon Go Back", other slogans were now added by the crowd to its repertoire. There were angry cries of "Angrez Murdabad" (Death to the British) and "Inquilab

Zindabad" (Long live revolution). A section of the crowd also took up the chanting of a rhyme which seemed to have been especially composed for the occasion.

Hindustani Hai hum, Hindustan Hamara,
Mur Jao Simon, Jahan Hai Desh Tumhara.
(We are Indians and India is ours. Go back Simon to the country that is yours).

The crowd was so thick and so closely packed that it prevented any forward movement on the part of the members of the commission. It seemed that if the crowd had their way they would put the commission back on the train and send it hurtling homewards. The police swung in to try and save the situation. They formed a closely linked chain and tried to push the crowd back with no success whatsoever; the crowd did not retreat even an inch. A dead end was reached with the crowd holding fast and the helpless police forming a barricade between the crowd and the members of the commission. It was at this stage of the impasse that Lala Lajpat Rai delivered a rousing speech. He said, amongst other things, "If the Government did not wish the commission to see the demonstrators, the best thing for it was to put blindfolds over the eyes of the members and take them straight to the Government house" (Quoted by Dr. L. P. Mathur, Bhagat Singh: The Prince of Martyrs, p. 52).

This speech was probably the proverbial straw that broke the camel's back. Seething already with anger and frustration at his helplessness and the fact that the situation was rapidly spinning out of control, Scott ordered a *lathi* charge on the crowd. The police too, reacted with uncharacteristic fury and the blows that were rained on the unarmed citizens were far harder than what the situation demanded. Surprised and alarmed at the ferocity of the attack, some of the people

ASSASSINATION OF SAUNDERS

standing in the front broke rank and ran helter skelter. "Don't run, stand firm," Lala Lajpat Rai called to the crowd. "We are all true Satyagrahis and know how to face these blows." Hearing the calm steady voice of their leader, the people regained courage and even those who had tried to escape to safety returned to take their place in the crowd. Scott's fury now found a single focus, the leader of the demonstrators. He ordered the police to attack Lala Lajpat Rai and his string of supporters. A few policemen struck half-hearted blows at the revered leader until Saunders, Scott's deputy, moved forward, snatched the baton out of the policeman's hand, and struck a severe blow at Lala Lajpat Rai, in order to please his boss. Scott, seeing blood, also raised his baton and struck a blow at Lalaji.

He was merciless both in the severity and the number of blows that he struck. Like General Dyer before him, it was as if Scott was giving expression to all his accumulated frustration and anger. Lala Lajpat Rai had become a symbol of all those who had dared to defy the British. By punishing Lajpat Rai so furiously, he wanted to punish all those who had stood up against the British in the past and to set an example for the future. On and on the attack on Lalaji continued. It did not stop even when there was blood flowing from Lalaji's injuries. There was blood flowing from his head and from his chest and yet the blows continued unabated. They only stopped when Lalaji fell to the ground.

A hush descended on the crowd as they watched with horror the gruesome brutality that had been unleashed on their beloved leader. They could not believe that a person of Lajpat Rai's eminence should be subjected to such callous and heartless treatment for no other reason than that of demonstrating peacefully against the Simon Commission.

Bhagat Singh had been close enough to see all that transpired.

137

SHAHEED BHAGAT SINGH

As we have seen, there was really by now no love lost between Lala Lajpat Rai and Bhagat Singh. But he did have the highest regard for Lala Lajpat Rai as one of the senior most leaders in the freedom struggle. He was possessed with anger that young English policemen like Scott and Saunders could heap such insult and indignity on the head of a revered Indian leader like Lajpat Rai. As a child of twelve he had visited the Jallianwala Bagh a day after the massacre and keenly felt not only the horror of the brutality that had been unleashed on the hopeless crowd but also the sheer humiliation of it all. He saw in this act the same humiliation of the Indian people.

The police ceased their beating and those closest to Lajpat Rai helped him to his feet. Almost the first words that Lalaji uttered were: "I suspend the demonstration." It was a strange order indeed—neither in keeping with the tradition of non-violence, which propounded that the more you were subjected to violence the greater should be your resistance, nor in keeping with the tenets of the revolutionary movement. The crowd was unhappy and Lalaji realised that unless he moved quickly an extremely time situation could develop. He once again exhorted the crowd to disperse. So great was his standing with the masses that though they resented doing so, they quietly dispersed, much to the relief of Scott and Saunders. There were a few pockets in the crowd managed by volunteers from the Naujawan Bharat Sabha who held on and continued to raise slogans of "Simon Go Home" when the rest of the crowd had dispersed.

Looking back after all these years there are just two reasons that one can offer for Lala Lajpat Rai's implacable decision, neither of them very satisfactory. Perhaps having borne the brunt of the police violence himself Lala Lajpat Rai did not want any of his followers to have to bear it too or perhaps he feared that seeing the injuries from the blows that had

138

been dealt to their leader, the mob would be incited to acts of violence which would in turn lead to a veritable blood bath.

In the Papar Mandi area of the city a few members of the Naujawan Bharat Sabha had been badly wounded. As part of the protest against the visit of the Simon Commission, the organisers of the protest had called for a complete *hartal* in the city. But some die-hard loyalists to show their support for the British had deliberately opened their business. Among these was one Rai Bahadur Laxman Das. When a group of revolutionaries led by Bhagwati Charan and Yashpal asked him to shut his establishment, a group of his goons attacked them and inflicted grievous head wounds. Lala Lajpat Rai's blood was not the only blood that was shed in the city of Lahore that day.

That evening a huge public meeting was held to condemn the brutal violence of the police and to reiterate the boycott of the Simon Commission. Addressing the meeting Lala Lajpat Rai said, "Every blow that was hurled at me this afternoon was a nail in the coffin of the British Empire." He went on to issue a warning to the British rulers: "I wish to warn the government that if a violent revolution takes place in this country, the responsibility for bringing it about will be on such officers as misbehaved today. If the government and the officers continue to behave as they did today, I would not wonder if the young men go out of our hands and do whatever they choose with the object of gaining the freedom of our country."

Manmathnath Gupta tells us that these words were spoken in English so that some Englishmen, who were listening, could clearly understand what was being said. At these words one of these Englishmen, O'Neil by name, burst into laughter. Sukhdev was watching this incident. This laughter was not only a symbol of the complete arrogance of the British but also of the complete ignorance of the forces that had been unleashed that afternoon.

The police had begun to suspect the activities of the HSRA and so kept a close watch on the homes of the members in order to keep an account of all the comings and goings. In order to thwart the efforts of the police, the association had hired a house at Mozang Road close to a burial ground to conduct their meetings. Almost immediately after the attack on Lala Lajpat Rai, Bhagat Singh returned to the building. He found Rajguru and Sukhdev, two of the senior members of the association already there. Sukhdev and Rajguru had not been present at the railway station but they had been present at the meeting in the evening and were aware of what had happened. Bhagat Singh provided them with a detailed firsthand account of exactly what had transpired. He also voiced his apprehension that Lalaji might not survive the attack. Sukhdev and Rajguru were beside themselves with indignation. Then Sukhdev told them about O' Neil's reaction to Lalaji's remarks. All three deeply felt the humiliation that had been heaped upon all Indians and discussed ways and mean to avenge the humiliation. Rajguru suggested that a pitched battle with the police would be a fit act of revenge. He was drawing his precedent from the example of Jatinder Nath Mukherjee, a revolutionary from Bengal, and four of his comrades. During the Second World War, Mukherjee and his four associates were taking delivery on the eastern coast of arms which had been carried by a German ship. They did not know that a force of armed policemen were on their tracks. But when they did come to know, instead of trying to escape they engaged the force in a gunfight in Balasore, Orissa. The fight lasted for seventy-five minutes. The revolutionaries were armed only with pistols while the far larger police force was equipped with the most modern

140

ASSASSINATION OF SAUNDERS

rifles. Jatin and another revolutionary were seriously injured, two revolutionaries were killed, while two were captured when their ammunition ran out. But the revolutionaries did succeed in inflicting untold casualties among the police. This incident fired the imagination of the Indians, and Jatin and his associates became folk heroes.

But Bhagat Singh pointed out that though the pitched battle would make a dramatic point it would not ensure the killing of either Scott or Saunders. "We need blood for blood," he pointed out and felt that only the shedding of blood of the two officers would be adequate revenge for the shedding of Lala Lajpat Rai's blood. No decision could be arrived at and it was decided to call a meeting of the HSRA the following month and take up the matter at this meeting. Chandra Shekhar Azad, the commander-in-chief of the HSRA who was still in hiding because of his role in the *Kakori Dacoity* case was sent an urgent summons to return to Lahore in time for the meeting.

Nehru looked upon the savage attack as an incident of national humiliation and insult and called upon the British government to make adequate atonement. Gandhi called upon the workers to turn the anger, which was the result of the attack, into dynamic energy to be directed towards the struggle for freedom.

The Simon Commission completed its scheduled rounds and left Lahore. On 17 November 1928, Lala Lajpat Rai died. Though the death occurred a few weeks after the *lathi* charge, everyone was convinced that the great leader had succumbed to the injuries he had received on that fateful day, 30 October, on the platform of the Lahore railway station because he had taken to his bed on 31 October and had never got to his feet again. It is estimated that over 1,50,000 people accompanied the body to the cremation grounds on the bank of the

Ravi, a good four miles from Lalaji's residence. The funeral procession set out at 10 a.m. and was stopped so often on the way by mourners seeking to catch a last glimpse of their beloved leader, that it reached its destination only by 4 p.m. Many of the great leaders accompanying the cortège wept openly and unashamedly at their great loss, amongst them Dr. Gopichand Bhargav. Customarily, once the funeral pyre has been lit, the mourners disperse. On this occasion, by the time the funeral pyre had been lit, darkness had descended on the cremation ground. Dr. Bhargav gave voice to his fear that if left unguarded the pyre might be subject to some form of sacrilege by the stooges of the British or by their hired goons. Bhagwati Charan and Yashpal braved the extreme cold of December and stood guard over the burning pyre all through the night till the body had been consumed by the flames. Shortly after Lala Lajpat Rai's death, Smt. Basanti Devi, the widow of C. R. Das made a public declaration. She said, "Some youth will avenge the death of Lala Lajpat Rai even before his ashes become cold." Her words were to prove to be prophetic.

Over the next week there was a smouldering fire that was lit in the hearts and minds of all Indians. The limit of their helplessness under British rule could not have been highlighted to any greater degree than by their failure to protect the life and honour of a revered leader like Lala Lajpat Rai. "The Lajpat Rai incident was probably the much needed spark to ignite the spirit of rebellion. The nation was transformed from a spectator to a participant. The Congress, and for that matter, even Gandhi, found more support from the people. It made the nation more indignant than ever before" (Kuldip Nayar, p. 23).

The meeting of the HSRA was finally held on 10 December 1928. No minutes of the meeting are available; perhaps the decision to be taken was of such a secret nature that it was best left unrecorded. As a result, we do not have an official version of what took place. But there are sufficient verbal and written accounts by some of the participants to help us piece together what actually happened with a great degree of accuracy. The revolutionaries, as has been established earlier, had been very critical of Lala Lajpat Rai when he had declared that he was going to retire from politics and also when he appeared to have thrown in his lot with the Hindu communalists. But in spite of this they still regarded him with respect as a man of great stature who had made considerable contribution to the cause of freedom in the past. His death and the manner of his death, was looked upon by them as the worst possible national insult that the British could have inflicted upon the Indians. They were unanimous in their agreement that the insult had to be avenged at any cost.

The meeting was presided over by Durga Devi or Durga *bhabhi* as she was often called, the wife of the party's ideologue, Bhagwati Charan Vohra, who had also written the manifesto of the party. Durga *bhabhi* had a standing in the party independent of her husband because she had proved over and over again that she was as much a revolutionary as any other member of the party. She had even served a three-year prison sentence in connection with a shooting incident.

Though the meeting had been called for the specific purpose of deciding what step was to be taken to avenge Lalaji's death, it was soon clear that the act of revenge was intended to serve a much larger and greater purpose: The murderer or murderers must, of course, be made to pay the price of shedding Lalaji's blood. But his killing must also serve to emphasise the bonafides of the revolutionaries, to establish in the minds of the people that the revolutionaries were no Gandhians. They would show no hesitation in shedding blood when they felt it was the only recourse open to them. The act of revenge according to them, must be so dramatic and startling that it would awaken the youth of the country from the lethargy that had been induced in them from the centuries of mind-numbing slavery that they had been subjected to and inspire them to participate actively in the movement to end both domination by a foreign power and the excessive exploitative practices of the landlords and the minified classes.

At this meeting Rajguru once again voiced the suggestion he had made when they had first met immediately after the incident. He was in favour of engaging the police in a pitched battle. There would be the sacrifice of the lives of a few revolutionaries in this engagement. But he felt that the sacrifice would be well worth it because those sacrificed would immediately become martyrs in the eyes of the people and would inspire, through their example, more and more young men to join the HSRA thus providing the revolutionaries with a larger army in their ongoing battle for freedom. Bhagat Singh argued convincingly that the most dramatic form of revenge would be taking the lives of those who were directly responsible for the death of Lalaji. Only then would the people at large see the immediate connection between what the revolutionaries proposed to do and the death of Lalaji; only thus would people realise that the revolutionaries had not taken the death of Lalaji submissively. Bhagat Singh's views were accepted by the majority of those present and a decision was taken to kill Scott as he had ordered the direct attack on the Indian leader. It has been suggested that a section of the members were also in favour of the execution of Saunders who had done most of the brutal and fatal hitting himself. But there is no evidence available in the statements of those present that this suggestion was really made or discussed. Perhaps this suggestion has been added on by some later writers to try and show that the killing of Saunders instead of Scott was not due to any bungling on the part of the revolutionaries and that Saunders was always on their hit list. Yashpal writes: "Jai Gopal's statement started the wrong notion that the party had decided to punish Scott but punished Saunders by mistake. Scott had ordered the attack but Saunders had inflicted the blows. Both deserved to be shot. There was also no room for a mistake—Scott always moved around in a small car while Saunders used a red motorbike. Scott did not visit his office regularly so he was to be shot in his bungalow while Saunders was to be shot in front of the DAV College."

As opposed to this Shiv Verma writes: "We intended to kill the Chief of Police Scott, but Jaigopal mistook Saunders for Scott. It is after the death of Saunders that we came to know that he was the real killer of Lajpat Rai." But Batuknath Agarwal writes: "Originally they had decided to shoot Scott but by mistake Saunders was murdered and so the original pamphlet had to be changed." And Sohan Singh Josh says that Bhagat Singh admitted to him after the assassination that "we had gone there only for him but the other devil came out" (Quoted by Manmathnath Gupta pg. 136, 137).

Be that as it may, none of the accounts of the meeting make any mention of Saunders' name being discussed as a possible subject of the retaliatory action proposed by the revolutionaries. The decision to kill Scott was further endorsed by the members at the meeting on the grounds of the prevailing tension in the country. The Bengal wing of the HSRA had in the recent past killed a few British officials. This had spread terror and panic amongst the British rulers and some officers had now begun to resort to the extreme step of sending their wives and children home, to safety in England. This had given a sense of great achievement to the revolutionaries and boosted their morale tremendously. The killing of another British official apart from the immediate objective of avenging Lalaji's death would also serve to aggravate this tension further and also further the cause of the revolutionaries.

Arriving at a decision as to the course of action that they had to follow was neither too difficult nor too time consuming. But the decision as to who would perform the action proved to be so. Durga Devi started the process by asking for volunteers and made the situation difficult by immediately raising her own hand. This led to a heated decision. She was greatly loved and respected by all the members of the group because she showered them with maternal love and supported them in everyway. She was also always beside them during their time of trouble and when they were feeling low. So when they all opposed her candidature emphatically, it was not on the basis of any gender bias. Their opposition was based solely on the assumption that while the killing of Scott could be performed by any one of a dozen revolutionaries, the role that Durga *bhabhi* played in the organisation could be performed only by her. It was too important and vital a role to permit her to undertake such a risky killing. After much heated discussion, Durga Devi accepted the unanimous will of all the other members and once again asked for volunteers. Almost everyone raised their hands.

After much deliberation the field was narrowed down to four: Bhagat Singh, Sukhdev, Rajguru and Chandra Shekhar Azad. Sukhdev wanted to take upon himself the task of firing the shot that would kill the despicable Englishman. But once again the majority opinion was against this. He was too important a member of the revolutionary network to be exposed to danger for one solitary revolutionary act. He was the mastermind, the strategist behind all revolutionary activities in the Punjab and played a very vital role in coordinating revolutionary activities all over the country and in bringing

146

revolutionaries together. It was agreed that he would play the part of the coordinator or arbiter in this revolutionary activity without being a participant.

Sukhdev accepted the role allotted to him and set about his task with his usual cool, practical sense. He chose for the task in hand, Bhagat Singh, Rajguru, Chandra Shekhar Azad and Jai Gopal, a newcomer to the party. He declared that Bhagat Singh would be the one who would take on the task of killing Scott. Sukhdev said that he was sure that Bhagat Singh was the one man who could be completely depended upon to carry out the task that had been assigned to him.

The moment Sukhdev announced Bhagat Singh's name there was whispering amongst some of the members. Shooting Scott was a very difficult and dangerous task but escaping from the police dragnet that would be immediately put into place would be impossible. It was as if Sukhdev was not only condemning Scott to death but was also assigning certain death to Bhagat Singh. There had been heated discussions between Sukhdev and Bhagat Singh in the past, which had created an impression that Sukhdev resented Bhagat Singh's growing popularity. Some members now whispered to each other that Sukhdev was sending Bhagat Singh to certain death to put an end to his great popularity so that he could emerge as the true leader of the party.

If Sukhdev heard this murmuring, he paid no attention to it and went on in quick sharp sentences to outline the plan that had sprung to his fertile mind with sudden and complete spontaneity. 17 December 1928 was fixed as the day for carrying out their plan. Bhagat Singh was to do the actual shooting, Rajguru was to stand close to him and provide him with the necessary cover. Azad was to assist in the escape which was to be affected as soon as they saw Scott fall. Jai Gopal was to let them know when Scott arrived at the spot.

The next week was spent in preparing for the event. Azad and Jai Gopal went over the route from Scott's residence to his office and back to ascertain what delays could possibly occur enroute and how much time Scott would take to travel the distance. They shared this with Bhagat Singh and Rajguru. 15 December saw what would now be called a "dry-run" of the assassination; they went through each move, timed each action and fixed positions. It had been decided that Scott would be shot as soon as he came out of the main gate of the Central Secretariat where his office was located. The exact spot from where Bhagat Singh would fire the shot had also been fixed. Azad had worked out the escape route. He showed Bhagat Singh and Rajguru that after firing the shots they would run to the DAV College to effect their escape. Jai Gopal, who had already learnt the number of Scott's car (6728), was entrusted the responsibility of signalling to Bhagat Singh and Rajguru, the moment Scott arrived at the police station. The plan had been formed and rehearsed meticulously and it did not appear at the time that with their training and resolve, the revolutionaries would not be able to carry it out with meticulous precision. In anticipation of this success Bhagat Singh drew up a poster with the headlines in red "Scott Killed". Four copies of the poster were prepared by Hans Raj Vohra, a quiet steady worker of the HSRA. Immediately after the shooting, these four posters would be put up at strategic points in the city. Little could Bhagat Singh know that the poster that he had written with so much pride would provide evidence against him in the *Lahore Conspiracy* case and, of course, no one could know that the quiet and steady Hans Raj Vohra would turn approver and provide vital evidence against his co-operators to the government.

In the poster that he designed for the occasion, Bhagat Singh took great care to emphasise the role of the armed wing of the HSRA. This would bring home to the people that they too now had an army fighting for their cause rather than against them as the imperial army was doing. This would in turn give birth to a surge of optimism and hope that one day their own army, the strong military wing of the HSRA, would be strong enough to take on the British army.

Already in September, in anticipation of a greater participation in revolutionary activities, Bhagat Singh had followed the party's order and shaved off his beard and cut his hair in order to make recognition by the police difficult. To escape official notice he had this done privately by a medical practitioner in September 1928 in Ferozepur. Unfortunately Jai Gopal had been present with him on the occasion and later, when he turned approver, he tendered this as a further piece of evidence to prove Bhagat Singh's involvement in the assassination.

The plan was as perfect as could be but had one major flaw. Jai Gopal, who was deputed to identify the victim and give the assassins a signal, had never seen Scott before. Inexplicably, Jai Gopal never voiced this ignorance, not to the leaders, not to any junior colleagues within the party. Perhaps as a newcomer he was so awed by the magnitude of the task he was involved in that he did not want to risk losing out on it by such an admission.

17 December arrived with nothing to indicate that it would be different in any way from any other day. The only difference, and an extremely important one at that, was that unknown to the conspirators Scott had not come on duty that morning. His mother-in-law was arriving that day and he had taken a day's leave to receive her and to make her feel at home. The conspirators were unaware of this. Jai Gopal, who had been entrusted with the task of reporting Scott's arrival at the police station to Bhagat Singh, had observed Scott's deputy,

SHAHEED BHAGAT SINGH

Assistant Superintendent J. P. Saunders arrive at the police station and had mistaken him for Scott. He duly reported Scott's arrival to Bhagat Singh. The conspirators took up their assigned positions at the appointed time. At about 4.30 in the afternoon, Azad was stationed at a vantage point near the gate of the secretariat waiting for Scott to emerge. Bhagat Singh and Rajguru, aware that the appointed time was close at hand, were casually moving towards the spot from where the shot would be fired. At that moment Saunders came out of the police station and made to climb onto his motorcycle. Rajguru took quick aim and shot him dead with a single bullet from his German Mauser pistol. Bhagat Singh had seen Rajguru pull up his pistol to take aim, realised the mistake that Jai Gopal had made, and called out, "No, he is not the man." But it was too late, the shot had been fired and Saunders was dead. To become party to the killing, Bhagat Singh fired some bullets into Saunders' body.

On hearing the shots Traffic Inspector W. J. C. Fern ran out of the police station. Azad, whose role was to provide cover to Bhagat Singh and Rajguru, quickly fired a volley of shots at him. As the bullets whizzed past his head, Fern turned and quickly retraced his steps into the safety of the police station. Head Constable Chanan Singh who had heard the shots ran forward to help Saunders. When he found that Saunders was beyond help he chased Bhagat Singh, Rajguru and Azad as they fled from the spot. Azad tried to get him to back off by waving his pistol at him and shouting: "No, we do not want to kill an Indian." But they had no effect and Chanan Singh continued his pursuit. Rajguru had no option but to shoot him dead.

As per plan, the three revolutionaries went into the compound of DAV College. They climbed the wall which divided the college from the hostel and stopped for a while at

150

the hostel to ensure that they had not been followed. Finally, assured that there was no one in the hostel, Bhagat Singh changed his trousers and coat and put on a felt hat. Then they walked out of the hostel as casually as they could. They picked up their bicycles, which, by prior arrangement Azad had placed against the toilet wall. Once again they checked to make sure that no one was on their trail. Finding everything safe they climbed onto the bicycles and leisurely pedalled to the home at Mozang Road. Anyone observing them would have assumed that they were three young men returning home after a long tedious day at work.

By the time the authorities learnt of the killing and raised an alarm, the three were safely ensconced in the retreat at Mozang Road, comparing notes on what had happened. Perhaps they were taken aback at the mistake that had been made due to Jai Gopal's ignorance. Perhaps they agreed that the death of Saunders, if not as dramatic in impact as the death of his senior would have been, also served their case. Because after all it was Saunders who had inflicted the maximum injuries on Lala Lajpat Rai, it was Saunders whom the people had seen, raising his police baton again and again to bring it down with sadistic pleasure on Lalaji's chest and head. Perhaps it was at this time that Bhagat Singh made the change in his poster and wrote Saunders' name in place of Scott's. We will never know what the three revolutionaries discussed at the time. But we do know that they were not even in a position to let Jai Gopal know of the mistake he had made because Jai Gopal, after informing them of "Scott's" arrival at the police station at 10.00 a.m. had quietly left for home.

The police learnt only late in the evening, hours after the incident, that some revolutionaries were seen to have fled into the DAV College complex immediately after the shooting. The college became the focus of their attention. It was surrounded by the police and a thorough search was made of the entire premises. A roll call was taken of all the residents and those not present were sent for and asked to provide an explanation for their absence. Not finding anything suspicious the police then ransacked the college and in turn failed to find any clue about the mysterious three. The adjacent premises of the DAV Middle School and the Agarwal Ashram were also searched and subjected to a thorough investigation. Every policeman in Lahore was summoned in to find some clue to the missing assassins. A number of people were taken into custody on suspicion but the interrogation provided nothing. All exits, both railways and roads, were sealed and heavily guarded. But in spite of all these activities, the authorities were not able to procure the evidence of the "crime". The needle of suspicion did point in the direction of revolutionaries but in the absence of any kind of evidence there was not much that the authorities could do.

The next day posters appeared all over Lahore. But the one that attracted the most attention was the one where Bhagat Singh had printed Saunders' name over Scott's name.

HINDUSTAN SOCIALIST REPUBLICAN ARMY NOTICE

J. P. Saunders is dead; Lala Lajpat Rai is avenged.

Really it is horrible to imagine that so lowly and violent hand of an ordinary police official, J. P. Saunders, could ever dare to touch in such an insulting way the body of one so old, so revered and so loved by 300 million people of Hindustan and thus cause his death. The youth and manhood of India was challenged by blows hurled down on the head of India's nationhood. And let the world know that India still lives; that the blood of youths has not been totally cooled down and that they can still risk their lives, if the honour of their nation

ASSASSINATION OF SAUNDERS

Bhagat Singh and the death of Saunders were discussed everywhere and gradually at first and then with the force of an avalanche Bhagat Singh's stature as a national hero, assumed gigantic proportions. The poster had clearly established that the killing was not the result of any personal enmity but an effort to restore the honour of the country. As a result he became a symbol of pride and the restoration of self respect for the entire nation. Even a moderate like Jawaharlal Nehru was to give due credit to Bhagat Singh for this act, violent as it was. "He became a symbol, the act was forgotten, the symbol remained, and within a few months each town and village of the Punjab and, to a lesser extent, the rest of northern India, resounded with his name. Innumerable songs grew up about him and the popularity that the man achieved was something amazing" (Jawaharlal Nehru, *Autobiography*, p.175-176).

Bhagat Singh, Azad and Rajguru stayed in the house on Mozang Road taking stock of their situation. Their task had been accomplished but they were fully aware of the consequences. The assassination of Saunders, the publicity that would attend it, and the humiliation that the British would feel at the assassins having got away, would ensure that the government would come down heavily on the Indians, especially on the revolutionaries. The longer they were successful in evading capture the greater would be the British effort to find some leads against them. They were sure of their immediate step. The only eyewitness of the assassination had been the head constable, Chanan Singh, who was now dead. There was no one who could identify them. But they knew that this fact alone was not enough to ensure their safety in the long run. Already the police would have swung into action and would be combing the city for any suspect, any lead. In their minds they could hear the knocking on the doors as the police went from the home of one revolutionary to the next,

155

SHAHEED BHAGAT SINGH

rounding them up, rounding up anyone who had at any time showed any sympathy for the revolutionary cause. There were so many of them and sooner or later one of them was likely to break under the third degree methods of interrogation of the police. Someone might reveal details of the plot, at the very least someone might reveal the address of the "safe" house on Mozang Road. As the hours stretched on, it became clear to the three that safety for them and their cause did not lie here, not in the home they were in, not in Lahore.

It seems strange now that while so much effort had gone into the planning and execution of the assassination, so little thought had been spared for the attempt to get away from Lahore. As Kuldip Nayar says, "It spoke well of their bravery, but not of their strategy" (p. 32).

At about 11 p.m. when the cover of dark was thick, Bhagat Singh and Sukhdev stepped out of the house at Mozang Road and made their way to Bara Ghara in the Islamabad locality where Sohan Singh Josh lived. He was alone in his home at the time as his family had gone to his ancestral village of Chetanpura in Amritsar district. Considering the predicament of the revolutionaries this was just as well. Josh narrates the encounter in his own words: "On the same night, a little after 11 p.m. somebody knocked on my door in Bara Ghara, Islamabad . . . I opened my door and to my utter surprise found Bhagat Singh and Sukhdev standing outside. I welcomed them but told them it was rather risky to have come to my house because the police might raid it any time. But Bhagat Singh said, 'Don't worry, we have made all arrangements.' They came in and said, 'We are hungry, give us something to eat.' I could only offer two chapattis, some vegetable and a glass of milk. I told them we could cook fresh food but they said, 'Nothing doing, we shall talk and sleep.'

"Bhagat Singh was wearing a hat and English style suit.

He was quite unrecognizable in those clothes. Sukhdev was wearing an English hat and suit. Bhagat Singh took off his hat and placed it on a table nearby. He hung his pistol on a peg above the cot. Then, after finishing the meagre meal, the first question he shot at me was, 'What is the reaction in general to Saunders' murder?'

'The youth are happy,' I replied. 'But they would have been much happier if Scott had been killed.'

'We had gone there only for him, but the other devil came out,' he said. 'And we could not go empty handed after all the pain taken for the preparation.' And then he added, 'Anyway, some beginning has been made . . .'

'What do you think of this action?'

'The panic is temporary, it will wear off soon.'

'I don't agree. This action will rouse the masses and strengthen the movement.'

"During this whole talk Sukhdev did not utter a single word. There were only two cots in the room. Sukhdev slept on one and Bhagat Singh and I shared the bigger one. He woke up a little before four in the morning to be ready to go. While going, Bhagat Singh borrowed a book: *Liberty and the Great Libertarian*. I did not want to part with the book, but Bhagat Singh had his way. He promised to return it after reading it."

Sohan Singh tells us of another meeting with Bhagat Singh within a week, this time in Calcutta. It was arranged in a suspicious manner and at great risk in a hair cutting salon where Sohan Singh with his turban and flowing beard would stick out like a sore thumb. Obviously Sohan Singh had arrived there to attend the all-India conference of the Workers and Peasants Party.

"I chided him for doing this foolish thing. He laughed and replied nonchalantly. 'Don't worry, nothing is going to happen. We have made all arrangements.' What arrangements he had made I do not know till today.

Then after some talk on the conference he said. 'You do the organizing of worker and peasants and we shall do the disorganizing of the British ruler. Let us have this division of work" (Sohan Singh Josh, *My Meetings with Bhagat Singh*, p.26).

The next rendezvous for the three fugitives was the house of Bhagwati Charan Vohra. Both Vohra and his wife Durga Devi were under police suspicion and their home was watched from 11 p.m. till 5 a.m. by the police. On that cold and frosty December morning, a little after 5 a.m. Durga Devi heard a knock at her door. She wondered who it could be at that very early hour and opened the door with a great deal of trepidation. She was surprised to find Bhagat Singh standing at the door with Rajguru and Azad close behind him. She let them in and bolted the door again. She congratulated them on having carried out the extremely dangerous task they had undertaken.

Bhagat Singh pointed out that it could not really be regarded as an unqualified success because they had shot Saunders instead of Scott by mistake. She said she knew about this and it made no difference at all as Saunders had been as responsible as Scott for Lala Lajpat Rai's death—in fact more so as he had inflicted most of the blows. In the eyes of the public shooting of Saunders was as great a blow to British imperialism as the shooting of Scott would have been.

They told her of the plan that Sukhdev had drawn up to facilitate their safe flight to Calcutta. The four friends were sure that till this point the British had not connected either Rajguru or Bhagat Singh with Saunders' killing though they would by now have concluded that it was the work of revolutionaries especially since the poster had appeared all over Lahore. But there was always the fear that some shred of evidence might appear during the investigation so it was thought best that they seek safety in far away Calcutta.

They were all to travel by the Dehradun Express from Lahore to Calcutta but they were not to travel together. Bhagat Singh would now don a disguise and assume the name of Ranjit. Durga Devi would travel as his wife and her three-year-old son, Sachin, would be passed off as their son. Rajguru was to assume the semblance of the servant accompanying the upper class couple on the long journey. Azad left the house to make his own arrangements for the journey. At this point Bhagat Singh admitted that he had no money and his efforts to borrow money from Sohan Singh Josh the night before had also been futile because Josh did not have any ready cash at home. Durga Devi smiled at Bhagat Singh's embarrassment and brought out five hundred rupees from the cupboard and held this out to Bhagat Singh. "Vohra Sahib left me this money in case of an emergency and what could be a greater emergency than this!"

Bhagat Singh, Rajguru and Durga Devi packed a number of boxes—upper class families in those days did not believe in travelling lightly. As was the practice with government officials of the day, each box was carefully labelled quoting the name of the passenger and the destination. Bhagat Singh's disguise was also designed to suggest that he was a government official. He donned a long overcoat belonging to Vohra and a felt hat which a visitor had forgotten. Durga Devi, in keeping with her role, wore an expensive sari and high heeled shoes. Rajguru, already well into his role, went out and brought a horse-drawn *tonga* for their journey to the railway station. Bhagat Singh and Durga Devi watched Rajguru load the boxes into the *tonga*. Durga Devi like a prudent housewife gave directions to the "servant" as to how and where each box was to be placed.

In the aftermath of Saunders' killing all entry and exit points of Lahore had been more or less sealed off. The railway station had become the prime focus and was so bristling with armed policemen that it became a veritable fortress. Through the blanket of suspicious and hostile security, the "government official" wearing smart European clothes, his "wife" immaculately dressed, carrying her baby in her arms and the servant supervising the coolies who were carrying their luggage, marched confidently to the first class carriage for which Bhagat Singh had brought the tickets. The actors played their roles to perfection and took their seats without having attracted any attention to themselves. In fact Kuldip Nayar tells us that as they entered their compartment, the policemen standing outside whispered to each other that this was a high ranking government official travelling with his family and moved deferentially aside to permit them to enter their compartment. The party must have been under tremendous tension and mental pressure all through the journey. Perhaps the only member who did not feel the tension too heavily was little Sachin. But at last the whistle blew, the guard waved the green flag, the train began to move and the three relaxed; they had done it, they had eluded the police without being challenged even once.

Chandra Shekhar Azad, on leaving Durga Devi's home, had joined a party of pilgrims who were on their way to Mathura to offer prayers to Lord Krishna. He dressed like one of them and joined in the singing of *bhajan*s and their chanting of "Hare Rama, Hare Krishna" with such enthusiasm that the police glanced at him only in a most perfunctory manner.

Even though no suspicion had attached to the departure, Durga Devi wanted to be absolutely sure of their safety and insisted that they break journey at Kanpur. Accordingly they disembarked from the train and stayed the night in a hotel close to the railway station. Durga Devi sent a telegram to her husband in Calcutta informing him about her impending

ASSASSINATION OF SAUNDERS

arrival. The telegram said that she would be accompanied by her brother. She had no brother and she hoped that Vohra would deduce from this that her companion was none other than Bhagat Singh. They boarded a train for Calcutta the next morning and were met by Bhagwati Charan whose curiosity had been aroused by Durga's telegram. He had deduced from this reference to a non-existent brother-in-law, that the person accompanying his wife was someone special. He had read about Saunders' assassination and had suspected that Bhagat Singh had played a part in it. So he had, as his wife had hoped, deduced that his "brother-in-law" might well be Bhagat Singh.

Before this episode, Bhagat Singh's association with Durga Devi had been a very superficial one. She was the wife of one of their most highly respected and revered colleague and as a result, was highly respected herself. He had been surprised by the lead that she had taken when she had presided over the special meeting of the HSRA when the decision to kill Scott had been taken. He had been surprised by her fearlessness in immediately agreeing to play the part that Sukhdev had allotted her in their escape from Lahore. But beyond this, there was little that they had known about each other. Now in their role of husband and wife they were thrown so closely together it was inevitable that they should share their thoughts and feelings and get to know each other well. Bhagat Singh especially, poured out all his thoughts and feelings. It was as if he had kept these pent up so long that now that he had a sympathetic listener they had burst the dam that had held them back for so long. He admitted to her that he found the violence that was a necessary part of revolutionary activity, extremely repugnant. But he had learnt to accept it because the violence seemed so trivial when compared with the violence with which the British rulers imposed their cruel rule

161

on the people. He expressed his conviction that no matter how severe and brutal the British rule, it would never be able to suppress the spirit of the people. Indian history was evidence to the immortal spirit of the Indian people. Wave after wave conquerors had come and conquered their beloved motherland but they had never been able to subjugate the spirit of India. In spite of all the raiders who had looted India's wealth and gone back, India's traditions and dignity and pride had remained intact. This was because of the sacrifice that its people were always ready to make and it was because of this that so many of the so-called conquerors had made India their home and become part of its composite culture, a culture which was made up of many strands. He expressed his sadness at the passive acceptance that was creeping into the Indian people, acceptance of poverty, acceptance of foreign rule, an acceptance which amounted to a resignation and it was this resignation he felt which could result in the defeat of India's indomitable spirit. He blamed Gandhi for encouraging this acceptance and resignation.

Bhagat Singh told Durga Devi about the various influences in his life which had shaped his revolutionary thinking. He told her about his joining the National College in Lahore where the first seeds of revolution had been planted in his mind, and the impact that their principal Chabildas had on them in fostering a spirit of patriotism and nationalism. He told her of the fiery words of Yashpal who had gone on to become an influential writer. Yashpal even at that young age had preached that to live meaningful lives, men should not allow themselves to be bound only in their private lives, their wives and their children. They must think beyond their home, of society in general and of mankind at large. It was perhaps Yashpal's thinking which had finally made him decide against marriage. He spoke of Sachindra Nath Sanyal who had told him that he would not become a revolutionary by staying at home—to become a true revolutionary he would have to abandon the comfort and security of his home. He spoke to her about the strong influence that Swami Ram Tirtha of Punjab and Swami Vivekananda of Bengal had had in moulding his thinking.

Sukhdev had earned a reputation of being a taciturn man, a man who held his peace and only spoke when it was absolutely necessary. Since she had rarely heard him speak Durga Devi looked upon Sukhdev as something of a mystery and asked Bhagat Singh about his relationship with Sukhdev. Bhagat Singh told her that Sukhdev and he had been contemporaries at the National College. They had been instinctively drawn to each other because their views on politics were at that time very similar. They were concerned about the lack of revolutionary spirit amongst the youth of India. Without their spirit they were convinced that neither the British colonial rule, nor the economic domination by the privileged and feudal classes, could ever be brought to an end. They were both frequent visitors to the Dwarkadas Library and read almost the same set of books that related mainly to the revolutionary movements of the world and to economic development. Their reading and intellectual interests centred on politics and economics and they discussed the books they had read and exchanged notes expressing their views on various topics. But at that time, they were not all fire and brimstone. They found time to enjoy music and art and the rich cultural life that Lahore offered. Even in this they shared the same tastes and would stay awake late into the night, discussing various aesthetic aspects of their cultural experiences. But over the years serious differences had crept up between the two because of a basic and implacable difference in their approach to revolution and revolutionary activities. Sukhdev was adamant

SHAHEED BHAGAT SINGH

that in the exercise of revolutionary principles there was absolutely no room for any feeling. Once the mind was put into play, the heart had to be turned to stone. Bhagat Singh differed on this and felt that this was the basic difference between terrorists and revolutionaries. To him, the heart and a sensitive compassionate nature were important because they prevented the revolutionary from indulging in senseless violence. While committing an act of violence, Bhagat Singh felt that the damage should be limited to the minimum. For Sukhdev, violence was violence and the extent of damage caused was inconsequential. Because of the basic difference in their thinking and approach there had been a drift between the two as far as their feelings for each other were concerned. Sukhdev made no secret of the fact that he regarded Bhagat Singh as a romantic—an attitude of mind which reeked of sentimentality and softened his revolutionary resolve. Bhagat Singh on his part, in spite of the difference, admired Sukhdev for the master strategist that he was and went along with all Sukhdev's wishes as far as their work as revolutionaries was concerned.

By the time they got off the train in Calcutta both Bhagat Singh and Durga Devi had learnt a great deal about each other, which they had not known before. They had discovered aspects of each other's personality and character that they had not known existed. He was touched by her warm sensitivity and she was reassured to find that behind the apparently forbidding demeanour of a revolutionary beat a compassionate and merciful heart.

The train at last drew into Howrah Station. Kuldip Nayar describes the normal hustle and hustle of the railway station in very vivid detail. Bhagat Singh was both relieved and disappointed to find that there was no anxiety or tension induced by the Saunders' murder. He was relieved because it ensured that their own arrival would not be greeted with undue suspicion, and disappointed because he had hoped that their daring act would induce at least some panic in the minds of their British rulers even here in Calcutta. Bhagwati Charan met them at the station and realised that it was indeed Bhagat Singh who had been travelling as his "brother-in-law".

Unknown to Bhagat Singh, there was indeed a sense of panic in government circles, stemming largely from the Saunders killing.

The escape of Bhagat Singh, Rajguru and Chandra Shekhar from Lahore had gone unnoticed mainly because the British authorities had no clue that they were in any way connected with the killing of Saunders. Till mid April 1929, the government did not have a single clue pointing towards the revolutionaries. The British expressed a strong sense of outrage that a British police officer could be murdered in broad daylight in the capital city of Punjab and that the murderer could escape with total impunity. There was tremendous pressure on the government of India and the Punjab government regarding the progress of the investigation.

On 19 December the Punjab government announced that the investigation had been placed under the direct supervision of the DIG of the CID and that Jenkins, SP, CID, had been given charge. Sixteen persons, most of them members of the Naujawan Bharat Sabha were arrested on suspicion of murder, abetment to murder and criminal conspiracy.

On 20 December the home secretary of the government of India, writing to the Punjab government, drew its attention to the inflammatory speeches that were being delivered all over Punjab regarding the death of Lala Lajpat Rai. It suggested to the Punjab government that action should perhaps, be taken against those making such inflammatory speeches. The names of Zafar Ali Khan, Satyapal, Muhammad Alam, Avinash

SHAHEED BHAGAT SINGH

Chandra Bali, and Gopi Chand were specifically mentioned.

On 29 December the viceroy informed the secretary of state about the lack of progress in the case. The secretary of state expressed his disappointment and enquired about the possibility of banning the Naujawan Bharat Sabha.

On 14 January 1929, the viceroy informed the secretary of state that all those arrested in the case had been released on bail on account of lack of evidence. He expressed the opinion that the killing of Saunders was a direct result of the death of Lala Lajpat Rai. At the same time, he offered some reassurance that the culprits would finally be caught. There was reason to believe that some of the arrested persons had been involved; there were some eye-witnesses who said they would be able to identify the culprits if they saw them. The fact that the DAV College was used as the route to escape, implied that the culprits had a first hand knowledge of the area. There was also every chance that they had been seen by some of the students. An examination of the used cartridges revealed distinctive markings which would help in identifying the weapons if they were recovered.

On 17 January, the Punjab government stated that there was, at the time, not enough evidence to warrant the banning of the Naujawan Bharat Sabha. It also revealed that Saunders had been involved in keeping Lala Lajpat Rai and other demonstrators back at the Lahore railway station on 30 October 1928. Since then a series of inflammatory speeches were being delivered which served to create an atmosphere for further execution of acts of such daring and fearless outrage.

Until 9 April 1929, the Punjab government did not have the faintest clue as to the identity of the killer of Saunders.

Chapter 5

BOMBS IN THE ASSEMBLY

Bhagwati Charan realised that since all revolutionaries were under suspicion for the Saunders assassination, the authorities would sooner or later be on the lookout for Bhagat Singh. The tracks at that moment led straight to him. In order to ensure the safety of Bhagat Singh, he felt it was prudent that Bhagat Singh should not stay with him and Durga in Calcutta. So he arranged for Bhagat Singh to stay in the sprawling mansion of a rich Marwari, Chajju Ram, who was a great admirer of all the revolutionaries and their acts of valour and sacrifice. The house was located in the exclusive suburb of Alipore, where only the rich and powerful lived and where a search by the police was highly unlikely.

Bhagat Singh had by now become quite adept in the matter of disguises and, while in Calcutta, assumed the disguise of a Bengali, dressing up in a dhoti-kurta with a shawl thrown carelessly over his shoulder. He went by the name of Hari. He also learnt Bengali from B. K. Dutt and became fairly fluent

SHAHEED BHAGAT SINGH

in the use of the language. While in Calcutta Bhagat Singh attended the session of the All India National Congress. He came away disgusted. The Congress was still going around in circles seeking nothing more than dominion status. It seemed to Bhagat Singh that the Congress continued to be controlled by the affluent sections of society. It seemed to want only to protect the interests of this group of society and showed little or no interest in the problems being faced by the workers and peasants. He was so disillusioned with the Congress session and what he felt was the meaningless ramblings of its leaders that he walked straight into a nearby movie theatre. The movie being screened was "Uncle Tom's Cabin", which touched upon the subject of the abolition of slavery. Going by his frame of mind at the time, we can be sure that he enjoyed the movie immensely.

Bhagat Singh also got a chance to meet almost all the prominent revolutionaries of Bengal and understood why they had not attended the all India meeting at the Ferozshah Kotla grounds. They had moved away from the path of anarchy and believed that the only way to achieve a revolution was through the motivation of the masses. Bhagat Singh was both surprised and hurt to find that so many of them were convinced that activities like the Kakori dacoity and the Saunders killing had failed to create any kind of revolutionary feelings and had not in any way carried the country forward in its struggle for freedom. In spite of this hurt and disappointment, Bhagat Singh was heartened to find two new developments amongst the Bengal revolutionaries. The Anushalin Samiti was an organisation of revolutionaries, which had been formed in 1894, with a staunch Hindu bias. Now there was a powerful faction that had broken away from the parent body, which made a clear distinction between religion and politics and was committed to secularism. The other development was that many of the revolutionaries were convinced that political freedom and democracy by themselves would be meaningless. To be truly free, all inequalities amongst men, including inequalities of wealth, and social and regional inequalities, would have to be abolished. "There could be no equality in politics and before the law as long as there were glaring economic inequalities. So long as the ruling class controlled jobs and the press and the schools of the country and all organs of public opinion . . . so long as laws were made by the ruling class, so long as lawyers who were private practitioners, sold their expertise to the highest bidder and litigation was exclusive and costly there would be only nominal equality before Law" (Kuldip Nayar, p.47). This echoed exactly Bhagat Singh's own firmly held belief.

Though most of the revolutionaries of Bengal had now come around to eschewing the bomb culture, Bhagat Singh left Calcutta with the firm conviction that a few of them would come forward to teach the revolutionaries of the north the techniques of manufacturing bombs. With this belief he now moved to Agra, which had become the new headquarters for the revolutionaries of Punjab, Bihar, and the United Provinces. Bhagat Singh, Rajguru, and Azad moved to two very ordinary looking houses in the Hing-Ki-Mandi area of the city which had been rented by the association. Here they were joined by Sukhdev and all the other revolutionaries who had been actively involved in planning the Saunders killing and who now needed to keep out of sight of the authorities in the Punjab. Bhagat Singh was not mistaken in his belief that the Bengal revolutionaries would assist them in the bomb manufacturing activities; soon Jatinder Nath Das and Lalit Mukherjee came over from Calcutta and joined them in the new headquarters. They had come with a specific purpose in mind. The houses in Hing-Ki-Mandi were ideally suited for this purpose. Close to the houses were dense, unspoilt forests stretching almost all the way to Jhansi and this provided a perfect location for testing the bombs that they would manufacture.

The revolutionaries were active once again. Not only was a bomb manufacturing unit set up in Agra, but once the revolutionaries had mastered the skill of manufacturing bombs efficiently, they also set up similar units in Lahore and Saharanpur with Sukhdev and Shiv Verma taking charge of these two ventures. Apart from taking an active part in the manufacture of bombs and the procurement of other arms and ammunition like pistols and cartridges, Azad took charge of organising finances. He proved to be a very effective fund raiser for the revolutionary cause. Amongst the regular contributors were some of the seniormost luminaries of the UP Congress, like Motilal Nehru and Purshottamdas Tandon. Many Indians who were in government service and could not be seen to be connected with the revolutionary cause in any way, sent regular contributions in cash through trustworthy emissaries. Surprisingly, Azad once received a bearer cheque from none other than the advocate-general of Bengal as a contribution to the revolutionary cause. Needless to say, he lost no time in encashing the cheque in order to eliminate any possibility of its being traced to its source.

The revolutionaries lived an extremely spartan life; as all the funds they managed to collect barely covered the expenses of their revolutionary activities, there was no money left for basic necessities like food, shelter and clothes. But they had long before learnt to live austere lives, learnt that physical discomfort was a small price to pay for the privilige of serving the motherland. They had already sacrificed family life and the comfort and warmth of their homes; this life of deprivation seemed an extremely insignificant addition to the sacrifices they had already made. The revolutionaries lived an isolated life. Other than their bomb making, there was little to occupy their time or their minds. They spent their time debating and discussing, often with much heat and passion, almost every little aspect of political, social, and economic orders both of the past and the present. Kuldip Nayar relates an incident to show that the revolutionaries were not beings entirely of the spirit but also of flesh and blood and that their life of long periods of inaction had begun to take its toll even on these men of steel. He tells us that one day Rajguru came across a picture of an extremely beautiful and sexy young girl in a bathing suit in an old issue of a foreign magazine. Hoping to add some colour and bring some relief to their otherwise austere lives, he tore out the picture and pinned it on one of the walls. Most of the others, all virile young men, looked appreciatively at the picture, their faces lighting up with broad smiles. But when Azad saw the poster he was seized with a violent fit of fury. He ripped the picture from the wall and tore it into shreds. He declared that they had chosen the difficult and grim path in their lives and they must not allow such trivialities to deflect their focus from the goal they had assigned to themselves. Rajguru was not present at the time but when he returned to the room, Azad told him what he had done and declared that he would destroy even something as beautiful as the Taj Mahal to ensure that they remained single-minded in their task. Rajguru was very hurt and is reported to have said, "We are out to make the world beautiful. How can he talk like this?" Azad's temper soon cooled. His flare-up, as he soon admitted, had been caused by the lack of action and their apparent failure to move forward. He graciously apologised to Rajguru and all the others for his unreasonable outburst. Inevitably, during their long discussions, the revolutionaries also indulged in a great deal of soul-searching and self-questioning. They debated whether all the tactics they had followed, all the action they had taken, had brought them any closer to their goals. They admitted that the killing of Saunders had not produced the results that they had aimed for. After the initial panic, things had settled down again. There was no longer an exodus of Britishers from India. In fact the British government seemed to believe that the killing of Saunders called for greater reprisals against the Indians. The revolutionaries came to the conclusion that bombs were necessary to rouse the attention of both the rulers as well as the suffering masses, but side by side with this it was essential to reach out to the minds of the people and to convince them that these bombs were part of a larger campaign to free them from the bonds of slavery. This conviction could only be achieved through reasoning and through personal example. For achieving this, Bhagat Singh felt that it was necessary to educate the masses so that a favourable atmosphere would be created and people would accept the social programmes which the revolutionaries felt were necessary for the emancipation of the common man.

Even while confined to the limits of their hideout, the revolutionaries kept abreast of all the latest political developments in the country. They were happy to note that the pressure on Gandhi to declare complete independence as his goal was mounting from influential quarters like Subhash Chandra Bose and Jawaharlal Nehru. They were also happy to note the rising tide of socialism in the country. The trade union movements were gaining momentum and more and more workers from factories and mills were coming forward to join these unions. This in turn had led to a series of labour strikes in many major cities. The British reacted sharply. On 20 March 1929, they arrested Sohan Singh Josh, S. A. Dange, Muzzafar Ahmed and thirty members of the Communist Party and the Kirti Kissan Sabha, in connection with what came to be called the *Meerut Conspiracy* case. Amongst those arrested were two Englishmen, Phillip Sprat and Bradley, who had come to India with the specific purpose of spreading communism in the country. It was now nine and a half months since Saunders had been murdered and the police had found no trace of the killer. But during the course of their investigations and interrogations, British intelligence sources and the police were alarmed to discover that in addition to the rapid spread of socialism and trade unionism, there was also a snowballing sympathy for the revolutionaries and their activities. They had learnt that many government officials were indirectly contributing to the revolutionary cause by secretly providing funds. The mindset about the harmlessness of Gandhi and the Congress persisted in the British government and they were sure that there was no real danger to the rulers from either of these two quarters. The immediate need was to deal with the revolutionaries on the one hand and the Socialists and Trade Unionists on the other. To fulfil this need the government proposed to introduce two bills in the Central Legislative Assembly. The first of these bills, the Public Safety Bill, sought to empower the government to arrest and detain anyone without assigning any reason and without bringing them to trial. The second bill, called the Trade Disputes Bill, was directed specifically against the Socialists and Trade Unionists because it sought to prevent trade unions from organising strikes. This was in direct reaction to the recent spate of strikes, which had forced mill owners to increase the wages of the workers. In keeping with their affinity for the rich and the feudal class, the British were determined to help the mill owners in their "war" against the workers and to keep the workers exactly where the British felt they belonged: in a state of complete bondage. Both the bills, when passed, would effectively curb the waves of revolution and socialism then sweeping through the country. The bills would effectively end all revolutionary and socialist activity.

The bills and their effect on the country were hotly discussed by the revolutionaries in Agra and a consensus soon emerged that there was need for urgent and drastic action against the bills. It was necessary, once again, to indulge in some direct action to bring the inequities of the proposed bills to the centre of public attention and to influence public opinion against them. The British, through their proposed bills, had thrown a gauntlet to the revolutionaries and this was a challenge that the revolutionaries were not going to ignore. Their work was already handicapped by their need for secrecy. Through the new bills the government was threatening to throttle them altogether. They decided to accept the challenge that the British had thrown at them by coming out into the open.

A formal meeting of the HSRA was convened to decide on the best course of action. It was unanimously decided that the central idea of any action that they decided to take was to express in the clearest possible way the strongest and loudest resentment against the two proposed bills. It was decided that whatever they decided to do must open the eyes and ears of the assembly members to the very real possibility that the two bills were only the beginning. As more voices were raised against the brutality of the British rule, more repressive measures in the form of bills and ordinances were sure to follow. A demonstration in the vicinity of the assembly was ruled out because the demonstrators would be arrested and hauled away even before they had had a chance to make their point. Since the bills were to be passed in the assembly, the revolutionaries came around to thinking that perhaps the assembly would be the most appropriate venue for whatever action it was decided to stage, to bring home to the people that

BOMBS IN THE ASSEMBLY

the bills were just one more step in the process of imposing an ever greater degree of tyranny on them. As Kuldip Nayar so aptly puts it: "They considered the Assembly a worthless place because it demonstrated the humiliation and helplessness of the Indian people to the world and gave credibility to the domination of an irresponsible and autocratic rule. Still the Assembly mattered because it put an official stamp on the illegitimate government" (*Without Fear*, p. 59).

It was finally decided that two members would be deputed to hurl bombs from the public gallery at the treasury benches, taking care not to hurt anybody. Azad proposed that just as he had organised the escape of Bhagat Singh and Rajguru after the Saunders killing, a similar escape plan should be organised for the two comrades who would hurl the bombs. Bhagat Singh proposed that this time, as they were not killing anybody, there should be no attempt to escape. They should use the occasion, both in the assembly immediately after the bombs were hurled and at the trial that was sure to follow, to explain why they had put their lives on the line to come into the assembly and hurl the bombs. They would use the occasion to apprise both the members of the assembly and the public about the sacrifices that the revolutionaries had already made in their fight against British oppression and their firm resolve to continue their fight in the future no matter what greater sacrifices were demanded of them. The other members agreed wholeheartedly with Bhagat Singh's suggestion and it was decided that after their arrest the two revolutionaries should use the court as a platform to explain their concept of revolution and justify everything that they were doing in its cause. This would serve the purpose that the revolutionaries had in mind, of not only drawing attention to the justness of their own revolutionary activities but also of mobilising public opinion against the bills. People would

175

ask why the revolutionaries had chosen the heavily secured assembly to make their protest and risk their lives. They would realise that the revolutionaries had chosen not to escape as a mark of protest against the tyranny of the British rule, best exemplified by the two bills that were now proposed.

Bhagat Singh had offered himself for the job and in the minds of all the members he would have made an eminently suitable spokesperson, not only to justify their action but also to explain their ideology and the inequities of the proposed bills during the trial. Azad, who was presiding over the meeting, firmly rejected Bhagat Singh's offer. He knew that in spite of the failure of the British to apprehend Saunders' killers, they had not given up the chase and there was a strong shadow of suspicion attaching itself to the revolutionaries including Bhagat Singh. He was afraid that Bhagat Singh's arrest, in case he was permitted to throw the bombs, would lead to the revelation of some evidence connecting him to Saunders' killing and this would result in certain execution. Finally, Batukeshwar Dutt and Ram Saran Das were selected for the task. B. K. Dutt and Bhagat Singh had been together in the early days in Kanpur and had found a great deal in common when they had shared their views on British rule and on revolution. Das had been convicted in 1915 and had, on his return from the Andamans, got in touch with Bhagat Singh and become an active member of the HSRA.

All this while Sukhdev had been in Lahore. He had not attended the crucial meeting in Agra where it was decided to hurl bombs in the assembly. But Bhagat Singh had sounded him on this as one of the courses of action that they could adopt. It had appealed to Sukhdev's nature and he had endorsed it wholeheartedly. But he had expected Bhagat Singh to be one of those who would hurl the bombs and when he discovered that Bhagat Singh was not one of the two, he was greatly incensed. He directed his ire at Azad who had rejected Bhagat Singh's offer to participate in this revolutionary activity. He argued that Bhagat Singh was best equipped to put forward the party's viewpoint to the country. This was a golden opportunity to explain to the people why they had been forced to resort to violence. This would be the only way to remove the stigma that had come to be attached to the revolutionaries in the common perception and make people realise that they were not killers and terrorists. They could have, through Bhagat Singh's propaganda in the aftermath of the bombs, once and for all removed the label that Gandhi had attached to them: "irresponsible young men". But even in the face of this onslaught, Azad remained obdurate and refused either to relent or take the matter to the HSRA for reconsideration. Having failed with Azad, Sukhdev turned on Bhagat singh. He accused Bhagat Singh of having become an egoist who believed that he was indispensable to the party. He accused him of being a coward, who, in spite of his many and repeated professions to the contrary, was afraid of death. He compared Bhagat Singh to Parmanand who had first been a revolutionary and had then become a staunch follower of the Hindu Mahasabha. The comparison was made on the basis of a reference made to Parmanand by a judge of the Lahore High court: "Although the brain and the spirit behind the party, he was a coward at heart, he sent others to the stake, himself remaining in the background." Sukhdev looked straight into Bhagat Singh's eyes and warned him that one day a judge would write similar words about him. In vain did Bhagat Singh try to explain what had happened and to try to convince Sukhdev that he had in all earnestness offered himself for the task. Sukhdev remained unconvinced. "You have so much influence with the other members. You are so highly respected. I know that if you had insisted strongly enough, your name would have been included." Finally in exasperation, Bhagat Singh raised his voice and said, "You are insulting me." Sukhdev smiled a small sad smile and said in a quiet voice, "I am just doing my duty to a friend."

The heaviness of heart that this encounter had induced in Bhagat Singh was further compounded at this time by a statement that Diwan Chamanlal had made. Chamanlal was the candidate in whose favour Bhagwati Charan and Bhagat Singh had campaigned when they had distributed the notorious "Lost Leader" pamphlets against Lala Lajpat Rai. Diwan Chamanlal, who probably knew of Bhagat Singh's involvement in the Saunders killing, now announced: "That an assassin killed Saunders makes me bow my head in shame." It was a statement that was given considerable coverage by the newspapers. To make matters even worse, Sukhdev hurled further insults at Bhagat Singh either out of a genuine desire to hurt him or only to induce him to perform the task that he was the one best suited to perform. "In any case you can be of no use to the revolution now, because you have allowed yourself to be ensnared by a woman." The reference was obviously to Durga Devi and the fact that they had travelled together and stayed together in Kanpur. It was no secret to the other member of the party that during this short period of togetherness, Bhagat Singh and Durga Devi had become very close to each other. Bhagat Singh was deeply hurt by this insinuation but despite Sukhdev's taunting he had held his peace. However, he was not able to come to terms with the accusation that Sukhdev had hurled at him and sought relief through a long letter that he wrote to him. In the letter he neither admitted nor denied his love for Durga Devi. He merely assured Sukhdev that when the time came he would be ready to sacrifice "all" like a true revolutionary. It is a wonderful letter because it reveals an extremely humane

178

and soft side of Bhagat Singh's character. Once again the exchange between Bhagat Singh and Sukhdev highlights the fact that though they had been through so much together, had so much in common, there was this one basic difference between them. Bhagat Singh points out that love is a positive force not be condemned or frowned upon or looked down upon. He cites the example of their common hero and role model, Mazzini. Mazzini's first attempt at revolution had failed miserably. Haunted by the thought of all his comrades who had laid down their lives in this failed attempt, Mazzini had seriously considered an escape through suicide. At this juncture he had received a letter from a girl whom he loved and this had not only saved him from committing suicide or losing his mind, but had steeled his resolve and determination to go on in spite of his first crushing defeat.

Love in itself can never be an animal passion. Love always elevates the character of man. It never lowers him, provided love be love . . . and I may tell you that a young man and a young girl may love each other, and with the aid of their love they overcome the passions themselves and maintain their purity . . .

I returned the love of one individual and that too in the idealistic stage. And even then, man must have the strongest feelings of love, which he may confirm to one individual and may make universal . . .

One thing I may tell you to mark, we, in spite of all the radical ideas that we cherish, have not been able to do away with the over-idealistic Arya Samajist conception of morality. We may talk glibly about all the radical things that can possibly be conceived, but in practical life we begin to tremble at the very outset.

Bhagat Singh, through this letter, reveals that he is first

SHAHEED BHAGAT SINGH

and foremost a revolutionary but he is also a man who is not devoid of the gentler, softer, human feelings. He thinks that as long as he does not allow his feelings to come in the way of his work as a revolutionary, Sukhdev must not begrudge him these feelings. But in spite of this rejoinder and the relief that it must obviously have brought to Bhagat Singh, Sukhdev's barb had left its mark true and deep. Bhagat Singh asked for the Central Committee meeting of the HSRA to be reconvened and this time was adamant that Ram Saran be dropped from the team and that he be included instead. No amount of reasoning by the other members or pleading by Azad would make him change his mind and finally, seeing his implacable determination, he and B. K. Dutt were nominated to hurl the bombs in the assembly.

Azad was particularly distressed by this development because he knew that this would be the end of the road for Bhagat Singh. They would never meet again and yet Azad could not bring himself to say goodbye to his friend after the decision was taken. But he did refer to what he knew was inevitable when he turned to Shiv Verma and said, "In a few days history will claim them (Bhagat Singh and Dutt) and only the legend will survive the corridors of time" (Kuldip Nayar, p. 68). The preparations were carried out with Bhagat Singh's usual meticulousness. Jaydev was deputed to stay in Delhi and arrange for passes to the assembly. He passed himself off as a student of the Hindu College. He was able to persuade some leaders of the Congress to get passes for him. He also did a reconnaissance of the building and its approaches and brought a layout plan back for Bhagat Singh. Dutt and Bhagat Singh spent the intervening days shuttling between Delhi and Agra.

In anticipation of the publicity that their action would generate and the fact that the papers would like to carry

180

BOMBS IN THE ASSEMBLY

their photographs once the bombs had been hurled, the two got themselves photographed at a studio in Kashmiri Gate. These were the photographs that would be later carried by the *Hindustan Times*, the *Pioneer* and the *Bande Mantaram* and it is this photograph which has provided the popular image of Bhagat Singh which endures in the public memory. On 6 April, two days before the event, Bhagat Singh and Dutt personally visited the assembly hall to ensure that they were familiar with the building. They wanted to visit the public gallery and look down into the hall and see where they should hurl their bombs to ensure that no one was killed. Manmathnath Gupta tells us that Bhagat Singh met Dr. Kitchlew who recognised him even without his beard and turban and offered him all possible help in his endeavour. Dutt and Bhagat Singh had also been kept busy preparing the posters and pamphlets that they would rain down on the members during the chaos caused by the exploding bombs. Bhagat Singh had written the text of these pamphlets and using the party letterhead, typed out thirty or forty copies on a machine which Jaydev had been able to procure. A few minutes before the session began on 8 April at 11 a.m., Bhagat Singh and Dutt came up to the entrance of the public gallery. By prior arrangement an Indian member of the assembly came up to them and gave them two passes and disappeared. Bhagat Singh and Dutt had taken great care with all the detailed arrangements.

Each carried his bomb in one pocket and the detonator in the other in order to avoid any chance of an accidental explosion. The gallery was overflowing with people who had all come to hear the viceroy's speeches in connection with the controversial bills. They would be passed easily. There was a sufficient number of toadies amongst the Indian members to ensure their smooth passage and even if by some miracle these members gave in to the stirrings of their conscience and voted against the bills, the viceroy had special powers to give the necessary clearance. The decision to throw the bombs had not been taken in the hope of obstructing the passage of the bills but to show how violently the Indians were opposed to them.

In the crowd in the gallery Bhagat Singh recognised Sir John Simon and the memory of that fateful day at the Lahore Railway station came rushing back into his mind, strengthening his resolve to do whatever he could against the British. Looking down into the well of the house, he also recognised important national leaders like Motilal Nehru, Mohammad Ali Jinnah, M. R. Jayakar and many others. Bhagat Singh tore up the two passes into tiny shreds so that they could not be traced back to the member who had arranged them.

Bhagat Singh had made up his mind as to the exact moment when he would hurl his bomb. The Trades Disputes Bill had been voted upon and passed, and the president of the assembly, Vithalbhai Patel, had declared that it had been carried. The Public Safety Bill had been taken up and passed by voting, but just before the president could give his ruling, Bhagat Singh hurled his bomb down into the well. After the loud explosion of the bomb, the hall became dark and was filled with smoke. A short while later, Dutt also threw his bomb. There was complete and utter confusion, not only in the hall but also in the visitors' gallery. People ran helter-skelter not knowing quite what had happened or what more was to come. Cries of fear rent the air. Some of the members in the hall found safety by hiding behind the wooden benches. There was such a rush of people trying to escape from the public gallery that the exits were jammed. At this juncture two pistol shots were heard and a terrified silence descended. It was in this silence that Bhagat Singh and Dutt raised slogans of "Inquilab Zindabad" and "Long Live Revolution". They

182

also threw down the pamphlets that they had brought with them, which now showered down on the members below. By now the smoke from the bombs had begun to clear. Gradually a feeling asserted itself that the worst was over and people began to return to their seats rather than risk the stampede at the exits. It was at this time that members began to pick up and read the pamphlets that were scattered all over the house. When people looked up at the gallery they saw two men in khaki shorts and shirts, with their hands up, reassuring everyone that they had no intention of harming anyone and were ready to give themselves up. In spite of this repeated assurance it took some time for the police to summon up enough courage to come and apprehend them. Bhagat Singh handed over his revolver to the police and then the two were handcuffed, searched, and led away. All through these proceedings the two raised revolutionary, anti-British slogans at the top of their voices. They were taken to separate police stations to be held in custody.

As the revolutionaries had intended, no one was killed in the explosions, though in spite all the precautions they had taken one member was severely injured and a few others sustained minor injuries. Orders were given that all copies of the pamphlets were to be collected and destroyed before their contents could be relayed to the general public. But in spite of these precautions, copies of the pamphlets did fall into the hands of the press. In the evening almost all the papers came out with a special edition which carried the full text of the pamphlets:

HINDUSTAN   SOCIALIST   REPUBLICAN
ASSOCIATION

NOTICE
"It takes a loud voice to make the deaf hear." With these

SHAHEED BHAGAT SINGH

immortal words uttered on similar occasion by Valiant, a French anarchist martyr, do we strongly justify this action of ours.

Without repeating the humiliating history of the past ten years of the working of the reforms (Montague-Chelmsford Reforms) and without mentioning the insults hurled at the Indian nation through this House—the so-called Indian Parliament—we see this time again, while the people, expecting some more crumbs of reforms from the Simon Commission, are ever quarrelling over the distribution of the expected bones, the Government is thrusting upon us new repressive measures like those of the Public Safety Bill and the Trade Disputes Bill, while reserving the Press Sedition Bill for the next session. The indiscriminate arrests of labour leaders working in the open field clearly indicate whither the wind blows.

In these provocative circumstances, the Hindustan Socialist Republican Association, in all seriousness, realising their full responsibility, had decided and ordered its army to do this particular action so that a stop be put to this humiliating farce and to let the alien bureaucratic exploiters do what they wish but to make to come before the public eye in their naked form. Let the representatives of the people return to their constituencies and prepare the masses for the coming revolution. And let the government know that, while protesting against the Public Safety Bill and the Trade Disputes Bill and the callous murder of Lala Lajpat Rai on behalf of the helpless Indian masses, we want to emphasise the lesson often repeated by history that it is easy to kill individuals but you cannot kill the ideas. Great empires crumbled but the ideas survived. Bourbons and Czars fell while the revolution marched ahead triumphantly.

We are sorry to admit that we who attach so great a sanctity to human life, we who dream of a glorious future when man will be enjoying perfect peace and full liberty, have been forced to shed human blood. But the sacrifice of individuals at the altar of the great revolution that will bring freedom to all, rendering the exploitation of man by man impossible, is inevitable.

Long Live Revolution!

Balraj
Commander-in-Chief

The viceroy issued a special statement about the incident in which he admitted that the revolutionaries could have caused complete havoc in the assembly if they had so desired. But obviously this was not their aim. They were targeting the institution and not the individuals. But in spite of this the police adopted their usual heavy-handed approach and charged Bhagat Singh under Clause 307 of the Indian Penal Code with attempt to murder. The authorities were suspicious of the motives of the revolutionaries in giving themselves up. In the confusion and pandemonium caused by the bombs, they could have so easily escaped. It was generally felt that the bomb explosions were only a precursor of things to come, that this would be the first of a series of revolutionary terrorist activities.

To arrive at the truth, Dutt and Bhagat Singh were lodged in different jails and subjected to intensive interrogation. Chaman Lal once again came out against the revolutionaries and declared that the hurling of the bombs was an act of madness. Though the throwing of the bombs had been planned with such meticulousness, Bhagat Singh had, in the entire episode, shown a strange carelessness, a total disregard for his own safety. He had left a wide open trail, connecting him directly to the Saunders killing. The CID and the police were not slow in getting on to this trail. The posters that had been distributed all over Lahore and pasted at prominent places immediately after the Saunders killing were remarkably

SHAHEED BHAGAT SINGH

similar to the pamphlets that had been dropped in the assembly. They were both printed on the same kind of pink paper. They were both on the letterhead of the HSRA. They were both signed by "Balraj" who called himself commander-in-chief. They both began with the word "Notice" and ended with the slogan "Long Live Revolution". On closer examination of the posters and pamphlets, other similarities were also found in style and wording. The last paragraph of the pamphlets, taken in conjunction with the last words of the poster distributed after Saunders' killing, left no room for doubt that both had emanated from the same source. The first of these two, as we have seen, read: "We are sorry to admit that we who attach so great a sanctity to human life, we who dream of a glorious future when man will be enjoying perfect peace and full liberty, have been forced to shed human blood. But the sacrifice of individuals at the altar of the great revolution will bring freedom to all."

The concluding words of the Saunders poster were:

"Sorry for the bloodshed of a human being; but the sacrifice of individuals at the altar of revolution that will bring freedom to all and make the exploitation of man by man impossible, is inevitable."

Until this time, the police, in spite of their best efforts, had failed to find any clue as to who had killed Saunders. In fact, a few days before the bomb incident, the viceroy had sent a telegram to the secretary of state for India, in which he had said, "The investigation in the Saunders murder case is not making much progress." Bhagat Singh had, through his carelessness, provided the British with a clue to his involvement with the Saunders killing, which they would, perhaps otherwise have never been able to obtain. Azad's worst fears were beginning to be realised, but only through the evidence that Bhagat Singh had himself unwittingly provided to the police. So while the trial of Bhagat Singh and Dutt in the *Assembly Bomb* case was in progress, the authorities were working on the evidence that had been provided and making all out efforts to establish Bhagat Singh's links with the Saunders murder.

On 22 April 1929, both Bhagat Singh and Dutt were transferred to the Delhi jail. Even though Gandhiji was the most highly revered and respected national leader of the times, it was Bhagat Singh and the other young revolutionaries who aroused passion among the people. His audacious act of hurling the bomb in the heart of the government machinery was regarded as an act of heroic daring and his willing surrender was regarded as an act of supreme self-sacrifice. Bhagat Singh and Dutt had become national heroes; everywhere one turned one saw pictures of them. The papers could find nothing else to write about and there was such a strong groundswell of support for the revolutionaries that the government did not dare to risk conducting the trial in an open court. It was decided that the trial would be held in the jail itself.

On 26 April 1928, Bhagat Singh wrote to his father telling him that the trial would be held in the jail itself. Unaware of the wide trail of evidence he had left behind him to link him to the Saunders murder, Bhagat reassured his father that everything would be all right and he should not worry on his account. Characteristically, he also asked his father to send him some books: *Gita Rahasya*, a biography of Napoleon, and a few good novels. He also conveyed his regards to the elder members of the family and love to all the youngsters (Dr. P. L. Mathur, p.91).

The revolutionaries were represented by Asaf Ali, a young Congress lawyer. In his first session with him, Bhagat Singh had requested him to convey to Chaman Lal that they were not terrorists but serious students of history, the conditions

SHAHEED BHAGAT SINGH

of their country, and its aspirations. The hearing of the case commenced on 7 May 1929. As a matter of abundant precaution, the roads to the jail were all heavily guarded by the police and the CID personnel in plain clothes. All those who entered the court room were subjected to a thorough search to ensure that no one was carrying any arms or explosives. Bhagat Singh's parents had come to Delhi and had been permitted to be present in the courtroom.

Bhagat Singh was determined to use the trial to get the maximum publicity for their cause and to this end he and Dutt entered the court with clenched fists raised in the air and shouting slogans of "Inquilab Zindabad" and "Down with Imperialism". The magistrate, P. B. Pool, in reaction, immediately ordered that they be handcuffed. They were duly handcuffed and sat down behind the iron railing which had been put up for the occasion.

On the first day the prosecution produced eleven witnesses. Sergeant Terry claimed that he had found a pistol on Bhagat Singh's person when he had arrested and searched him, which was not true because Bhagat Singh had surrendered the pistol to him even before his arrest. Other prosecution witnesses claimed that they had actually seen Dutt and Bhagat Singh hurl their bombs. This was again not true because other eyewitnesses, who were not summoned, said that everything had happened in such a whirl that there had been no time to register what was going on till much later. Bhagat Singh knew that the court would convict him and Dutt, and would go to any lengths to secure this conviction. This is what he told his parents too when he talked to them during the lunch break. When Bhagat Singh was finally allowed to speak, he asked for the provision of his newspapers in his cell, a request which was immediately turned down. It was clear that the prisoners were to be treated as petty criminals.

BOMBS IN THE ASSEMBLY

The next day when the accused were brought to court, they again came in shouting revolutionary slogans. Bhagat Singh answered the questions put to him in a roundabout way, thus denying the court the information that it sought to elicit from him through the questioning. Dutt refused to answer any questions on the plea that since Bhagat Singh was the leader at the time of hurling the bombs, he must be the spokesperson for both of them and he would rather leave all the answering to be done by him. The court then went on to do what it had obviously made up its mind to do even before the start of the hearings: it framed charges against them under Section 307 of the Indian Penal Code and Section 3 of the Explosives Substances Act. They were both accused of hurling bombs to "kill or cause injuries to the King Majesty's subjects". Both were committed to the sessions court. The court once again asked the accused to make a statement but they resolutely refused to do so.

The trial started in the first week of June 1929 at the Sessions Court, which was presided over by Judge Leonard Middleton. Prosecution witnesses were produced to testify that Bhagat Singh and Dutt had been seen actually hurling the bombs. Witnesses were also brought forward to say that they had seen the two firing pistols. Both Bhagat Singh and Dutt were angry because they had not fired the shots. It seemed to them that false accusations were being made to push them into a corner in order to make them reveal information about the plans and activities of the revolutionaries. At this stage, after consultations with their lawyer, Asaf Ali, Bhagat Singh decided to make a statement which was read out in the court by the lawyer. Amongst other things, the statement said:

It was necessary to awaken England from her dreams. We dropped the bombs on the floor of the Assembly Chamber to register our protests on behalf of those who had no other means left to give expression to their heartrending agony. Our sole purpose was to make the deaf hear and give the heedless a timely warning . . .

We have only marked the end of an era of Utopian non-violence of whose futility the rising generation had been convinced beyond the shadow of doubt.

He justifies the violent activities of the revolutionaries thus: "It was the only effective method of solving the great social problems of the times—the problem of bringing economic and political independence to the workers and the peasants, constituting the mass of people."

He makes a reference to the Trade Disputes Act which was the immediate trigger for their action: "None whose heart bleeds for them, who have given their life-blood in silence to the building up of the economic structure, could repress the cry which this ruthless blow had wrung out of our hearts."

He reiterates what the viceroy had said: "We repeat that we hold human life sacred beyond words, and would sooner lay down our own lives in the service of humanity than injure anyone else . . . Our practical protest was against the institution, which since its birth, has eminently helped to display not only its worthlessness but its far-reaching power for mischief."

Though this statement has passed into Indian folklore and taken its rightful place in the history of India's struggle for freedom, it left the judge totally unmoved. The court held Bhagat Singh and Dutt guilty of endangering life, and punishable under Section 3 of the Explosive Substances Act. In his statement the judge declared, in contradiction to what the viceroy had held, that he was sure that the acts were deliberate and that he did not believe that the accused had done everything to prevent any casualties because they held human life sacred and with this in mind had used only low intensity explosives in the bombs. He pointed out that this contention by the defendants was negated by the fact that the bomb had shattered the wood panelling of the assembly hall, which was one and a half inches thick. He sentenced them both to life imprisonment.

Though Bhagat Singh knew that the British had made up their minds to punish him to the maximum and an appeal would have no effect on the outcome of the case, he decided to file an appeal only because he hoped that the longer the case was dragged out in the court, the greater would be the publicity that it would receive, which in turn would help in awakening the masses and would motivate them to rise against their condition of slavery. The appeal was rejected.

Two of the four assessors had held that the accused could not be held guilty of an attempt to murder because there was obviously no intention of causing death, their intention had only been to cause destruction. But from the way in which both these opinions were ignored and the haste with which the trial was conducted, it was obvious that there were other forces at work behind the scenes. In fact, during the trial the sessions judge had even hinted that Bhagat Singh was connected with another case. It was obvious that the British had made the connection with Saunders' killing. Perhaps the British had realised that the pistol surrendered by Bhagat Singh was one of the two pistols from which shots had been fired at Saunders. They were sure of a larger conspiracy at work and had moved quickly against the HSRA. The premises of the association and the homes of its members were raided and searched intensively. During the raids at Saharanpur and Lahore the police recovered bombs, pistols and cartridges. From Bhagwati Charan's residence in Lahore alone, the police found twenty-six bombs. Bombs were also found in Jhansi. Sukhdev, Jai Gopal and Kishori Lal were arrested from Lahore.

SHAHEED BHAGAT SINGH

From the precision with which the raids were conducted and the recoveries made, it was obvious that the British had found a weak spot in the HSRA network. Bhagat Singh was to learn later that both Jai Gopal and Hans Raj Vohra had turned approvers. It was from the evidence collected during the raids and the information gained during the interrogations that the British were able to collect enough material to institute what later came to be called the *Lahore Conspiracy* case. The authorities were able to marshal six hundred witnesses against Bhagat Singh. The execution of the punishment in connection with the *Delhi Assembly Bomb* case was kept in abeyance and he was charged with involvement in the killing of Saunders and Head Constable Chanan Singh.

Having been denied mileage from his trial when his appeal was turned down, Bhagat Singh looked for an occasion to keep his case alive in the minds of the people. Even while the sentence was being pronounced, it seemed he had decided what to do. During his brief stint in prison in 1927, he had been appalled by the conditions under which prisoners had to live and had tried to draw the attention of the authorities to this condition without success. He was sure that the conditions would not have improved in the intervening two years and decided that on reaching prison he would mount a mass hunger strike and keep interest in his case alive. He decided that both Dutt and he would go on hunger strike on 15 June. But since he had been sentenced to jail in Mianwalli and Dutt in Lahore, and they were being transported in different compartments from Delhi, Bhagat Singh did not know how to convey this decision to Dutt. Fortunately, he found the British officer who was escorting him to be of a kindly disposition. He begged him to let him spend a few, brief, farewell moments with Dutt because there was every chance that they would never meet again since they were being

192

confined to different jails. He added that since they were both handcuffed, there was little chance of them attempting to escape. After some initial hesitation, the officer agreed to the meeting, and in the few moments that they were able to share together, Bhagat Singh was able to pass on the idea of the hunger strike to Dutt.

One of the first things that Bhagat Singh did on reaching Mianwali jail was to mount a systematic instigation of the other inmates against the deplorable living conditions in the jail. He showed them the lists of the amenities provided to the Indian prisoners and those provided to the European prisoners and pointed out the glaring differences between the two. He pointed out to them that not only was the food virtually inedible but the prisoners were treated like animals. He proposed a hunger strike in protest. He stopped eating any food from 15 June and a few of the other inmates followed his example. He was using this platform to make the statement that the revolutionaries were committed not only to violent methods but would use every weapon to wage their war on the British even if it was the Gandhian weapon of non-violent protest.

On 17 June 1929 he wrote to the inspector-general of police, Punjab: "Despite the fact that I will be prosecuted along with other young men arrested in the Saunders shooting case, I have been shifted to the Mianwali Jail from Delhi. The hearing of the case is to start from 26 June 1929. I am totally unable to understand the logic behind this kind of shifting. Whatever it be, justice demands that every under trial should be given all the facilities which will help him in preparing and contesting the case. How can I appoint a lawyer while I am here? It is difficult to keep contact with my father and other relatives" (Quoted by Kuldep Nayar, p.87).

He also drew the attention of the inspector-general

of police to the fact that even though he was a political prisoner he was not being given the amenities that he was entitled to. He pointed out that he had been on complete hunger strike since the fifteenth and had already begun to lose a noticeable amount of weight. He wrote another letter on the same day to the superintendent of the Mianwali jail pointing out the discrepancies in the amenities provided to the Indian prisoners when compared with those provided to the European prisoners, and the fact that the Indian prisoners were denied even the amenities that they were entitled to.

In the meantime, Dutt, now lodged in the Lahore jail, had also written a similar letter to the superintendent of Central Jail, Lahore, and gone on hunger strike from 14 June. At first only Dutt and one other inmate had joined the strike but by July 1929 a large number of prisoners had joined in including revolutionaries like Sukhdev, Jatinder Nath Das, Rajguru, Shiv Verma, Ajay Kumar Ghosh, Gaya Ram, and B. K. Sinha. Bhagat Singh's letter seemed to have the desired effect and he was shifted to Lahore. He was not to know that the British had an ulterior motive in making the move. Before being taken to the jail, he was brought to the police station to enable the prosecution witnesses that the police were preparing to take a good look at him so that they could identify him in the "identification parade" that would be held later.

Kuldip Nayar tells us that Bhagat Singh was met by Udham Singh in the Lahore jail, who told him that he would be going to London with the specific purpose of killing Michael O'Dwyer, who had been the lieutenant-governor of the Punjab in 1919 at the time of the Jallianwala Bagh massacre, because as the administrative head of the province he must bear the responsibility for the terrible carnage and pay the price for it. He took his time but fulfilled his promise by shooting O'Dwyer dead in 1940, thus extracting revenge for

BOMBS IN THE ASSEMBLY

the unspeakable tragedy.

Bhagat Singh continued his fast in the Lahore jail and soon the hunger strike was taken up by inmates in jails all over the Punjab. Worried about this growing agitation, the British authorities tried to bring the *Lahore Conspiracy* case to trial as soon as possible. News of the hunger strike quickly spread beyond the walls of the courtroom and the jail. There were nationwide protests. Motilal Nehru published a statement in which he condemned the negative and indifferent attitude of the British authorities towards the hunger strikers. The strike continued from day to day and then from week to week. With the government remaining adamant in its stand, there seemed to be no end in sight. The authorities adopted all kinds of nefarious steps in an attempt to break the strike. In the garb of medicines, they fed the hunger strikers with liquid food. They also went so far as to fill up the water pitchers with milk, so that Bhagat Singh and his colleagues would be forced to quench their thirst by drinking milk and thus, in effect, break their strike. Those on hunger strike retaliated by breaking all the pitchers. Finally the jail authorities resorted to forced feeding. On 5 July 1929, Jawaharlal Nehru issued a statement in which he expressed sympathy for the hunger strikers. He said, "I have learnt with deep grief of the hunger strike of Bhagat Singh and Dutt. For twenty days or more they have refused all food and I am told that forcible feeding is being resorted to." He added that no Indian could refrain from admiring their great and voluntary suffering.

Meanwhile, the hunger strikers lost weight rapidly. On 15 June 1929 Bhagat Singh had weighed 133 lbs. On 9 July 1929 he was reduced to 119 lbs. The agitation in support of the demands of the inmates of the jails gradually gained momentum. Jawaharlal Nehru visited Lahore jail at the beginning of August to meet Bhagat Singh and the others

SHAHEED BHAGAT SINGH

who were on hunger strike. After his visit he issued another statement: "I was very much pained to see the distress of the heroes. They have staked their lives in this struggle. They want that political prisoners should be treated like political prisoners. I am quite hopeful that their sacrifice would be crowned with success" (Quoted by Kuldip Nayar, p.88). Mohammad Ali Jinnah also drew public attention to the hunger strike by raising the matter in the Central Legislative Assembly. In the face of this growing pressure from all quarters in support of the prisoners, the authorities chose to maintain a studious silence. When they did break this silence it was to show a superficial concern for the deteriorating health of those on hunger strike and not to show any concern for their demands. This only served to fuel the public anger even further. The hunger strike became the focus of national interest and many people in all walks of life went on prolonged fasts to express their sympathy for, and solidarity with, the prisoners. Public meetings were held to express concern and sympathy with those on hunger strike. Inevitably, these meetings also expressed anger against the British authorities. Kuldip Nayar tells us that at a public meeting held in the Jallianwala Bagh in Amritsar, the administration was warned that it would be held responsible if anything untoward happened to any of the prisoners who were on hunger strike. At a meeting in Lahore, solidarity was expressed with the prisoners by a show of ten thousand hands. In a further show of this sympathy and solidarity a nation wide "Bhagat Singh Day" was celebrated. Newspapers took to publishing a daily bulletin, devoted exclusively to the health of the prisoners.

In an effort to break the strikers, the government announced that it would give better facilities and food to some of the hunger strikers on medical grounds. But no one was fooled by this announcement. The prisoners spurned the offer and continued the strike. Finally the British were forced to appoint a Punjab Jail Enquiry Committee under the chairmanship of Duni Chand to look into the prisoners' demands. The committee promised that special facilities and diet would be provided to all political prisoners. It assured the prisoners that it had been authorised by the government to make this promise. On the basis of this assurance some of the hunger strikers broke their long fast. But this assurance was regarded with scepticism because a note was given to the chairman that on the basis of the assurance given by the committee the prisoners were only suspending their strike and not abandoning it. Should the government renege on its promise the strike would be resumed. Events were to prove that this scepticism was not unfounded.

On 10 July 1929, the proceedings of the *Lahore Conspiracy* case began. Twenty-eight persons were charged with a battery of charges. Some sources like Dr. Mathur put the number of people thus charged at twenty-one. The court was presided over by first class magistrate, Rai Sahib Pandit Sri Krishen. On the opening day of the trial, the courtroom was strongly barricaded by the police. The general public was not allowed in and even counsel for the defence had to insist on the legal rights of their clients before they were allowed into the courtroom. Bhagat Singh's parents were among the very few who were able to get entry. The revolutionaries had decided that since there was absolutely no hope of getting justice from a court set up by the British, there was no point in fighting the charges that had been levelled against them. Indians in general, and more particularly the prisoners, had lost all faith and respect for the British and their sense of justice. So it was decided that the best course to adopt under the circumstances was to treat the trial with total indifference and to boycott the proceedings. And yet they decided to go through with

SHAHEED BHAGAT SINGH

the trial because they wanted to utilise this opportunity to the maximum to stir up public opinion against the British. By this time J. N. Das had lost so much weight that his health was in a critical state. He had remained steadfast in his resolve to fast to the very end even in the face of the assurance put out by the jail committee and his condition deteriorated rapidly almost by the hour. Bhagat Singh and the other prisoners watched in total helplessness. Seeing how rapidly he was declining, the committee had recommended that he be released unconditionally. But the authorities felt that his release at this point of time would appear to be an act of surrender and submission, and agreed only to his release on bail. Bail was almost immediately deposited by a supporter but Jatin refused to accept the British offer. It is said that by this stage he had become so weak that he found it difficult to turn in bed. The British made a last ditch attempt to deflect some of the strong support and sympathy that Jatin's case was eliciting by announcing that he had refused the British offer of release on bail because he was demanding that all the prisoners on hunger strike should also be released along with him. But no one was fooled by the announcement. By now everyone knew clearly that the aim of the hunger strike was one and only one: the improvement of the jail facilities. All the prisoners had taken care to keep this aim completely separate from the trial. Jatin's ordeal stretched for sixty-three days and shortly before the end he said, "I do not want any obsequies to be performed at Kali Bari in the orthodox Bengali fashion. I am an Indian." He died on 13 September 1929. Subhash Chandra Bose immediately dispatched money to defray the expenses for the transport of his body from Lahore to Calcutta. Offers of similar kind of help came pouring in from all over the country. The news of Jatin's death shocked the country. The nation was stunned into silence and yet there was a sense of great pride in the resolute courage that Jatin had displayed and the ultimate sacrifice that he had made. He became a symbol for the country, a rallying point, as one who had remained undefeated even when pitted against the might of the British.

The funeral procession started from Borstal Jail at four in the evening. It was accompanied by eighty eminent Punjab Congress leaders. On the way, shops downed their shutters as a mark of respect and hundreds joined the procession. At every station that the train carrying the body passed through, hundreds of people lined the platform with heads bowed and hands folded in silent respect. Over six lakh people waited at Howrah station to receive the body and crowds of people lined the route to the cremation ground, showering the body with flowers as it passed. The viceroy reported to the secretary of state in London: "The procession in Calcutta is stated to have been of a record size and to have consisted of five lakhs of people. The crowd was undoubtedly enormous . . . Meetings of sympathy with Das and condemnation of the government have been held in many places, but no report has yet been received of any clash with the authorities" (Quoted by Kuldip Nayar, p. 96).

Tributes poured in from every quarter. In the Punjab, Mohammad Alam and Gopichand Bhargava resigned from the Punjab Legislative Assembly. At the centre, Motilal Nehru proposed that the House should be adjourned to register a censure of the government's inhumanity towards the prisoners. The motion was passed by 55 votes against 47. The sad and tragic loss of Jatindra Das heightened the revolutionaries' resolve to face the proceedings with a well thought out strategy to convey to all of India their determination not to cave in to the British pressure. Bhagat Singh, Sukhdev, and B. K. Sinha, who were the strategists, decided that on some days of the

SHAHEED BHAGAT SINGH

trial, they would not attend court in order to convey that they did not recognise the authority of a foreign appointed court to try them. On some other days they would attend court but would disrupt the proceedings by the non-stop raising of revolutionary slogans and the singing of patriotic songs. On other days they would simply reiterate their resolution that only through revolution could the country gain deliverance. On still other days they would use the courtroom to expound their ideology—that liberation from foreign rule was only the first step on the country's road to freedom. Political freedom by itself would have little meaning unless it was followed by the transformation of the nation to a socialist society. All exploitation, whether British or Indian, had to go. Only then would the country be really free. The court proceedings were also often disrupted by the crowds of students from nearby colleges and schools who would crowd around the courtroom waiting for a glimpse of Bhagat Singh and his colleagues. As soon as they spotted them, they would raise revolutionary slogans and, following the revolutionaries' example, burst into song. Finally it was Bhagat Singh's father who intervened and persuaded the prisoners to end their hunger strike. The All India Congress, saddened by Jatindra Das' death and worried about the deteriorating health of the other prisoners, had passed a resolution urging the prisoners to give up their hunger strike. A copy of the resolution was sent to Bhagat Singh's father with a request that he use his good offices to persuade the prisoners to relent. The revolutionaries disagreed with the ideology and policies of Gandhi and the Congress, but they had the deepest respect for both. They admired Gandhi for the awakening that he had brought to the Indian masses, and the Congress for its tremendous contribution to India's freedom struggle. It was decided to accept the Congress resolution and to suspend the hunger

200

BOMBS IN THE ASSEMBLY

strike. On 5 October 1929, on its 116th day, the hunger strike was suspended. At the end of the strike, Bhagat Singh and Dutt sent the following message to the Congress:

In obedience to the resolution of the All India Congress, we have today decided to suspend the hunger strike till the final decision of the government in regard to the question of the treatment of political prisoners in Indian jails. We are very anxious that all those who went on hunger strike in sympathy with us should also discontinue it forthwith.

(Quoted by Kuldip Nayar, p. 99)

Chapter 6

THE TRIAL

Right from the time of his arrest, even during the preliminary hearings, Bhagat Singh had adopted a strategy of prolonging the proceedings as much as possible in order to build up awareness in the minds of the public. The intermittent hunger strikes and the refusal on many days to attend the hearings had resulted in one adjournment after another. In fact, the case had been progressing at such a snail's pace that it had earned some contempt for the court in the eyes of the public. In order to extract itself from this ridiculous situation, the government of India issued an ordinance, published in the Gazette of India Extraordinary from Shimla in May 1930, to say that the *Lahore Conspiracy* case would now be tried by a special tribunal. The sentence passed by the tribunal would be final and there would be no appeal against the sentence. The High Court would have no authority over the functioning of the tribunal. It was under this ordinance that the chief justice of Punjab constituted the three member tribunal with Justice

THE TRIAL

Coldstream, Justice Agha Haidar and Justice J. C. Hector as the members. The appointment of the tribunal suggested clearly that the British were determined to crush the challenge that Bhagat Singh and the other revolutionaries posed for them.

In the run up to the trial, some of those arrested had been subjugated to torture. Jai Gopal broke after eight days in police custody and became a police witness. Hans Raj Vohra, the youngest of the accused, was misled into believing that Sukhdev had betrayed them when he was shown a statement purported to have been written and signed by Sukhdev. In the face of this statement he felt there was no point in holding out any further and he became an approver. Five other accused were also "persuaded" to turn approvers.

The trial began on 5 May 1930 on what was to be remembered as a fiercely sweltering day with the mercury touching 106.3°F. Poonch House, where the trial was to be held, was guarded so heavily that it had become a veritable war zone. The British intelligence had reported that there would be a bid to rescue Bhagat Singh and the government was in no mood to take any chances. Visitors who had hoped to see their hero were turned away in such large numbers and subjected to such harassment that when the tribunal entered the courtroom, there were only forty people attending the trial, among them Bhagat Singh's father, Kishan Singh.

When the revolutionaries entered the courtroom a few minutes later shouting revolutionary slogans, the spectators all rose to their feet as a mark of respect. The revolutionaries then burst into the patriotic song "Sarfaroshi ki Tammana". Many visitors joined in the song and those who could not sing clapped their hands and stamped their feet in accompaniment. Justice Coldstream lost his temper and threatened to clear the court.

Once some semblance of order was restored, one of

the accused asked for an adjournment on the grounds that the constitution of the tribunal was illegal and he needed time to prepare his arguments against it. This request was refused. A petition was then handed to the judge asking for an adjournment to permit them to make arrangements for their defence. This petition was also rejected. At this stage Rajguru rose and made a speech in Hindi, which two of the judges could not understand. It was explained to the court that Rajguru was asking for an interpreter, as the language in which the proceedings were being held was as alien to him as the language in which he had spoken was to the judges. The court acceded to this request and ordered the appointment of an interpreter.

At 11 a.m. the government advocate, Carden Noad, began the opening speech for the prosecution and charged the revolutionaries with conspiring to murder, and waging war against the king. He said they were all members of the Hindustan Socialist Republican Association, which was committed to using arms, bombs and other explosives against the government, for which activities they had raised funds from abroad. He accused them of raiding banks and trains to raise money for their nefarious activities. He referred to the murder of Saunders, terming it part of a wider conspiracy. He then went on to read out the names of the eighteen accused, informing the court that of the twenty-eight accused, five were still absconding and five had turned approvers.

The prosecution case received a mild setback when G. T. Hamilton Harding, SSP, stated that he did not know the facts of the case and had filed the FIR under the directions of the chief secretary to the government of Punjab. Carden Noad attempted to lessen the impact of the statement by saying that the SSP's life was under threat from the five who were absconding, thus implying that it was the fear of this threat that had prompted the SSP to make this statement absolving himself of any direct responsibility in the case.

At this point, Jatinder Nath Sanyal, without waiting for permission from the judges, began to read out a speech on behalf of four other accused as well, in which he launched a virulent attack on the British government. The tribunal stopped the reading of the speech on the grounds that it was highly seditious in nature. A copy of the speech was then handed over to the tribunal and special attention was drawn to the last paragraph, which read: "For these reasons we decline to be party to the farcical trial and henceforth we shall not take any part in the proceedings of the case" (Quoted by Dr. L. P. Mathur, p. 128). All hell broke out at this point and the case was adjourned to the next day.

Bhagat Singh and his colleagues were convinced that the trial was a sham and that they could expect no justice at the hands of the British. Even Inspector W. J. C. Fern, who was perhaps the only reliable eye-witness of the Saunders murder, had not been able to recognise Bhagat Singh during the identification parade held in the jail. The British attitude made Bhagat Singh more than ever determined that they should continue to treat the proceedings of the court as a complete and utter farce and with the mockery that they deserved. He was, however, reassured by the wholehearted support of the visitors and was convinced that his purpose had been served.

On 6 May 1930, Bhagat Singh, who said he would conduct his own defence, asked for a legal adviser who would observe the course of the proceedings and advise him as to the line he should adopt from time to time. He asked for Duni Chand to be appointed as his legal adviser. To ensure that the role of the adviser would be completely nominal, he asked that the legal adviser should not be permitted to cross-examine any witness or address the court. The court gave its assent to this

SHAHEED BHAGAT SINGH

appointment.

At this point of the proceedings the defendants were asked if they would like a defence lawyer to be appointed by the court. Nine said an emphatic no to the question, five did not reply, and only four accepted the offer, though they imposed the condition that they could only name the lawyer they wanted after consulting the Defence Committee which had been set up by Kishan Singh. Over the next few days the proceedings were brought to a virtual standstill by the slogan shouting and singing of patriotic songs by the accused.

The hearing on 12 May began like all the other hearings but this time Justice Coldstream tried to retain control of the situation. He ordered the guards to handcuff the prisoners and remove them from the court. In an attempt to carry out this order, the overzealous Pathan policemen beat up the accused with their batons and even with their shoes. In the process many of the prisoners were injured, some of them grievously. They were dragged out of the court and forced into a van, which carried them back to the jail.

Agha Haider, the Indian member of the tribunal recorded a note: "I was not party to the order of the removal of the accused from the court to jail and I was not responsible for it in any way. I disassociate myself from all that took place today in consequence of that (Coldstream's order)" (Kuldip Nayar, p.122). In the court the next day he again publicly reiterated his stand. The shape of things to come was clearly defined by the tribunal's decision not to identify the accused. The contention was that since the identification had already been conducted in the magistrate's court, the same identification could be adopted by the tribunal as well. This glaring lacuna established once and for all that the trial was only being conducted as a formality and that the outcome had already been decided upon.

206

THE TRIAL

On 13 May 1930, all the accused except Sukhdev refused to come to court. Each of them was asked individually if he would attend and each of them refused. The reason they gave was that after the previous day's happenings, unless the president of the tribunal apologised and assured them that such behaviour would not be repeated, there would be no point in their being present in the court. As expected, there was no apology from the tribunal. Instead there was a statement that the court, though anxious that the accused should have an opportunity to defend themselves and that the trial should be fair, was also committed to the smooth and uninterrupted conduct of the trial and to ensure this it would take every possible step, even the removal of the accused from the court.

As a consequence of this attitude of the tribunal, the accused, including Sukhdev, refused to attend court. From then on the jail authorities reported each day that the accused had refused to attend court and the tribunal duly recorded this report and did not deem it necessary for the accused to be present in the court. Kuldip Nayar quotes a typical order issued by the president. It is dated 18 June 1930 and says: "Both Bhagat Singh and B. K. Dutt refused to attend court. Both were brought to the main gate where the police inspector took each of them by the arm and ordered them to come to court, whereupon they each refused to come" (ibid., p.123).

There was no indication that given the circumstances, the tribunal might consider it proper to suspend the proceedings. The trial had indeed been reduced to a sheer mockery of justice. The attitude of the tribunal aroused an indignant disgust in almost everyone connected with the trial. Most of the Indian lawyers reacted strongly and disassociated themselves from the case. The press too boycotted the proceedings. But these strong reactions had no effect on the tribunal—it went ahead

207

SHAHEED BHAGAT SINGH

and recorded the statements of the approvers.

The prosecution based its case almost entirely on the stories of three of the approvers: Phanindra Nath Ghosh, Jai Gopal, and Hans Raj Vohra. All three had been associates of Bhagat Singh. Jai Gopal and Hans Raj Vohra had both been members of the Central Committee of the HSRA and had been party to all the happenings in the Mozang Road house. They had both already made lengthy confessions to the police. These confessions were the only source of information that the government had about all the activities that the revolutionaries had planned and executed. Ghosh, not being a member of the inner circle and having no first-hand information about the *Saunders* case, focussed in his story on the welding of all the revolutionary parties into a single revolutionary party, the HSRA. Jai Gopal concentrated on the details of the Saunders murder and Vohra supplied details of the other revolutionary activities of the party. It was clear from this careful segmentisation that the British were orchestrating the evidence of the approvers, that they were carefully building up a framework for the "conspiracy" against the government that they were trying to prove.

Jai Gopal's betrayal must have been particularly bitter as far as Bhagat Singh was concerned because he had always had a high regard for him and for his contribution to the party. Carden Noad played upon Jai Gopal the way a maestro would play on his instrument and over ten long days drew out the story and a pile of evidence from him. He told the tribunal that he had been present at the party headquarters at Ferozepur in September 1928 when Sukhdev and Bhagat Singh had come in. Bhagat Singh had cut off his hair and shaved his beard and donned a *dhoti-kurta*, the traditional clothes of someone belonging to UP. It was obvious that in doing so he was attempting to escape detection.

He also narrated an incident that bore witness to the fact that Bhagat Singh and his associates, in order to secure funds for their revolutionary activities, raided banks and indulged in other criminal activities. It was decided to rob the branch of the Punjab National Bank in the city. He recounted the meticulous planning that had gone into the proposed raid. But the robbery had to be postponed because the taxi in which they were to make their getaway after the event could not be arranged in time. Referring to other robberies, Jai Gopal said that the revolutionaries usually left a receipt for the amount that had been stolen with the remark: "You can encash it after Independence" (ibid., p. 125).

Since he had been an active participant in the *Saunders* case, he was able to provide all the details. He told the tribunal that the original design was to murder Scott, the senior superintendent of police, because he had not only ordered the brutal attack on Lala Lajpat Rai but had also actively participated in it. Jai Gopal said that he had been asked to identify Scott's car (No. 6728) and watch Scott's movements for a few days. 17 December had been fixed as the day for Scott's murder. He also told the court that the posters Bhagat Singh had made had been printed with red ink on thin paper on behalf of the HSRA. He revealed that the original posters had carried the legend: "Scott is dead. Lalaji is avenged."

After identifying Sukhdev, he told the court in some detail about the influence that Sukhdev had had upon him, due to which he had been motivated to join the secret society whose avowed aim was to overthrow the government. He remembered that he had once stolen a book titled *Manufacture and Use of Explosives* for Sukhdev from the school library. Jai Gopal also narrated an incident, which though inconsequential in itself was perhaps added to authenticate his narrative. He said that four days after the killing of Saunders he had been walking towards the canal bridge along the Ferozepur Road

SHAHEED BHAGAT SINGH

with Sukhdev and Kishori Lal, when they saw Scott. Jai Gopal suggested to Sukhdev that if he wanted he could easily shoot down Scott right there. According to Jai Gopal, Sukhdev smiled and shrugged his shoulders and said that since fate had spared his life once, there was no point in their trying to kill him.

After the hearing was over copies of the trial proceedings were provided to Sukhdev, Rajguru and Bhagat Singh in their cells. Sukhdev made as many as two hundred and forty-one comments in the margins of his copy, most of them regarding the unreliability of the witness or the falsity of his statements. In Jai Gopal's case Sukhdev wrote in the margin against the last clause that this was utter nonsense, he could never have said this. "I believed him too much. Many a time I disclosed before him what I should not have" (ibid., p.126).

Next it was Hans Raj Vohra who testified before the court. Vohra's turnaround was very painful for the other revolutionaries because he had always appeared to believe passionately in the cause that they were fighting for. Like Jai Gopal, Vohra too had been pardoned by the magistrate. Hans Raj had been too naive to understand the trick that the police practised in all such cases and had revealed everything he knew, including the locations of all the safe houses, the ammunition dumps, and the bomb factories. Vohra had asked to be permitted to give his testimony in English because he had a better command over English than over Hindi, a request that was readily granted. Vohra revealed that he was related to Sukhdev—Sukhdev was the brother of his wife's uncle. He stated that in his meetings with Sukhdev their talk would invariably turn to the futility of the methods that the Congress adopted to secure the freedom of the country from British rule. They had come to the conclusion that under the circumstances not only was it necessary but it was also

210

THE TRIAL

justifiable to adopt revolutionary methods to achieve freedom. Vohra said it was Sukhdev who had enrolled him into the party. As a member of the party it had been his responsibility to propagate revolutionary ideas, especially among the students and the youth of the country. This was done through the wide circulation of revolutionary literature.

He too provided details of the Saunders killing. He said that Sukhdev had called him to the Lawrence Gardens on the evening of 1 December 1929, from where he too had gone to the Mozang Road house. In spite of the fact that he had already been pardoned by the magistrate, Vohra still tried to minimise his own knowledge and involvement in the killing. He said he was in the house for about twenty-five minutes and all he knew was that some action was being planned for which some members had been called from UP. At this stage Jai Gopal was brought in and Hans Raj was asked to identify him. In the face of this confrontation Hans Raj was forced to amplify his earlier, rather bald statement. He admitted that Bhagat Singh had revealed to him the party's decision to murder Scott to avenge the humiliation that Lala Lajpat Rai had suffered, though he had not been told where the murder would take place. He also revealed that on 15 December, Bhagat Singh had shown him some posters typed out on pink coloured paper. The lower edge had the date in one corner and in the other the designation "Commander-in-Chief". The heading of the poster was: "Scott is dead. Lalaji is avenged."

After Vohra two other approvers gave their testimony. Then Khan Bahadur Abdul Aziz, who, as superintendent of police, Montgomery, had been in charge of the investigation of the *Dussehra Bombing* case, was called to the witness stand. He had now been given charge of investigating the *Lahore Conspiracy* case. He testified that during his investigation of the *Dussehra Bombing* case, Bhagat Singh and Babu Singh, a member of the Naujawan Bharat Sabha, had come to his notice. While questioning Babu Singh, the latter had offered to sell him some information. It was Babu Singh who had informed him that Bhagat Singh had killed Saunders and also provided him with details about the formation of the society. He had immediately ordered the arrest of Bhagat Singh but the order could not be carried out because by that time Bhagat Singh had disappeared and surfaced in Delhi on 8 April 1929. He told the court of his discovery of the bomb factory set up by the HSRA in Lahore and the raid on it on 12 April 1929, during the course of which a great deal of incriminating evidence was discovered and Sukhdev, Kishori Lal, and Jai Gopal were arrested.

On 30 May 1930, Ram Saran Das, one of the approvers, retracted his earlier statement of 11 June 1929, claiming that it had not only been made under duress but it had also subsequently been changed and he had been forced to sign this statement by the police. In spite of the startling disclosures made by Jai Gopal and Hans Raj Vohra, the trial still seemed to have no legitimacy in the eyes of the public because of the continued absence of the accused. The British, painfully aware of this, wanted somehow to get the accused to attend the hearings. Since Bhagat Singh and his colleagues had repeatedly stated that they would attend court only when Justice Coldstream was removed, the government compromised by sending the presiding judge on long leave. The government took this opportunity to drop Agha Haidar who had been so open in his dissent to the order of the chairman of the tribunal. Hilton took over as the chairman and the two new members appointed were J. K. Tapp and Abdul Qadir. The accused immediately raised an objection that Hilton should not be appointed as chairman as he had been party to Coldstream's controversial order. The objection

212

THE TRIAL

was, quite expectedly, overruled. In spite of this, when the tribunal met the day after it was reconstituted six weeks later, all the accused, with the exception of Agya Ram, attended the proceedings. Agya Ram was adamant that he did not recognise either the tribunal or the court. After two days of attending the hearing, the accused were convinced that the reconstitution of the tribunal had made no difference, that there was little to choose between the two tribunals. As a result they refused to attend any further hearings. On 24 June, thirteen accused did not attend and on 25 June none of the accused attended. The tribunal reverted to its original pattern of proceeding with the hearings even in their absence.

Not only was the legitimacy of the case in question because of the absence of the three prime accused—Bhagat Singh, Rajguru, and Sukhdev—but the British were also aware that the evidence of the approvers by itself was not enough to secure conviction unless it was supported by corroborating evidence from an outside source. Without this, the evidence of the approvers had no credibility. In spite of all the efforts by the authorities no such corroboration could be obtained. In the face of this failure, the tribunal had no other option but to declare that there was no reason why the approvers should not be believed.

On 10 July 1930 the tribunal issued an order informing the accused that their pleas, if any, on the charge, copies of which were attached, would be taken up on the following day. In spite of this order, on 11 July the accused again refused to be produced in the court. The accused also ignored an order passed on 11 July requiring their presence in order to state whether they wished to cross-examine the witnesses. Again the accused refused to attend the court and resisted being forcibly taken to court. The tribunal then recorded that none of the accused had appeared in court or expressed a desire to

SHAHEED BHAGAT SINGH

cross-examine the witnesses.

There were no further hearings till 4 August when the evidence of the medical officer was recorded to say that all the accused except two were on hunger strike and too weak to appear in court. On 11 August the court recorded that though Bhagat Singh, Sukhdev and Rajguru were well enough to attend court, they had refused to do so. On 26 August the public prosecutor closed the case from his side. The court was adjourned to the next day and gave the accused an opportunity to present any questions to the court. The court also passed an order asking all the accused to attend the proceedings on the following day. A copy of the order was sent to each of the accused in jail but none of them appeared in the court on the following day. The tribunal was adjourned, something that was done again on the following two days.

On 5 September, in a dramatic development, Amolak Ram Kapur appeared on behalf of the two revolutionaries, Bijoy Kumar Sinha and Ajay Kumar Ghosh. He moved for a recall for cross-examination of all forty-five prosecution witnesses and also asked for the five approvers to be summoned. Jai Gopal was actually summoned and stood in the witness box but Kapur declined to cross-examine him on the plea that there had been no instruction in this regard from his clients. Kapur also presented an application from his clients seeking a week's adjournment before cross-examining the prosecution witnesses—a request that was denied.

The trial ended on 10 September 1930. It was by now clear that Bhagat Singh would receive the death sentence. The trial had been completely one-sided, with the dice heavily loaded against the accused right from day one. The tribunal, in the way it had conducted itself, had violated all norms of justice and ignored even a basic sense of decency. Every law had been bent and broken with the sole purpose of pronouncing

THE TRIAL

the sentence of death, which had obviously been decided upon even before the trial began. The entire evidence had been based on the statements of the approvers, which cannot stand up in the eyes of the law without corroborating evidence from another source, or on the statements of proven perjurers. Apart from the statements of the seven approvers and confessions from three unknown accused, the prosecution claimed that there were as many as four hundred and fifty eyewitnesses who said they had identified the accused at various places and at various times. There were specialists of all kinds who presented evidence in support of the case— handwriting experts, printing experts, and experts on arms and ammunitions. Long before the trial drew to its close, the string of false witnesses produced by the prosecution in court had proved that the government had one and only one aim in mind—the execution of Bhagat Singh.

Seeing the writing on the wall and despairing for his son's life, Bhagat Singh's father was persuaded by his friends and relatives to submit a petition to the tribunal and the viceroy, even though he knew that by so doing he would be going against everything that his son believed in and everything that he stood for. In his petition, amongst other things, he drew attention to the fact that on being brought from Delhi to Lahore, instead of being taken straight to jail, Bhagat Singh had first been taken to the Lahore Cantonment police station, thus making it possible for the police to let the prosecution witnesses see him so that they could later identify him in the identification parade. He also pointed out that Fern, the only reliable eye-witness, had failed to identify Bhagat Singh. He stated what the court and the world at large already knew, that no faith could be reposed in the testimony of the approvers. He pointed out that most of the witnesses for the prosecution were brought in at a very late stage in the case

215

SHAHEED BHAGAT SINGH

and that the provenance of the witnesses was suspect. Before any faith could be put in the statements of these witnesses the police had to tell the court how they were able to trace these witnesses. Finally, he stated that Bhagat Singh had not been in Lahore on the day of Saunders' death and he had, in fact, been in Calcutta. In conclusion he pleaded that his son be given a chance to defend himself.

As was to be expected, Bhagat Singh was so shocked and angered by this move on the part of his father that he wrote a strong letter to him and asked him to make this letter public so that his own stand on the matter would be clear. In this letter, which was published in the *Tribune*, he wrote:

I was astounded to learn that you had submitted a petition to the members of the special Tribunal in connection with my defence. This intelligence proved to be too severe a blow to be borne with equanimity. It has upset the whole equilibrium of my mind. I have not been able to understand how you could think it proper to submit such a petition at this stage and in these circumstances. In spite of all the sentiments and feelings of a father, I don't think you were at all entitled to make such a move on my behalf without even consulting me . . .

I hope you can recall to yourself that since the very beginning you have been trying to convince me to fight my case very seriously and to defend myself properly. But you also know that I was always opposed to it. I never had any desire to defend myself . . .

You know that we have been pursuing a definite policy in this trial. Every action of mine ought to have been consistent with that policy, my principles and the programme . . . I had only one idea before me throughout the trial i.e. to show complete indifference towards the trial in spite of the serious nature of the charges against us. I have always been of the

216

THE TRIAL

opinion that all the political workers should be indifferent and should never bother about the legal fight in the law courts and should boldly bear the heaviest sentences inflicted upon them. They may defend themselves but always from purely political considerations and never from a personal point of view. Our policy in this trial has always been consistent with this principle. Whether we are successful in that or not is not for me to judge. We have always been doing our duty quite disinterestedly.

In the statement accompanying the text of the Lahore Conspiracy Case Ordinance, the viceroy had stated that the accused in this case were trying to bring both law and justice into contempt. The situation afforded us an opportunity to show to the public whether we were trying to bring law into contempt or whether others were doing so . . .

Father, I am quite perplexed. I fear I might overlook the ordinary principle of etiquette, and my language may become a little bit harsh while criticizing or rather censuring this move on your part . . .

In the end, I would like to inform you and my other friends and all the people interested in my case, that I have not approved of your move. I am still not in favour of offering my defence . . .

I want that the public should know all the details about this application and, therefore, I request you to publish this letter.

(Quoted by Dr. L. P. Mathur, p. 134-136)

Charges were finally framed against fifteen of the accused. The case against B. K. Dutt was withdrawn as he had already been sentenced to life imprisonment and transportation for life in the *Assembly Bomb* case. Hearing of this, Bhagat Singh wrote a letter to Dutt in which he said, "You will live,

217

while living, you will have to show to the world that the revolutionaries not only die for their ideals but can face every calamity. Death should not be a means to escape the worldly difficulties. Those revolutionaries who have by chance escaped the gallows should live and show to the world that they can not only embrace the gallows for the ideal, but also bear the worst type of torture in the dark, dingy, prison cells"(Kuldip Nayar, p. 134).

On 7 October 1930 the tribunal delivered its judgement. Twelve of the accused were convicted. Three were acquitted—Ajay Ghosh, Jatinder Nath Sanyal, and Des Raj. Three of those convicted—Bhagat Singh, Sukhdev, and Rajguru were sentenced to death by hanging, while the other nine were sentenced to varying degrees of imprisonment from transportation for life to three years' rigorous imprisonment. Bhagat Singh's conviction was based on the evidence of various eyewitnesses, the statements of the approvers, and the poster that he had designed. While delivering its judgement, the tribunal said, "Having regard to the deliberate and cowardly murder in which he (Bhagat Singh) took part and to his position as a leading member of the conspiracy, he is sentenced to be hanged by the neck till he is dead" (Quoted by Dr. L. P. Mathur, p. 137).

The tribunal was of the opinion that it was Sukhdev who was behind the conspiracy and had master-minded the entire plot. Not only had he been responsible for recruiting new members to the Revolutionary Party and detailing the plots both for Saunders' murder and the throwing of the bombs in the assembly, but he was also responsible for setting up bomb factories in Agra and Lahore and for organising the making of bombs. The tribunal felt convinced that Rajguru had been recruited because he was an expert marksman—it was he who had fired the first shot at Saunders, the shot that had brought

Saunders down, after which Bhagat Singh had fired many shots from his automatic pistol at almost point-blank range at the helpless and wounded police officer. Since the accused had resolutely boycotted the proceedings through the entire trial they were not present in the court when the judgement was delivered and did not hear personally of their conviction and the different punishments that had been awarded to them for their crimes. A special messenger was sent to the jail to bring them the orders of the court regarding their conviction. Kuldip Nayar tells that the order for the execution of Bhagat Singh, Rajguru, and Sukhdev was marked with a black border.

There was widespread anger at the internment of so many of the heroes of revolution, which was further aggravated by the high profile trial of the *Lahore Conspiracy* case. A few attempts at revolutionary retaliation against the government were made, but in the absence of any leadership worth the name, all these attempts ended in failure. Two revolutionaries in Lahore hatched a conspiracy against the government, but before anything could come of their efforts, they were arrested and tried. An unsuccessful attempt was made near Delhi to destroy a special train carrying the viceroy on 23 December 1929. In March 1930, the superintendent of police in Jullundhur learnt of a plan by the revolutionaries to use bombs to kill the British officials in the city. The inspector general of police was able to nip this plan in the bud. The police raided the houses in which the revolutionaries, who were to perform the task, had found sanctuary. A bomb factory was found in one of the houses raided by the police and Mulk Raj Danda and six others were arrested, though Ujagar Singh, the brain behind the plot, managed to escape.

During the trial, one of the attempts to help Bhagat Singh to escape involved the throwing of a bomb at the main gate of the Lahore Jail when Bhagat Singh was being brought to the court. Bhagwati Charan Vohra was entrusted with the task of hurling the bomb. In a trial run it was decided to first test one of the bombs manufactured for the purpose. Bhagawati Charan, Sukhdev Raj, and Vishwanath were to carry out this test. They carried the bomb on bicycles, crossed the Ravi by boat and found a suitable place in thick forest for carrying out the test. Unfortunately, the bomb burst in Bhagwati's hands and he was fatally injured. He succumbed to his injuries. His colleagues secretly cremated him at the site where the bomb had burst. Another raid by the police yielded yet another bomb factory near Sitaram Bazaar in Delhi, where bombs were found in various states of preparation which suggested that the revolutionaries had not given up their efforts. The fact that almost their entire leadership was under arrest left no one to give a focussed direction to their efforts and bring them to fruition.

Almost immediately after the sentence had been pronounced, the three condemned men, Bhagat Singh, Rajguru, and Sukhdev, were lodged in solitary cells in the Central Jail in Lahore. These cells were death row cells and were referred to in the jail as "Phansi Ghar". Bhagat Singh was the occupant of cell no.14. After a few days they were allowed communication with other prisoners and even a few short meetings with their relatives.

The sentence of death had not come as a surprise to Bhagat Singh and his inner circle of friends. From the time that he had insisted on hurling the bomb he had known that he would become the main target of British revenge and by throwing the bomb he would in effect have signed his own death warrant. So when the warrant with the black border had been handed over to him, it was a mere ratification of a sentence that he had accepted a long time ago. Chandra

Shekhar Azad and other revolutionaries had also known that once Bhagat Singh had taken on the responsibility of hurling the bomb it would be the end of the road for him. As a result Bhagat Singh accepted the sentence with equanimity and remained calm and at peace with himself, even at the prospect of his impending death, which he had known all along was inevitable in the light of his deep involvement with revolutionary activities. In fact, it seemed to those who had the good fortune to come into contact with him during this period that he welcomed his death. In a letter written to B. K. Dutt in November 1930, he said, "Besides me, there are many other guilty persons in the cells, who are waiting for their execution. These persons are praying that they may somehow or the other, escape the execution, but among them I am the only man who is impatiently waiting for the day, when for my ideals, I would be fortunate enough to be hanged" (Quoted by Dr. L. P. Mathur, p. 142). He went on to say that by showing how much he welcomed the death that would be coming to him shortly and by showing a joy while the act of execution itself was being carried out, he would show to the world the revolutionaries can sacrifice themselves willingly and with courage, for their ideals.

As was to be expected, the news of the death sentence that had been passed against the three national heroes evoked a strong and spontaneous reaction. There was a show of solidarity by people from all walks of life, all over the country, which found expression in strikes and processions and meetings in which slogans were raised against the sentence and impassioned speeches were delivered condemning the British for this action. The British, alarmed by this strong show of protest and afraid that the situation would again snowball out of control, immediately reacted by imposing Section 144 of the Criminal Procedure Code, making the assembly of more

SHAHEED BHAGAT SINGH

than a specified number of people unlawful. But even this measure failed to produce the desired effect and in blatant defiance people continued to meet and march in processions in hundreds and thousands. The British resorted to violence to disperse the "unlawful" gatherings. So much so that even gatherings only of women were subjected to *lathi*-charge by the police.

It was the students who took the lead in Lahore, where quite understandably the protests were the strongest. All colleges were closed indefinitely with the exception of the Government College. This was a college patronised by the elite, most of whom had benefited by remaining loyal to the British government and now thought it prudent to make a further display of loyalty by disassociating themselves from the anti-British protests. Unable to close this pro-British college, the protesting students took to setting up pickets just outside the college gates. Meetings were held at many places where hundreds of young men and women came forward to express their admiration for Bhagat Singh and all that he had done for the nation. The biggest and most successful of these meetings, held at Mori Gate, was quite befittingly presided over by Lala Lajpat Rai's daughter.

Appeals were made to Gandhi to intervene from many diverse sources including the under-trials in the *Chittagong Army Raid* Case. A resolution was also passed by the Bengal Revolutionaries, detained at the Buxar Camp, requesting the viceroy to commute the death sentence. A public petition making the same request and signed by thousands of people was also sent to the viceroy.

All through October, November, and December, the protests continued gaining strength from day to day but remained essentially peaceful in nature. On 23 December 1930, the first violent incident took place when two students who

THE TRIAL

were among a group of protestors took it upon themselves to express their anger by firing six shots at the governor of Punjab when he came to preside over the annual convocation of the Punjab University. One of the two students went on to shoot himself rather than be captured. The other was arrested. The governor escaped without any injuries.

On 14 February 1931, the greatly revered leader, Madan Mohan Malviya, sent a telegraphic appeal to the viceroy requesting him to use his powers and commute the death sentence of Bhagat Singh, Rajguru, and Sukhdev. On 18 February 1931 a memorandum was submitted to the viceroy pointing out that the trial was not conducted as per the normal practice of law but was held by a special court in the absence of the accused; that the accused were not permitted to appeal the judgement in the High Court, which was also against the normal practice of law; and finally, that Bhagat Singh's father had been denied permission to produce evidence in the *Saunders* case. On the basis of these three grounds the memorandum appealed to the viceroy to commute the death sentence. On 19 February, in violation of Bhagat Singh's clearly and strongly expressed wish, Vidyavati, his mother, also submitted a petition to the viceroy, making a very strong plea for the commuting of his death sentence to one of life imprisonment.

On 17 February the much awaited talks between the viceroy, Lord Irwin, and Mahatma Gandhi began. Very high hopes were pinned on the outcome of these talks because it was generally perceived that if anyone could influence the viceroy to commute the death sentence, it was Gandhiji.

There is a strong controversy surrounding Gandhi's contribution towards attempting to secure a commutation of Bhagat Singh's death sentence during his meeting with Irwin. Much has been written on the subject both by historians and

223

lay writers. The issue of Gandhi's attitude to Bhagat Singh has been deeply discussed and debated though the pages of the weekly *Mainstream*, and as V. N. Datta points out, not only has this debate added greatly to the growth of historical knowledge on the subject but has also proved that Bhagat Singh continues to occupy an eminent position in the public mind.

The first view is that Gandhi did make a serious effort to persuade Irwin to commute Bhagat Singh's death sentence. The strongest advocate of this viewpoint is Anil Naurya. Naurya refers to the diary of Mahadev Desai and other primary sources to substantiate his claim. He says that for Gandhi the plea for a commutation of Bhagat Singh's sentence was one major reason for agreeing to hold talks with Irwin. In fact, Naurya claims that Gandhi even sent Tej Bahadur Sapru, M. R. Jayakar and Srinavas Shastri to the viceroy to plead for the commutation of the sentence, thus making his effort in this direction a multi-pronged one. Andrew Roberts in his biography of Irwin says that Gandhi did make a very strong plea for the commuting of Bhagat Singh's sentence and argued strongly that such a move would have a good effect on the minds of the Indians and mitigate, to some extent, the mounting hostility against the British. But after pondering on this vital issue through the night, Irwin decided against the commutation. In a letter addressed to the viceroy dated 23 March, Gandhi did make a last desperate effort to save Bhagat Singh's life. He wrote:

Popular opinion rightly or wrongly demands commutation. When there is no principle at stake, it is often a duty to respect it.

In the present case the chances are that, if commutation is granted, internal peace is most likely to be promoted. In the

THE TRIAL

event of execution, peace is undoubtedly in danger.

Seeing that I am able to inform you that the revolutionary party has assured me that, in the event of these lives being spared, that party will stay its hands, suspension of sentence pending cessation of revolutionary murders becomes in my opinion a peremptory duty.

Political murders have been condoned before now. It is worthwhile saving these lives, if thereby many other innocent lives are likely to be saved and may be even revolutionary crime almost stamped out.

Since you seem to value my influence such as it is in favour of peace, do not please unnecessarily make my position difficult as it is almost too difficult for future work.

Execution is an irretrievable act. If you think there is the slightest chance of error of judgement, I would urge you to suspend for further review an act that is beyond recall.

If my presence is necessary, I can come. Though I may not speak, I may hear and write what I want to say "Charity never faileth."
(Quoted by V. N. Datta: *Gandhi and Bhagat Singh*, p. 42)

The second viewpoint that emerges is that with his own commitment to non-violence and his desire to save the pact with Irwin, Gandhi's plea and support for the commutation of Bhagat Singh's death sentence was, at best, lukewarm. This viewpoint finds the largest number of supporters, among them A. G. Noorani, S. R. Bakshi, D. S. Deol, D. G. Tendulkar, and General Mohan Singh of the INA. Some writers like Manmathnath Gupta even go so far as to accuse Gandhi of being double faced—showing great sympathy for Bhagat Singh in public, but not making any effort in his meetings

225

with Irwin to have the death sentence commuted. Allan Campbell Johnson, another Irwin biographer, tells us that the issue was discussed at the meeting, and Gandhi and Irwin arrived at an agreement. He writes: "Sir Herbert Emerson, the Home Member, who was called upon to play a prominent role in Delhi negotiations records listening with amazement to Irwin and Gandhi after agreement had been reached by them that Bhagat Singh must be executed, engaged in a prolonged decision not as between statesmen but as between two saints on the sanctity of human life" (Allan Campbell Johnson, *Viscount Halifax: A Biography*, p. 316, quoted by V. N. Datta, p. 5).

The third viewpoint is that Gandhi and Irwin did reach an agreement that Bhagat Singh's sentence would be commuted, but this information was recklessly made public by a member of the Congress Working Committee, which in turn unleashed a strong reaction from a veritable army of British officials all of whom threatened to resign. The viceroy, in the face of this threat, was left completely helpless and, succumbing to the pressure, reneged on his commitment to Gandhi. Supporting this viewpoint, Prem Basin writes: "Gandhi had succeeded in obtaining a private assurance from the Viceroy that the death sentence would be commuted and Gandhi conveyed this assurance to the working Committee . . . a member from Punjab divulged it to a section of the press, which led to a revolt by the Steel Frame with threat of mass resignation, and Irwin had to bow down to the pressure" (Prem Basin, "Bhagat Singh and Gandhi's Truth", *Mainstream*, 27 July 1996, p. 19-23, quoted by V. N. Datta, p. 9).

Danial Latifi, a well-known advocate, also subscribed to this view and said that the understanding was that the announcement of the commutation would be made after the pact had been ratified. In the euphoria created by

THE TRIAL

the ratification, the commutation would be more readily acceptable. Unfortunately, the premature release of the news put an end to this possibility and Irwin had to go back on his commitment. But as V. N. Datta points out, this possibility is highly unlikely—Irwin makes no mention of a deal regarding Bhagat Singh in his memoirs nor does Robert Bernay, who was the most reliable witness of the talks.

This entire debate, heated and extensive as it has been, becomes purely academic in character when we consider whether Bhagat himself would have accepted a commutation of his sentence. Bhim Sen Sachar, was to become a prominent leader and politician in free India and who was, even at that time, a noted Congress worker, went to meet Bhagat Singh in 1930 while he was on death row. During the course of their conversation, Bhim Sen Sachar suggested that a commutation of Bhagat Singh's sentence would be a far better option for the nation as it would enable Bhagat Singh to continue working for the nation while in prison even if in a limited manner. To which Bhagat Singh's reply was prompt, clear, and firm: "No, the country will be served better by my sacrifice." He felt that his execution would provide a strong impetus to the revolutionary movement and motivate other young men to gather up enough courage to join in the struggle for India's freedom.

During this time, a Defence Committee was constituted to appeal to the Privy Council against the sentence. As was to be expected, Bhagat Singh, Rajguru, and Sukhdev were firmly against the move but finally Bhagat Singh gave his consent. He had no illusion about the outcome of the appeal, but he hoped that the hearing of the appeal would make people in England aware of the existence of the HSRA and bring to their knowledge the travesty of a trial that had been conducted in order to secure his conviction.

227

The appeal was heard by a five judge bench. The points on which the appeal rested were that the ordinance, which had brought the special tribunal into power to conduct the trial, was invalid. With the setting up of the special tribunal, the accused were deprived of their right to appeal to the High Court which the law permitted them. The government's argument rested on Section 72 of the Government of India Act 1915, which vested the power of setting up a special tribunal in the governor-general.

The farcical trial that had been conducted against the accused had aroused public opinion amongst liberal-minded Englishmen. They were strongly incensed against the illegality of the proceedings which had made a mockery of the very foundation on which the British judicial system rested. As a result of this, eminent legal personalities like D. N. Pritt stepped forward to argue the case for the defendants before the Privy Council. Pritt argued that though the governor-general was empowered to set up a special tribunal, this power was bound by three conditions: there must be an emergency, the ordinance must be passed in the interest of peace, and the ordinance must pertain only to the points that were within the power of the Indian legislature. Pritt pointed out that at the time of the issue of the ordinance for setting up a special tribunal to try the accused, none of these conditions prevailed. Neither was there an emergency as defined by Section 72 nor was there the mention of an emergency in the governor-general's statement which had accompanied the ordinance.

As was expected by almost all sections of the thinking public, including the defendants, Pritt's plea was dismissed. The bench answered Pritt's argument by saying that it was not always possible to define an emergency. An emergency implied that a state of affairs existed which called for extreme action and the only person who could decide if such a state existed

THE TRIAL

was the governor-general. It also added that the governor-general was not bound by law to explain the reasons which had led him to issue the ordinance. This verdict was arrived at five days before the commencement of the Gandhi-Irwin talks. The secretary of state for India had informed the viceroy that an appeal on behalf of the three convicted revolutionaries had been heard by the Judicial Committee of the Privy Council and that the committee had decided to recommend to the King that the petition be dismissed. In the light of a possible political compromise between Gandhi and the viceroy, it was decided not to make this decision public. When it was finally made public, it evoked no surprise in any quarter. It only served to confirm, if further confirmation was indeed needed, that the Indians could never hope for or expect any fairness in their dealings with the British.

Oblivious of the attempts being made on his behalf, oblivious of the protests and demonstrations that were being staged all over the country, Bhagat Singh pursued with single-minded devotion what had become an obsession—the reading of books. He had established a very good relationship with the warden, Chattar Singh. As a result Chattar Singh connived with Kultar Singh, Bhagat Singh's brother, to smuggle all the books that he wanted to read into the prison. Most of these books were borrowed from the Dwarkadas Library, which as we know had become a repository for revolutionary literature.

We know of the books that Bhagat Singh read at this time from what has come to be known as the "Jail Notebook" or the "Jail Notes". K. C. Yadav, one of the editors who prepared these notes for publication, tells us that the notebook was bound in red cloth and was beautiful to look at. It had 404 pages of about 21cm by 16 cm size, tied together with a long thread. The pages must originally have been white in colour, were of a very good quality and texture, and weighed 90 gsm. With the passage of time the pages had turned a beautiful antique cream in colour. Each page was stamped with the page number on the top right-hand corner in black. An entry on page one of the notebook tells us that the book was handed over to Bhagat Singh by the jail authorities on 12 September 1929. Barring four couplets in Urdu, all the entries are in English. The pen used is obviously a very good fountain pen, probably made available to him through the generosity of Chattar Singh. The handwriting is careful and neat, and easy to read.

The notebook contains short entries from most of the books that Bhagat Singh read during this time in prison. Obviously these were points that he was impressed by and felt were worth recording. These quotations confirm what we already know of Bhagat Singh's character. He had an enquiring mind and always wanted to learn. He devoured books with an insatiable appetite especially books that he thought could help to solve the many problems that the country faced. The listings in his notebook not only reveal an extremely wide and broad range of interests but also his special bent of mind. There are, among others, passages in the notebook from Aristotle, Plato, Descartes, Hobbes, Locke, Rousseau, Trotsky, Bertrand Russell, Karl Marx, Engels, Lajpat Rai, Socrates, Victor Hugo, John Bodin, Thomas Aquinas, Edmund Burke, Thomas Paine, J. S. Mill, Spinoza, Karl Kautsy, Dostoevsky, Nikolai Bukharin, Lenin, Valentine Chirol, and Upton Sinclair. He was also very fond of poetry because the notebook contains extracts from Rabindranath Tagore, Byron, Tennyson, Omar Khayyam, and Arthur Clough. The notebook consists of four parts, each part devoted to a particular theme. There are blank pages at the end of each part, obviously leaving provision for extracts from future readings in that particular subject.

THE TRIAL

There is a deep poignancy to these blank pages, because one cannot help feeling a churning of the heart at the thought of what words would have filled these pages if Bhagat Singh had lived.

We can see from the notes that Bhagat Singh was attempting to understand the struggle that had waged from time to time and the theories and strategies of social evolution that had been propounded over the years in an effort to make the world a better place to live in. He also seems to be attempting to understand in simple terms, the reality, meaning, and purpose of life.

On 3 March 1931, the jail authorities permitted members of Bhagat Singh's family to meet him. A question mark hung over the meeting. Would it be the last meeting before the execution? No one knew the answer and as a result Bhagat Singh went to it prepared to treat it as the final meeting. Once again it is Kuldip Nayar who gives us an extremely poignant and moving account of the meeting. As Bhagat Singh was led by Chattar Singh to the meeting place, he walked past the barred cells of Rajguru and Sukhdev. No one had come to meet them. Bhagat Singh must have felt that if this was to be their last meeting with their loved ones, it was indeed sad that no one had come forward to give emotional and moral support to his comrades.

When he came face to face with his family, he realised how fortunate he was to have his entire family turn out to attend what could be their final meeting. He had especially requested his family not to meet him with tears. But the enormity of the situation and the distinct possibility that this might be the last time they were seeing him was too much for them to bear. Arjun Singh, his grandfather, wept inconsolably and Kishan Singh's copious tears streamed down his cheeks and into his flowing grey beard, unheeded. His mother and his

SHAHEED BHAGAT SINGH

three sisters, Amar, Sumitra, and Shakuntala wept so much into their dupattas that they were soon soaking wet with their tears. Kulbir, the younger brother, tried to put up a brave front by wiping away the tears that sprang into his eyes. But it was of no use because in an instant fresh tears sprang up to take the place of the ones he had wiped away. Kultar, the youngest, sobbed so deeply that it seemed that he would choke on his sobs.

Bhagat Singh made every effort to control the situation. He pleaded with his mother to stop crying or else, moved by her intense grief, he too would not be able to hold back his tears. It would not behove either of them for the world to say that they had shed tears at the prospect of his execution. At this Vidyavati gathered up enough strength to check her tears. She looked intently into her son's face, as if eager to store each fold, each curve of those beloved features in her mind. She reached up and caressed his hair; hair which he had permitted to grow long again now that there was no further need of disguise. At last she found the courage to smile through her tears and said,"Everyone has to die one day. But the best deaths are the ones the entire world can cherish" (Kuldip Nayar, p.155).

Kishan Singh indicated to his son that Irwin and Gandhi, between them, had agreed that if the three young men were to be hanged, the execution should take place before the all-India Congress session, which was due to be held towards the end of March in Karachi. The time permitted for the meeting was soon over and Chattar Singh, the head jail warden, gave quiet indications that it was now time for Bhagat Singh to go back to his cell. But for once, Bhagat Singh, too overwhelmed by his love for his family, was hesitant to end the meeting. According to Dr. L. P. Mathur, the deputy superintendent of the jail, Khan Bahadur, who was present on the occasion, was

THE TRIAL

also too overcome by the situation to insist that the meeting be brought to a close. At last Bhagat Singh knew that any further extension of the meeting would amount to taking advantage of the kindness of both Chattar Singh and Khan Bahadur and might create trouble for them. His family embraced him in turns and he bent down and touched his mother's feet. His sisters lost control once more and began to sob. Little Kultar wept as if his weeping would have no end. He clung to Bhagat Singh and buried his face in his brother's kurta, till the kurta too was drenched with tears like the ladies' dupattas.

On his way back to his cell, Bhagat Singh paused long enough at the cells of Sukhdev and Rajguru to tell them that the execution would be any day now. Back in his cell, the image of little Kultar and that final burst of grief haunted him, and he sat down and wrote a letter to him in Urdu: "Dear Kultar, I was deeply grieved to see tears in your eyes. Your words today were full of pain. I cannot bear your tears Darling, go on pursuing your studies with determination and take care of your health. Don't lose heart. What more can I say?" He then went on to quote some couplets which he hoped would give the little boy courage and strength to face the impending tragedy (Kuldip Nayar, p. 161). It was left to Barkat, the jail barber, to carry the news from ward to ward and cell to cell that Bhagat Singh had had the last meeting with his family and that the executions could be any time now.

On 22 March 1931, the revolutionaries who were being held in ward number 14 of the Central Jail were able to smuggle a note to Bhagat Singh in his cell, desperately seeking his sanction to set in motion some last ditch effort to save him. His reply, typical as it was, personified everything that Bhagat Singh stood for:

Comrades, I should have a natural wish to stay alive. I do

SHAHEED BHAGAT SINGH

not wish to hide this fact. But there is a pre-condition which would have to be satisfied before I do anything to stay alive. I do not wish to stay either in prison or under restriction . . . My name has become symbolic of the Indian Revolutionary Party. The ideals and sacrifices of the members of the Revolutionary party have uplifted me to such a height that I cannot go higher by staying alive.

As things are, my weaknesses are not evident to the people. If I am saved from the gallows, these weaknesses would become obvious and the revolutionary tide would begin to ebb, perhaps even sink into stillness. But I go to the gallows fearless and smiling. India's mothers will give the example of Bhagat Singh to urge their children to be like him. The number of people ready to sacrifice themselves for the country's freedom would increase and their number would continue to enlarge so much that the devilish power of the imperialists would not be able to hold down the progress of revolution.

But there does come to my mind one thought that what I had set out to do for the country and the humanity has not been accomplished even to a thousandth of my wish. If I had been able to stay alive I might have utilised the opportunity to do all I wished to accomplish.

But for this one reason I have never had any other desire to save myself from the gallows. Who can count himself more fortunate than I? I have these days much pride in myself. Now I am impatient to meet the test. I wish it would come soon.

(Quoted by Dr. L. P. Mathur, p.162)

At noon on 24 March 1931, the district magistrate, Lahore ,issued a general notice which read: "The public are hereby informed that the dead bodies of Bhagat Singh, Rajguru, and Sukhdev, who were hanged yesterday evening (March 23),

THE TRIAL

were taken out of the jail to the bank of the Sutlej, where they were cremated according to Sikh and Hindu rites and their remains were also immersed in the water."

But long before the notice was issued, the public was already aware of what had really happened the previous night. Early in the morning, two witnesses from Ferozepur had arrived and brought the news of the hurried and half-hearted cremations. A procession was formed starting from Neela Gumbad, close to the spot where Saunders had been murdered. It is estimated that the procession stretched over three miles and all the three communities, Hindus, Muslims, and Sikhs, in large numbers formed part of it. Some reports say that there were over thirty thousand participants; about five thousand of them were women. As a mark both of respect and of mourning, many women wore black saris and men wore black arm bands. Slogans were raised in praise of Bhagat Singh, Rajguru and Sukhdev.

> In the entire area black flags fluttered in large numbers. Passing through the Mall, the procession halted in the middle of Anarkali Bazaar. The crowd was hushed into silence, when an announcement was made that the party that had gone to Ferozepur had now returned with the remains of the three martyrs. Three hours later, the three flower bedecked coffins, followed by Bhagat Singh's parents and Sukhdev's and Rajguru's mothers, joined the procession. People were weeping openly and loud cries rent the sky. The procession reached the banks of the Ravi, where the authorities had wished in the first instance to cremate the bodies twenty four hours earlier.
>
> (Dr. L. P. Mathur, p. 176)

There was a complete hartal in Lahore. Even shops selling essentials downed their shutters. All schools and colleges except the Government College were closed. British officials

235

were advised to remain indoors and fearing acts of vandalism and destruction of government property, police pickets were set up all around public buildings and at the Civil Lines, where the British officers lived. Inevitably the news of the execution, when it spread, resulted in a state of national mourning. All over the country condolence meetings were held and there were hartals and processions in almost every city and town. Many people fasted to express their solidarity with the martyrs. Tributes and praise were showered on the martyrs from every quarter.

Nehru was the first among the Indian political leaders with his tribute. Amongst other things he said that all through his short life Bhagat Singh had displayed passionate zeal for the country. "He was like a spark that grew into a flame in a short time and spread from one city of the country to another, illuminating the darkness everywhere" (Kuldip Nayar, p. 171). Gandhi was also quick to shower praise on the three martyrs for the extreme courage that they had displayed. "Bhagat Singh and his companions have been executed and have become martyrs . . . I join in the tributes paid to the memory of these young men. Bhagat Singh and his associates have been hanged. Many attempts were made to save their lives . . . Bhagat Singh did not wish to live. He refused to apologise and declined to file an appeal. If at all he would agree to live, he would do so for the sake of others, if at all he would agree to it, it would be in order that his death might not provoke anyone to indiscriminate murder . . . " (Kuldip Nayar, p. 171-172).

But the praise did nothing to dispel the hostility that had built up against Gandhi. It was commonly perceived that he had been in a position to save the lives of the three young men but had not asserted himself sufficiently in this direction. In Karachi, on 26 March, three days before the start of the

Congress session, people demonstrated against Gandhi. There were shouts of "Down with Gandhi" and "Gandhi go back". At the Karachi session of the Indian Congress, which began on 29 March, all the young men wore black armbands in protest against what they perceived was Gandhi's failure and lack of will. They felt that if he had threatened to break off the Gandhi-Irwin Pact, the sentence of the three martyrs would have been commuted to life imprisonment. Robert Bernays, who was present at the session, wrote: "An Indian carrying a flag, rushed at him (Gandhi) and struck his head with the flag pole" (Robert Bernays, *Naked Faquir*, p. 235). Subhas Chandra Bose was to openly say that he had advised Gandhi that if necessary he should break the pact in order to guarantee the lives of Bhagat Singh and his comrades. But Bose qualified his statement by adding that Gandhi had tried his best in this regard. Kuldip Nayar quotes a statement that the Mahatma made in Gujarati to support Bose's contention that Gandhi did his best to save the three lives: "I have tried to persuade the Viceroy with all the methods of persuasion that I had . . . After my last meeting with the relatives of Bhagat Singh . . . I wrote a personal letter to the Viceroy in which I had poured in my whole being—heart and soul—but it has all gone in vain."

In an effort to soften the anger against the revered leader, many stories were circulated seeking to shift the blame from his shoulders. One story doing the rounds, as we have already seen, was that the news of the agreement on the commutation of the sentence had been leaked out and as a result all the senior British ICS officers had threatened to resign en bloc, forcing the viceroy to go back on his word. Another farfetched story was that the viceroy had sent a telegram to the authorities of the Central Jail ordering a commutation of the sentence but interested bureaucrats had delayed the telegram to ensure that

SHAHEED BHAGAT SINGH

it reached the jail authorities only after the hanging.

A further effort was made to contain the anger of the crowd by Sardar Patel, who was to take over as president of the Congress the following year. He paid glowing tributes to Bhagat Singh and his comrades. Nehru moved a resolution which had been drafted by him with help from Gandhi, and which was seconded by Madan Mohan Malviya. Gandhi chose Nehru for this purpose, because he among all the congress leaders was most popular with the youth. The resolution sought to place on record its admiration for the bravery and great sacrifice of Bhagat Singh and his comrades. The resolution also expressed great sympathy for the families of the martyrs and shared in their grief. It termed the execution as an act of deliberate vengeance and of ignoring the nationwide demand for a commutation of the sentence. It went on to say that the government, by not commuting the sentence, had lost a golden opportunity of promoting goodwill which was absolutely essential at this stage of the political process. But the resolution qualified all this by stating at the beginning that the Congress disapproved of political violence in any form and disassociated itself from any such violence. There was an immediate reaction to this qualifier and a few delegates, most notably Lal Bahadur Shastri, moved an amendment seeking to revise the opening qualifier. Before the movement for the amendment could gain strength a quick closure was called for and a vote was cast. The resolution was passed without the amendment.

In the issue of *Young India* dated 11 June 1931, Gandhi stated that he had put his whole being into the task of getting the death sentence commuted. In a moving speech at about the same time, he said that he would have willingly and gladly surrendered his own life, if it could have saved that of Bhagat Singh and the others.

238

THE TRIAL

If a catharsis was at all achieved and the hostility against Gandhi somewhat softened, it was not through the efforts of any of the Congress leaders but by a moving speech made by Sardar Kishan Singh, Bhagat Singh's father. So moving was this speech that most of the listeners wept openly and unashamedly. He spoke of Bhagat Singh's legacy and the message he had left for the youth of the country. He spoke of the cruelty and barbarity of the British rulers which was so extreme that it had not permitted the members of Bhagat Singh's family to meet him a day before his death, which was a privilege allowed to all condemned men. He concluded his speech by fervently appealing to all his listeners: "You must support your general (Gandhi). You must support Congress leaders. Only then will you be able to win independence for your country" (Kuldip Nayar, p.18).

The Annual Conference was still in session when a letter written to Gandhi by Sukhdev a few days before his execution was delivered to Gandhi's private secretary, Mahadev Desai, by Sukhdev's brother, Mathura Das. In his letter Sukhdev drew Gandhi's attention to the enormous amount of support and sympathy that had been shown by the public towards the prisoners of the *Lahore Conspiracy* case. He pointed out that the three of them were a small minority when compared to the scores of revolutionaries who were still confined in jail, a few of them awaiting execution. He referred specifically to the large number of revolutionaries arrested during the Ghadar Party's rebellion, the Babbar Akali Movement, the *Kakori Conspiracy* case and the dozen or so conspiracy cases that were being pursued in various cities of the country. He made a fervent appeal to Gandhi to work to secure the release of these revolutionaries. Sukhdev also questioned Gandhi's call to the revolutionaries to abandon the movement. Sukhdev said that by doing so, Gandhi was making common cause

239

SHAHEED BHAGAT SINGH

with the bureaucracy, which was doing everything possible to crush the revolutionaries. Sukhdev suggested that Gandhi should meet with some of the prominent revolutionaries, who were not men without reason, and convince them of the futility of their movement.

Sukhdev had asked for a public reaction from Gandhi to his letter, and in his speech, Gandhi reacted to it by saying that the writer of the letter was one of a few exceptional men because most men did not seek the gallows in their quest for freedom. No matter how worthy of condemnation political murder maybe, it was virtually impossible not to recognise and admire the courage and the love of the country which had led to the committing of such wrong deeds. He said that in his appeals to the revolutionaries he had advanced arguments to show why they should call off their movement. Because the Revolutionary Party worked in such complete secrecy, the only approach he had to its leaders was through public appeals. As far as support to the bureaucracy was concerned, Gandhi pointed out that it did not need any support because it reacted with crushing force even to non-violent protests. On the question of working to secure the release of political prisoners, Gandhi said he wanted them all to be released. He would make every effort in this direction.

Glowing tributes to the martyrs poured in from many sources, including Bejoy Kumar Sinha, Shiv Verma, the Hindustan Ghadar Party in San Francisco, Subhas Chandra Bose, and many others. In order to perpetuate the memory of the martyrs, an All India Bhagat Singh-Rajguru-Sukhdev Memorial Committee was set up in Lahore. A meeting was held at the Bradlaugh Hall on 28 April 1931, in which several leaders from different political parties took part and a number of decisions regarding the setting up of the proposed memorial were taken. Anand Kishore Mehta

THE TRIAL

approached Gandhiji for advice and support in this venture. Gandhiji firmly declined to be associated with the project in any way. In his letter dated 26 June 1931 addressed to Mehta, the general secretary of the memorial society, Gandhiji wrote: "I have your letter dated 13 instant. A memorial erected in honour of anybody undoubtedly means that the memorialists would copy the deeds of those in whose memory they erect the memorial. It is also an invitation to posterity to copy such deeds. I am therefore unable to identify myself in any way with the memorial" (Quoted by V. N. Datta, p. 90).

The government of India too realised that the proposed memorial could become a strong motivational device for similar revolutionary crimes and moved swiftly and with ruthless efficiency to nip the proposal in the bud. It advised the government of the Punjab to take every possible action against the erection of the memorial or any other programme connected with it. According to the government, the only claim of the three hanged convicts for a memorial was that they had murdered British police officers. The Punjab government immediately banned the issue of any appeals in connection with the proposed project and confiscated copies of appeals that had already been printed before they could be circulated. As a result of this prompt action, the decisions taken at the meeting of the memorial society remained only on paper. It was only after independence that the three martyrs got what was long overdue to them and an appropriate memorial was built at the site at which they had been cremated.

241

BIBLIOGRAPHY

Bernays, Robert, *Naked Faquir*, London, 1931.

Bhargava, G. S., *Bhim Sen Sachar: An Intimate Biography*, New Delhi, 1977.

Datta,V. N., *Gandhi and Bhagat Singh*, New Delhi, 2008.

Deol, Gurdev Singh, *Shaheed-e-Azam Sardar Bhagat Singh*, Patiala, 1978.

Dwyer, Sir Michael, *India as I knew It*, London, 1925.

Ghosh, Ajoy, *Bhagat Singh and his Comrades*, Calcutta, 1945.

Gupta, Manmathnath, *Bhagat Singh and his Times*, New Delhi, 1977.

Josh, Sohan Singh: *My Meetings with Bhagat Singh*, (Punjabi), Delhi, 1972.

————— . *The Tragedy of Komagatu Maru*, New Delhi, 1975.

Khullar, K. K., *Shaheed Bhagat Singh*, New Delhi, 1981.

Mathur, Dr. L. P., *Bhagat Singh: The Prince of Martyrs*, Jaipur, 2002.

Nayar, Kuldip, *Without Fear: The Life and Trial of Bhagat Singh*, New Delhi, 2007.

Noorani, A. G., *The Trial of Bhagat Singh: Politics of Justice*, New Delhi, 2005.

Puri, Harish, *Ghadar Movement, Ideology, Organisation and Strategy*, Amritsar, 1983.

BIBLIOGRAPHY

Rana, Dr. Bhagwan Singh, *Bhagat Singh: An Immortal Revolutionary of India*, New Delhi, 2009.

Saigal, Omesh, *Shaheed Bhagat Singh*, New Delhi, 2002.

Sandhu, Virendra, *Shaheed Bhagat Singh*, Delhi, 1974.

Sanyal, Jitendra Nath, *Sardar Bhagat Singh*, Allahabad, 1931.

Singh, Bhagat, "Why I am an Atheist".

Singh, Swaran, *Path of Revolution: A Biography of Shaheed Bhagat Singh*, New Delhi, 1998.

Thakur Gopal, *Bhagat Singh: The Man and His Ideas*, New Delhi, 1961.

Waraich, Malwinderjit Singh, *Bhagat Singh: The Eternal Rebel*, New Delhi, 2008.

Yadav, K. C., Babar Singh (eds.), *Jail Notes of a Revolutionary*, Gurgaon, 2007.

ABOUT INDUS SOURCE

Indus Source was founded in 2003 with the objective of celebrating the diverse traditions of the world and recreating the wealth of spiritual teachings, culture, and history in a contemporary format. To this end, Indus Source is engaged in publishing books for adult as well as young readership. As a niche publishing house, all our books are created with personal interest and attention to detail. Indus Source aims to promote understanding of the Self as well as understanding between faiths and cultures, and to provide positive, spiritual insights for harmony and better living.

Visit our website www.indussource.com for more details.

Indus Source Books
PO Box 6194
Malabar Hill PO
Mumbai 400006
India
www.indussource.com
info@indussource.com